JEREMIAH:

HIS LIFE AND TIMES.

BY

REV. T. K. CHEYNE, M.A., D.D.,

ORIEL PROFESSOR OF THE INTERPRETATION OF HOLY SCRIPTURE AT OXFORD,
CANON OF ROCHESTER.

WIPF & STOCK · Eugene, Oregon

Wipf and Stock Publishers
199 W 8th Ave, Suite 3
Eugene, OR 97401

Jeremiah
His Life and Times
By Cheyne, T. K.
Softcover ISBN-13: 978-1-7252-9745-6
Hardcover ISBN-13: 978-1-7252-9746-3
eBook ISBN-13: 978-1-7252-9747-0
Publication date 1/18/2021
Previously published by Anson D. F. Randolph, 1888

This edition is a scanned facsimile of
the original edition published in 1888.

TO

PROF. EBERHARD SCHRADER,

Author of

"THE CUNEIFORM INSCRIPTIONS AND THE OLD TESTAMENT,"

A FOREMOST PUPIL OF EWALD

AND PIONEER OF ASSYRIOLOGY,

AS A MEMORIAL

OF PLEASANT PERSONAL INTERCOURSE

IN FORMER DAYS.

CHRONOLOGICAL TABLE

(*Supplementary to Table in Driver's "Isaiah" in this series*)

B C.
685–641	Reign of Manasseh.
640–639	,, Amon.
638–608	,, Josiah.
608	,, Jehoahaz.
607–597	,, Jehoiakim.
597	,, Jehoiachin.
596–586	,, Zedekiah.

⁎ These dates are taken from Kamphausen's "Die Chronologie der hebraischen Konige" (Bonn, 1883)

PREFACE.

JEREMIAH is one of the central figures of an exciting period which has to be reconstructed by a combined effort of criticism and imagination. It is nearly twenty years since I first began to prepare for a commentary on Jeremiah, and since then the book and its author have retained an interest for me. The exposition in the "Pulpit Commentary" (1883-1885) is a most fragmentary realization of my original plan, and I was glad to take up the pen once more. In the summer of 1887 I preached a course of sermons on Jeremiah in Rochester Cathedral, similar to a course which I have printed on Elijah.[1] These sermons are the germ of the present volume.

In these two biographies I have entered on a field which is new to me—the literary and yet critical treatment of those Old Testament narratives which from my childhood I have loved. With faltering steps I have sought to follow Arthur Stanley, who regarded it as his mission "so to delineate the outward events of the Old and New Testament, as that they should come home with a new power to those who by long familiarity have almost ceased to regard them as historical at all." It is hoped that this volume may be an appropriate companion to Dr. Driver's critical and yet both reverent and popular study on the Life and Times of Isaiah.

I regret that, since Deuteronomy had to be brought in at all hazards, it was impossible to discuss the question of the text of Jeremiah, that of the arrangement of the prophecies, or that of the origin of Jer. x. 1-16, and (see p. 168) l, li. I should now probably modify what I have written on these subjects in

[1] "The Hallowing of Criticism" (Hodder and Stoughton, 1888).

the "Encyclopædia Britannica" (art. "Jeremiah"), and in the "Pulpit Commentary," and should have to discuss them in connexion with the larger question of the method of the editor of Jeremiah, who, I suspect, dealt more freely with his material (yet not so as to injure its true prophetic inspiration) than some of the other editors of the prophecies. I have thought it best on this occasion not to assume more than the most assured results of criticism. The reader must make allowance for the narrow limits prescribed to the volumes of this series. The Book of Jeremiah itself is full of exegetical interest; the character of Jeremiah is a fascinating psychological problem; the times of Jeremiah are among the most important in Old Testament history. On each of these subjects I have tried to throw some light from various sources, and at the same time to kindle in the reader that same reverential sympathy which I hope I feel myself for this great prophet.

Sept. 18, 1888.

CONTENTS.

PART I.

JUDAH'S TRAGEDY DOWN TO THE DEATH OF JOSIAH.

CHAPTER I.

                 PAGE

GOD COMMANDS TO TAKE THE TRUMPET 1
 The narrative of Jeremiah's call; its biographical and spiritual value.

CHAPTER II.

FRIENDS IN COUNCIL 13
 Jeremiah and his friends—Reformers before the Reformation.

CHAPTER III.

HOPES AND FEARS QUICKLY REALIZED 21
 Jeremiah's early discourses, and the historical inferences warranted by them—The quiescence of the reforming party—The sign granted at length—The threatened Scythian invasion.

CHAPTER IV.

MORNING-CLOUD GOODNESS 37
 The crisis and its effects—Religious reaction.

CHAPTER V.

"HE THAT SEEKETH, FINDETH" 48
 The finding of the book of Divine instruction—The national covenant—Jeremiah, a preacher of Deuteronomy.

CONTENTS.

CHAPTER VI.

THE ANCIENT LAW TRANSFORMED 60

The publication of the first Scripture, its significance—The leading ideas of Deuteronomy—The effects of the recognition of the Lawbook.

CHAPTER VII.

FRAUD OR NEEDFUL ILLUSION? 69

Criticism of the narrative in 2 Kings xxii.—The Mosaic authorship of the Lawbook, not tenable—Reasons for this—Notes on the allusions to Egypt in Deuteronomy, and on the finding of the Lawbook.

CHAPTER VIII.

"HIS REMEMBRANCE IS LIKE MUSIC" (ECCLUS. XLIX. 1) . . 87

David's "last words" fulfilled in Josiah—His thirteen golden years after the great covenant—Jeremiah's comparative happiness—His friends among the wise men—Pharaoh Neco profits by the weakness of Assyria—Josiah's defeat at Megiddo, his death—The national mourning—The tragedy of his life, and of Israel's history.

PART II.

THE CLOSE OF JUDAH'S TRAGEDY.

CHAPTER I.

THE CLOUDS RETURN AFTER THE RAIN 102

Consequences of Josiah's death—Jeremiah's changed attitude towards Deuteronomy—His visit to Anathoth.

CHAPTER II.

ON THE VERGE OF MARTYRDOM 114

Jeremiah's sermon in the Temple—The fate of Shiloh—The prophet's trial and acquittal—The martyrdom of Uriah.

CHAPTER III.

KEEP THE MUNITION, WATCH THE WAY! 125

Progress of Neco—Accession of Jehoahaz, and soon after of Jehoiakim—Fall of Nineveh—Neco's defeat by Nebuchadrezzar—Dread of Babylon at Jerusalem—Jeremiah's new peace of mind—His prophecy on Egypt, &c

CONTENTS.

CHAPTER IV.

THERE BE GODS MANY, LORDS MANY 139

Jeremiah's verdict upon the later kings — Nebuchadrezzar crosses the border—Duel between Jeremiah and Jehoiakim.

CHAPTER V.

BRIGHT VISIONS IN THE DEATH-CHAMBER 148

Jeremiah's Wartburg period and its results—The drought—The problem of Israel's spiritual condition—The new covenant—Jehoiakim's rebellion—The Rechabites—Two symbolic actions—Jehoiachin's captivity—His character and Nebuchadrezzar's.

CHAPTER VI.

IF THOU HADST KNOWN, EVEN THOU! 165

Zedekiah ; his accession and character—Ezekiel, the prophet of the exiles—The lower prophets at home and in Babylonia—Zedekiah's revolt—First siege of Jerusalem—Imprisonment of Jeremiah—His purchase of family-property—He is again in danger of his life—Cast into the cistern—Ebedmelech's help—Fall of Jerusalem—Book of Lamentation.

CHAPTER VII.

A PASTOR'S STRANGE FAREWELL 182

Gedaliah becomes viceroy—The prophet stays with him at Mizpah—Ishmael's outrages—Flight from Mizpah—Migration into Egypt—The heathen festival—The stormy colloquy.

CHAPTER VIII.

PER CRUCEM AD LUCEM 200

Legendary accounts of Jeremiah's death—His sufferings and compensations—Jeremiah compared with Milton and Savonarola—The spring foreseen by the Israelite and the Italian still future.

PART I.

JUDAH'S TRAGEDY DOWN TO THE DEATH OF JOSIAH.

CHAPTER I.

GOD COMMANDS TO TAKE THE TRUMPET.

The narrative of Jeremiah's call ; its biographical and spiritual value.

THE peculiar importance of Jeremiah, both as a man and as an actor in an unique tragedy, is too visible upon every page of his writings to need explanation at the outset. His life resembles no other life ; his character and his experiences are full of surprises which stimulate thought on great moral and religious problems. The introductory paragraph (i. 1), due perhaps to his faithful secretary Baruch, is of itself of a somewhat startling nature. Is it not strange that the herald of the Church of the New Covenant should have been a hereditary member of the sacerdotal order? There is nothing however to indicate that he ever performed priestly functions. Ezekiel very possibly did ; he was not called so young as Jeremiah, and was evidently well acquainted with and keenly interested in the traditions of the priesthood. Still, Jeremiah had a true priestly heart in the deepest sense of the word. By intense sympathy, he so identified himself with his people as to feel their sins and sufferings his own, and bear them on his heart before his God. He was a priest, not merely by birth, but by the grace of God ; and his life, as a critical view of the Psalter proves, was a fertile seed of similar Christ-like self-forgetfulness.

It was not all at once, indeed, that Jeremiah attained the heights of saintly heroism. There was a time when no more than Moses (Exod. iv. 13) could he deny that he had sought to evade a pastor's grave responsibilities (comp. xvii. 16), when he agonized, as in a Gethsemane, confessing the divinity of the impulse which stirred him, but painfully conscious of his own natural infirmity. He tells us so himself in his book, parts of which might fitly be called "The Confessions of Jeremiah;" for, admitting that later experiences may have coloured the form of the introductory narrative, a solid substratum of fact must, even on psychological grounds, be assumed. It was the thirteenth year of King Josiah when three distinct heavenly voices reached the youthful Jeremiah—reached him, that is, not from a God without, but from the God within him; or, in Western language, he passed through three separate, though connected, phases of consciousness, which he could not but ascribe to a direct Divine influence. I cannot say more about this belief of Jeremiah's in this place; those who will, may accuse what I have said of vagueness; the phenomena of Biblical religion cannot be brought under the clear, cold definitions of Western orthodoxy. A fresh and openminded re-examination of the religion of the Old Testament is urgently called for, and a sketch of the life and times of a single prophet is not the place to insert one of the chapters in such an exposition. Suffice it to say that Jeremiah must have had inner experiences at a still earlier age, which made these phases of consciousness in a psychological sense possible. A veil may conceal them from view, but of what prophetic experiences (in the wider sense) must not the same confession, to some extent at least, be made? We may at least be sure that, as with St. Paul, so with Jeremiah, there was a "gracious proportion between the revelation vouchsafed and the mental state of the person receiving it." In both cases there is some material for conjecture, but I doubt if the main object of this book will be served by an attempt which might reasonably enough be made in a critical survey of Old Testament prophecy. I prefer therefore to confine myself now to the distinct statements of the Biblical record.

The first Divine truth of which Jeremiah became conscious may be summed up thus—Jehovah hath foreordained thee to be a prophet[1] (Jer. i. 5). To understand this we must read the

[1] Observe—*to be a prophet*—not a *Nazirite* as well (Plumptre). The two classes are evidently distinguished (Amos ii 11, 12). Jeremiah's sorrowful experiences may have made him an ascetic, but such an one needed no outward rules Nor, probably, was his life, even after his call, one of *unmixed* gloom

GOD COMMANDS TO TAKE THE TRUMPET.

139th Psalm. Every man's career is written in the book of God; but, if possible, there are some careers more legibly written than others. To some it is only given to see God's "purpose" (lxxiii. 24) concerning them at the end of life; while others, like Abraham (Gen. xviii. 19), Cyrus (Isa. xlv. 4), and Jeremiah, are assured from the very first that the personal God has distinguished and selected them (*I knew thee*, means all this) to perform a special work for Him. It inspires them with double energy and enthusiasm, and is a part of the secret of their success. The belief in predestination, as Ewald truly observes, was a " powerful lever in Hebrew prophecy[1];" and though "prophet," "religious reformer," and (much less) "saint," are not absolutely synonymous terms, we may well appropriate the lesson that (in the words of Milman) "he who is not predestined, who does not declare, who does not believe himself predestinated as the author of a great religious movement, he in whom God is not manifestly, sensibly, avowedly working out his pre-established designs, will never be saint or reformer."[2] This did not, however, become Jeremiah's conviction without an attempt at resistance.

And I said, Alas, O Lord Jehovah! behold, I cannot speak; for I am (still) young (like a young man); i. 6. It is a cry of pain Jeremiah is too warmhearted to regard with any complacence the office of a censor; it hurts him to say that which will give pain to others. He would fain live at peace with all men, and one of his saddest complaints in later life is this—*Woe is me, my mother, that thou hast borne me, with whom all the world has strife and contention* (xv. 10). It is also a cry of alarm. How can one who is not yet of mature age—in Oriental society a young man has no *rôle* to play—expect to be listened to, especially by those who have been already fascinated by more flattering orators? And even if his credentials were accepted and his prophetic message received, is it not too likely that, through the malice of those whom he provokes, his career will be cut short when it has scarcely begun?

And so a man uniquely qualified to promote it was well nigh lost to the cause of spiritual religion. There were hundreds of

[1] "Die Lehre der Bibel von Gott," ii 208.
[2] "History of Latin Christianity," 1 112 Perhaps some may wish the word "saint" away from this fine passage, for are not all Christians *called to be* (not, to become) *saints* (κλητοὶ ἅγιοι)?

stationary and unprogressive religionists who exercised the sacred office of prophet; there were few indeed to be compared with Jeremiah. There were Zephaniah and Habakkuk, and we shall be indebted to these prophets later on for illustrations but, if we may judge from Jeremiah's account, the main drift of prophetic influence was downwards and not upwards. The *young man* is only too conscious of this, and in his pain and alarm almost makes the "great refusal"—to apply once more the phrase (Dante, "Inf." iii. 60) which has been so variously interpreted. His first impulse was insufficient to carry him away, and so the God of revelation caused a second, which, translated into words, could be expressed thus—

Say not, I am (still) young; for to whomsoever I send thee, thou must go, and whatsoever I command thee, thou must speak. Be not afraid because of them; for I am with thee to deliver thee, saith Jehovah (i. 7, 8).

God had his own method for overcoming Jeremiah's hesitancy. First, he heightened the young man's consciousness of a Divine call. He made him feel that the work to which he was summoned was not his own but God's—that the youth would be lost in his message. How could he be disobedient to the voice which came indeed from above, but which he heard within himself? *The lion roareth—who will not fear? the Lord Jehovah hath spoken, who can but prophesy!* (Amos iii. 8; cf. Hos. xi. 10). The path of duty was the path of safety—above all for one called to be a prophet. As another prophetically-minded writer says in lyric verse—

> I have set Jehovah before me continually;
> With him at my right hand, I cannot be moved (Psa. xvi. 8).

Did Jeremiah think of God's early promise of deliverance, as he went through his last brief agony? Did his heart tell him that God could be better than his promise, and even in death could "deliver" him from the songless, praiseless world of the shades? But we must not anticipate too much, though here as elsewhere it is true that "coming events cast their shadow before."

While Jeremiah is pondering, a third voice reaches him,—

Behold I put (or, I have put) my words in thy mouth (i. 9); that is, whenever the occasion to prophesy arises, Jehovah will supply the fitting words, just as Jesus Christ said to His disciples, *When they deliver you up, be not overcareful, for it is not ye that speak, but the Spirit of your Father who speaketh in you* (Matt. x. 20). But how is this? Does the Biblical record sanction the later Hellenistic view of inspiration, which impressed itself so firmly on traditional theology, that, as Hooker says, "so oft as God employed them (the prophets) in this heavenly work, they neither spake nor wrote any word of their own, but uttered syllable by syllable as the Spirit put it into their mouths, no otherwise than the harp or the lute doth give a sound according to the discretion of his hands that holdeth and striketh it with skill"[1]? No; this would be to degrade Jeremiah to the level of a μάντις or a προφήτης (Plato, "Timæus," 72 B), or—since we are speaking of a Semitic and not an Aryan religion—of an Arabian *kâhin* whose personality is entirely absorbed in that of the genius or divinity who speaks through him.[2] Jeremiah's book is too full of human nature to allow us to imagine this for a moment. *I have put my words in thy mouth*, cannot, of course, mean anything poor or commonplace. But who can say that such a paraphrase as this gives an unworthy or inadequate meaning—"I promise never to leave thee in uncertainty as to thy message; I will guide and overrule the natural promptings of thy heart and intellect as that thou shalt convey the only true conception of my will which the language can express or the people of Israel comprehend."

But this is not all. The voice adds—

See, I set thee in charge this day over the nations and over the kingdoms, to pluck up and to break down, to destroy and to overthrow, to build and to plant[3] (i. 10).

It may seem strange that Jeremiah could thus early realize

---

[1] "Works," ed. Keble, iii. 662; comp. Philo, II. 417, and other passages Lee's "Inspiration," 1st ed pp. 54-57. Hooker, however, does not, like Philo, represent unconsciousness as an essential condition of the prophetic inspiration. According to him, the prophets both sympathize with and understand the words committed to them, according to Philo, "the understanding goes away from home" (ἐξοικίζεται ὁ νοῦς).

[2] See Wellhausen, "Skizzen und Vorarbeiten," Heft 3, p. 133.

[3] Sirach quotes this passage in his eulogy of great men, but apparently explains it, in the sense suggested by Jer xxxi. 28, of the pulling down and building up of Israel. In the original context, it applies at least as much to the non-Israelitish world as to Israel

the wide range appointed for his ministry, and some will suspect that, writing perhaps twenty-three years afterwards, he may have transferred his later conviction to those early days when the state of his own country must have been the absorbing theme of his meditation. Modern parallels to such a case will at once suggest themselves—how constantly for instance Goethe violated strict historical truth in re-editing and rearranging his various works! But why need we go beyond the king of the Hebrew prophets? If at the opening of his ministry Isaiah had really become certain (see Isa. vi. 9, 10, that his preaching would only confirm his people in its blind obstinacy, could he have had courage to work as cheerfully and as sympathetically as he did? Must not his later experience have cast a deep shadow over his recollections of the past? Psychologically, this is quite conceivable; and it is certain that the prophets were in no hurry to express their burning thoughts and words in literary style. At any rate, it seems more than probable that the phraseology of Jer. i. 10, 12 is modelled upon a passage in one of Jeremiah's subsequent prophecies (xxxi. 28), and these verses cannot be taken alone—the whole context must equally have been affected by the prophet's later experience.[1] And yet—may not *the truths which underlie this verse* have been already present to the mind of Jeremiah, though he may have not fully realized their application to his own case? For what do the solemn words, *I set thee in charge over the nations*, mean? Surely this—that it is not the necessary result of certain physical laws when an institution, or a dynasty, or a people, is overthrown and perishes. The forces of nature are, according to this passage, but ministers of Jehovah, "fulfilling His word." The one absolute Power in the universe is God's "wisdom," or thought, or purpose, or word—a Power which, both in the sphere of creation and in that of government, has two aspects—a destructive and a constructive, so that the world is a mysterious scene of blended production and destruction. Between this great Power and ordinary mankind the prophet is the link; he has in a certain sense to co-operate with God by pronouncing words which are in a secondary sense forces.

---

[1] Possibly, too, *vv.* 18, 19 may be a development of xv 20, 21, though Ewald regards the latter verses as a (shortened) "repetition" of i. 18, 19.

> " 'Tis not in me to give or take away,
>   But He who guides the thunder-peals on high,
> He tunes my voice, the tones of His deep sway
>   Faintly to echo in the nether sky.
> Therefore I bid earth's glories set or shine,
>   And it is so ; my words are sacraments divine."[1]

If Jeremiah had already grasped the truth that Jehovah was the God of the whole earth—and is there any reason to doubt this ?—why should he not have had at least a presentiment (1) that to the world at large, as well as to Israel, he had a prophetic mission ; and (2) that if he was called to destroy and to overthrow, this was only that he might, as a fellow-worker with God, plant and build up ? The former conviction without the latter would have been a source of deepest anguish. One who as a prophet, was set in charge even over a single nation needed all the strength and comfort which could be conveyed to him. Why should not He, " by whose holy inspiration we think those things that be good," have suggested to Jeremiah's mind a bright though as yet vague vision, not of Israel alone, but also of the other nations, emerging regenerate from the temporary chaos of political ruin. At a later time the vision reappeared (xxxi. 28), and became the subject of earnest meditation, though doubtless it is for God's " first-born son," Israel, that Jeremiah is chiefly concerned.

I have spoken of this experience of the young prophet as an inward experience. So it mainly was. But it was accompanied with imaginations which were as real to him as if they had been visible to the outward eye. They partook of the nature of visions, but, unlike many recorded visions, were unaccompanied, as we must infer, with morbid, moral, or physical phenomena. I mention this to distinguish them from the vision which attended the only inward experience analogous to our prophet's with which extra-Biblical history acquaints us—the vision of Mohammed on Mount Hirâ. From a historical point of view, Mohammed must be called the Prophet of Islam, and his prophetic career was introduced by a vision which is alluded to in the opening lines of the 96th Sura of the Korân. But the mingled character of Mohammed's prophetic ministry is foreshadowed by the morbid elements in the phenomena of his call. " From youth upwards," says the late Professor Palmer,

[1] *Lyra Apostolica*, cxxiv., "Jeremiah" (by Keble).

"[Mohammed] had suffered from a nervous disorder which tradition calls epilepsy, but the symptoms of which more closely resembled certain hysterical phenomena well known and diagnosed in the present time, and which are almost always accompanied with hallucinations, abnormal exercise of the mental functions, and not unfrequently with a certain amount of deception, both voluntary and otherwise."[1] One cannot, however, be sure that we have the visions of the prophets exactly as they were experienced, if they were written down a long time afterwards, and the plays upon words which occur in Jeremiah's account of his own visions,[2] warn us not to build too much on the literal historical accuracy of the narrative. It will be pardonable if some reader should doubt whether Jeremiah meant us to believe that he had really had any vision at all— whether he does not presume that his readers will take these so-called visions as pure literary fictions, such as have been recognized in all great literary periods. The decision depends on the range which each person allows to the quality of reverence. For my part, I prefer to believe that one who is so candid as Jeremiah in his descriptions of himself really did experience a vision at this crisis of his inner life, like Isaiah before him ; but I lay no stress upon this, because the opposite view is possible, and Jeremiah's principal object in writing verses 11–16 of chap. i. is to bring strikingly before us the grand though not the only themes of his prophetic discourses.

The first visionary experience of Jeremiah is described in the words, *And Jehovah put forth his hand and touched my mouth* (i. 9). Just as God so often employs the letter of Scripture as the channel of spiritual illumination, so here He repeated a scene in the grand inaugural vision of Isaiah, because His servant, by frequent study of that revealed vision, was prepared to understand a similar experience. Jeremiah's inner eyes were opened (2 Kings vi. 17), and he saw a Form, which he does not attempt to describe, approach him and touch his lips. What this meant could only become clear by the Divine guidance of the prophet's reasoning powers. Isaiah had been led to interpret a similar action, performed by one of the sera-

[1] "The Qur'ân" (Oxford, 1880), Part i., Introd , p. xx.
[2] These plays upon words remind us of Amos viii. 2, which was probably Jeremiah's model.

GOD COMMANDS TO TAKE THE TRUMPET. 9

phim, of the purification of his "unclean lips" (Isa. vi. 9); Jeremiah, however, understands the Divine touch to mean the revelation of a truth—the communication of a message from Jehovah to Israel. No longer could he complain, like Moses, of inability to speak; He who gave the theme would so lift up his whole being that the most appropriate words would rise unsought for to his lips.

Two more visions are recorded in the same chapter, which the prophet, with intuitive certainty, interprets—that is, with which he connects a truth impressed upon his mind with Divine power. The first is of the rod of an almond tree (i. 11). The Israelites, with the unconscious natural poetry of primitive times, called it *shâqēd*, or the "*wakeful*" tree, because it blossoms in Palestine as early as January, when all the rest of the plant-world seems asleep. So, thought Jeremiah (it was God who suggested the thought), Jehovah will *be wakeful over his word;* that is, will break through the winter of man's careless sleep by a sudden but not premature fulfilment of the purpose which His prophets have announced (comp. xxxi. 28; xliv. 27). The second is a *seething cauldron with its front turned from the north* (i. 13). The fire of war is a frequent image in Arabic literature. Thus one poet says—

"Their sternness remains unflagging, though they be roasted,
Again and again in War's most flaming furnace;"[1]

and another, speaking of fierce warriors, long used to the helmet—

"White are our foreheads and worn; for ever our cauldrons boil;"[2]

in commenting on which the scholiast quotes a verse from another poem in which, still more distinctly, the boiling cauldron seems to mean the desolation caused by war. In Isaiah, too, fire is an image for war, but of war regarded as a judgment sent from Jehovah (Isa. ix. 19; x. 17, 18). The cauldron in Jeremiah's vision is on the point of boiling over, and the seer's intuitive interpretation (intuitive, and therefore Divinely sanc-

[1] Lyall, "Ancient Arabian Poetry," p. 8; "Hamâsa," ed. Freytag p. 13, l. 4.
[2] Lyall, p. 18; "Hamâsa," p. 47, l. 7.

tioned)[1] is, *Out of the north shall the evil seethe* (*i.e.*, come seething), *over all the inhabitants of the land* (i. 14). "The evil" means that which Jeremiah has already learned to expect, as a thinker trained in the school of Amos and Isaiah —" the evil" which sin, when it is mature, necessarily produces, by a law of God's moral government. And why "out of the north"? Does it mean that the threatened invaders will be a northern people (comp. v. 15 with Ezek. xxxix. 2), or simply that the road which they will take will lead them through the north of Palestine? We must leave this question until Jeremiah's own prophecies supply us with the means of answering it.

It is needless to say much more on this opening chapter, the remainder of which is of little biographical use for this, the earliest stage of Jeremiah's ministry. It contains three ideas. (1) That Jeremiah is to say out frankly and fearlessly whatever message may be given him; (2) That he will encounter great opposition; and (3) That Jehovah's protection will render His prophet invincible. Two of these ideas are repeated from the first part of the chapter; the third is one which can hardly have been realized by Jeremiah as fully as the words would imply. I think we shall gain something if now and then we read the first fourteen verses by themselves. They give us a striking picture of what Jeremiah was by nature, and what Jehovah would have him become, and will, I hope, prepossess us in favour of the prophet and the book which he and his disciples have left us. Shall we not let this favourable bias have full play, and allow Jeremiah some influence in forming our character, remembering that "whoso receiveth a prophet in the name of a prophet shall receive a prophet's reward." Prophets are few and far between, even if the term be stretched to include all great moral and religious teachers; but of those who "receive a prophet," in the highest sense of the phrase, by embodying the truths which he teaches in their life and character, there may and should be many. We cannot all be Shakespeares, but we can all take up some part of Shakespeare into

[1] Does not this parenthesis justify the self-confidence of prophets like Hananiah (ch. xxviii.)? It explains it, I would rather say As a prophet's God, so his prophetic intuitions. A false or at least inaccurate conception of God was as virtually powerful for the lower prophets as a true conception was for the higher prophets like Jeremiah.

GOD COMMANDS TO TAKE THE TRUMPET.

ourselves. We cannot all be prophets, but we can all be disciples of the prophets, and receive a prophet's reward.

As the earnest of such a reward, may we seek to have the inner experiences which Jeremiah had in his early manhood ! May we open our ears to the still small voice of God's Spirit ! May we never thrust ourselves into any post without the sense that we are providentially called to it ! On the other hand, may we never reject a true call from any earthly consideration ! A call to a position of comparative poverty may be just as truly Divine as a call to riches and prosperity. Who so happy as he who deliberately sacrifices a brilliant prospect for the sake of his conscience? May we learn to submit our personal wishes and aspirations to that supreme authority whose oracle is within us, and whose living voice is known to the obedient disciple as the shepherd's voice is known to the sheep ! When langour or depression creeps over us, may the thought of duty revive us, and be to us an inspiration ! In circumstances of danger, may God's Spirit teach us how to speak and how to act ! May our natural graces be transformed into supernatural, and even our natural disqualifications be overruled to the profit of ourselves and our work ! And may we learn something even from that part of Jeremiah's "vision" which speaks of "destroying" and "building up"—learn, that is, to trust God more boldly, not only for ourselves, not only for society, but also for the Church, remembering that Christ's religion is not bound up with this or that form or system, is not indeed properly a form nor a system, but a spirit and a life, and that the gospel lives and thrives upon honest inquiry, and delightedly assimilates fresh truth. Christ is the great Reconciler both in the spiritual and in the intellectual sphere, both in the individual soul and in society at large, and all outward changes and painful revolutions are but the disguised ministers of His all-reconciling Love.

Need I offer an excuse for this appeal addressed to myself as much as to my readers. If so, why, let me ask, should books on the Scriptures be written solely in the academical or historical style? Is there not a human nature common alike to the historical critic and to the ordinary reader of the Bible? Why is it that the patristic commentators still possess an attractiveness for many students? They are deficient in that self-projection into a different order of ideas which is necessary for the historical realization of distant times, but they see the permanent elements in Scripture-teaching, even if they exaggerate them. "Their whole soul is stirred and penetrated with words which to them are manifestly full of the words and Spirit of God; their reading leaves them aflame with the enthusiasm of admiration, delight, awe, hope" (Dean Church). Is it impossible that, among the many new developments of the Christian life for which Providence is preparing us, this may be one—the union of the critical with the devotional and with the social spirit? Are there not even now some examples of this union, like the first ripe fruit in prophetic imagery, "wise master-builders" (1 Cor. iii. 10) of the Church of the future?

CHAPTER II.

FRIENDS IN COUNCIL.

Jeremiah and his friends—Reformers before the Reformation.

THE conflict between Jeremiah and the constituted authorities referred to at the end of Chapter I. belongs properly to the time of Jehoiakim and his successors; but surely not less important is the earlier period during which his character was formed, and his hold upon fundamental truths became assured. However scanty then may be the records concerning it, we must make the most of them, and not refuse the help of imaginative inference or conjecture. The dangers of an undisciplined imagination are undeniable; in the regions of science and in those of history beacon-lights enough have risen to view within the recollection of our generation, and far be it from me to encourage the intrusion of a sensational element into the hallowed study of the records of revelation. But the fact that the imagination is a bad master does not nullify its usefulness as a servant—say rather, as God's appointed minister for enabling us to realize the significance and the beauty of His words and works in the past. A biography with an element admitted to be imaginative may have less of photographic accuracy than one based entirely on so-called fact, but more of essential fidelity, both to the ideals and to the achievements of a life. One is often tempted to ask, What have we gained by the biographies of the present day, which give us countless details but without a breath of realizing imagination. Useless indeed would a "Life of Jeremiah" be, if no attempt were made in it to reconstruct what may, or must have been, the course of the prophet's development, by the help of the imagination.

The only facts that we know as yet are that Jeremiah was called to be a prophet in the thirteenth year of the reign of Josiah (say, B.C. 618, or 617), that he was then under the age at which it was usual for men to venture an opinion in public,[1] and that he at first timidly drew back from so weighty an office, but gave way to Jehovah's repeated injunctions, which were coupled with promises of protection and visionary disclosures of the appointed subject-matter of his prophecies. But how had Jeremiah been prepared to be thus distinguished? What had been his education? Who had been his friends? If we dip into his book we are at once struck, first, by the warmth of his sympathies, and next by the isolation in which he would seem to have lived. His tender heart overflowed with sympathy. To apply the words of psalms which may, perhaps, present an idealized view of Jeremiah, "when others were sick, he clothed himself with sackcloth,"[2] and yet "when he looked for sympathy himself, there was none,"[3] so that he felt in his loneliness as if the patriarch Jacob's lot were his—as if "bereavement had come upon his soul."[4] He had, in fact, felt the truth of those warnings of Jehovah. *The whole land, kings, princes, priests, and people, shall fight against thee;* [5] *even thy brethren and the house of thy father, even they have dealt treacherously with thee.*[6] *Take ye heed every one of his friend, and trust ye not in any brother.*[7] Nor had he that soothing compensation which many a persecuted Christian has found in family joys; for he had received this express injunction:— *Thou shalt not take thee a wife, neither shalt thou have sons or daughters in this place.*[8] What, then, became of that sympathy in which Jeremiah's nature was so rich? Did its precious waters run wholly to waste, like the neglected overflow of some Eastern river which once irrigated a smiling country, and now stagnates in pestilential marshes? The psalmist, indeed, who gives us, as some think, Jeremiah idealized, craves from his God that recompense of love which

---

[1] He calls himself "a boy" (i. 7), somewhat as Solomon calls himself "a young boy" (1 Kings iii. 6, comp xi. 4), though probably as much as twenty years old

[2] Psa xxxv 13. [3] Psa lxix. 20. [4] Psa xxxv. 12.
[5] Jer. i 19 (comp. 18). [6] Jer. xii. 6. [7] Jer. ix. 4. [8] Jer. xvi. 2.

was denied him by men—*let my prayer* (for them) *return* (*i e.*, be recompensed) *into mine own bosom.*[1] But must we—can we believe that Jeremiah was so utterly without responsive human love? That his own strong sympathy with his people only served to call forth its opposite—hate? Can human nature in the land of Judah have been so base as this? Must we take Jeremiah at his word?

In reply it may be said that none of the prophets are artists in moral portraiture; they do not, like even the saddest of our recent novelists, express the lights as carefully as the shades of the social picture; and Jeremiah most of all was liable to exaggeration through the very intensity of his character. He has left us some inestimable pages of confessions, supplemented by notes of important episodes in his career, but not a complete autobiography. It is allowable therefore to hold that he did, at some period in his life, enjoy the privilege, as successively disciple and teacher, of communion with other minds, and that we should have found some allusion to this in his works, if twenty-three years had not elapsed before his first public addresses received a permanent form? I am the more inclined to this view because it appears certain that Jeremiah often somewhat exaggerates the spiritual insensibility of his people —he himself even now and then confesses that it is composed of two very different elements (see xv. 19, xxiv. 5–7). Surely some like-minded men must have gravitated towards Jeremiah; presently, the names of a few such may occur to us.

This conjecture will gain much in plausibility if we fix this fact in our minds that the new movement of religious reform probably began earlier than is sometimes supposed. If so, Jeremiah must have had friends, for he too (I will justify the phrase presently) early became a religious reformer. But did the new reform-movement begin before the eighteenth year of the reign of Josiah? Certainly; and one may add that it *must* have begun earlier. Just consider the state of things when the young king came to the throne. We know but little of the long reign of Manasseh (a good critical view of it will be found in Ewald[2]), but we do know what Manasseh's next

[1] Psa. xxxv. 13.
[2] "History of Israel," iv 206–213. Perhaps, however, this great critic (whom an American writer has strangely mis-named "the great denier") may have erred in some of his details, *e g*, he may have placed the Book of Job a little too early But we will return to this later. Ewald's

successor but one found. He found the friends of a comparatively pure religion deprived of many of their natural leaders, including, as legend asserts, the aged Isaiah, by the persecution of Manasseh; and, as we shall see, the venerated sanctuary at Jerusalem polluted by a number of imported heathenish rites. But he did *not* find pure religion friendless,—indeed, among its friends, as the event proved, were many of the princes and even of the priests of Jerusalem, and some of these would seem to have obtained the guardianship of the eight-years-old[1] prince Josiah on the death of his father (himself but a young man), Amon, son of Manasseh. This was of the greatest importance to the plans of the as yet quiescent reforming party. Manasseh had ascended the throne when on the verge of manhood, and fell at once into the hands of reactionary advisers; Joash, on the other hand, who became king at seven, was (in spite of a too probably polytheistic queen-mother) completely under sacerdotal influence, and, accordingly, "did that which was right in the eyes of Jehovah, all his days wherein Jehoiada the priest directed him" (2 Kings xii. 2). It is most unfortunate that our sources of information are so silent as to the period of Josiah's minority; but none, I hope, will object to the "imaginative inferences" which I venture to draw from the facts which have reached us.

But where shall we find even a scanty basis of fact? The earlier and more documentary of our two narrative-books merely says that in the eighteenth year of Josiah's reign he began a course of reforming measures which, by their drastic nature, threw those of Hezekiah completely into the shade. The second book of Chronicles indeed states[2] that the young

account of Manasseh may be compared with the modest and instructive, though not too critical, sketch in Edersheim's "History of Israel and Judah," vii. 169-177.

[1] Provisionally, I follow the ordinary view that the unidiomatic expression, "eight year" instead of "eight years" in 2 Kings xxii. 1, (Hebrew text) is an unimportant accident (2 Chron. xxxiv. 1, has "eight years"). Klostermann, however, thinks that the original document used by the compiler had "eighteen year", this would be idiomatic, but would involve a revision of the chronology of the kings. In Arabia it was a local principle that no minor could be elected caliph.

[2] 2 Chron xxxiv 3. It is doubted by conservative scholars whether *vv* 4–7 describe what Josiah did (or at least began to do) in his twelfth year, or whether they are an awkward anticipation of facts to be told more fully later.

king began his reformation, not in the eighteenth year of his reign but in the twelfth, and as early as the eighth began to seek after the God of David his father. But can we altogether trust this assertion, considering the late period of the Chronicler, and his evident determination to judge the kings of Judah by the orthodox standard of his own times? This would be too bold; and yet I think there is something to learn from the Chronicler. *He* perhaps reconstructs history on the basis of inference: *we* may follow him in his inferences, though we may be vaguer and less dogmatic in our historical reconstruction. Certainly it is difficult to conceive that Josiah's adoption of reforming principles was really so sudden as it is represented in the Second Book of Kings. An observation of God's ways both in nature and in the soul of man justifies the conclusion that events which we call sudden have been long since prepared by unobserved agencies. The call of Jeremiah, for instance, must, psychologically speaking, have been preceded by inward experiences, the nature of which we can only conjecture. And so it is but reasonable to suppose that Josiah had—not indeed all at once shocked his people by what would seem to their unprepared minds arbitrary iconoclasm, but nevertheless given early and serious consideration to the lessons of the past and the needs of the future. The premature death of his idolatrous father Amon may well have appeared to him in the light of a judgment, and the reforming zeal of Hezekiah may have fired him with a noble emulation. Nor can he have been unacquainted with those bold prophecies of Isaiah which supplied a Divine sanction to the not very successful attempt of his great ancestor; of Isaiah, not less than of Jeremiah, may it be said, that by their pen they accomplished more than by their speech. And yet, if we may venture to carry on the method of inference—reading and meditation cannot have satisfied a mind of so practical a bent. Josiah would naturally seek for living teachers and congenial religious friends. Isolation is as unfavourable to practical ability as to personal religion. The ideas of Isaiah needed to be developed and supplemented before they could be applied to present circumstances. And even if none of Josiah's contemporaries was ready as yet to show how this could be done, yet it would be no slight gain if Josiah and some likeminded friends could ponder the lessons of history together, and build each other up in the truths of prophetic religion. He had, no doubt, his "tutors and governors," but he must also, unless human nature has changed since his time, have needed youthful associates. Among such would naturally be Jeremiah and others of the same generation. What happy days the destined prophet must have had at this period, for what friendship so delightful as that which is cemented by common principles and a common object of ambition? I could willingly believe that it is Jeremiah who takes that melancholy retrospect (almost the sweetest-saddest passage of the Psalter), in which those touching words occur—

> "But it was even thou, mine equal,
> My companion, and my familiar friend;
> We took sweet counsel together,
> And walked to the house of God as friends "—PSA. lv. 14.

Alas! this was not "the friend that sticketh closer than a brother." Worse than Demas, who forsook Paul out of mere worldliness, this bosom-friend became an apostate first and a personal enemy of his old associate afterwards.

Shall I startle the critical, nineteenth-century reader if I remark that Jeremiah is already revealed in these circumstances as a true though incomplete type of Him to whom all prophecy points? Let me assure such an one that the theory which underlies this remark involves no unfaithfulness to a strict historical method. It is simply a corollary from the fundamental Christian doctrine of Providence. No doubt the theory may be pressed too far. "Types" which satisfied, and were personally intended by the guiding Spirit to satisfy, earlier ages do not and cannot satisfy our own. But as long as the belief in Providence and a sense of biographic analogies last, there will be many who are not afraid to recognize "adumbrations" (a synonym of which Mr. Max Muller has lately reminded us) of Jesus Christ in the great men of ancient Israel There will even be some who, with a personage in "John Inglesant," can go further, and maintain that, " as the innocent and heroic life of Socrates, commended and admired by Christians as well as heathens, together with his august death, may be thought, in some measure, to have borne the image of Christ; and, indeed, not without some mystery of purpose, and preparation of men for Christianity, has been so magnified among men" (vol. i. p. 36). I have said elsewhere[1] that I belong to this class of religious thinkers, and that I account Jeremiah a striking historic type of that Servant of Jehovah, who is himself a grand *poetical* type of the Saviour of Israel and the world. Certainly Jeremiah "knew the fellowship of Christ's sufferings," and it is pleasant to hope that his Christlike sympathy with his people was accompanied by some Christlike friendships in which he, not less than more commonplace persons, began to practise on a small scale the Divine virtue of love. "It is enough for the disciple," says Jesus, "that he be as his Master" (Matt. x. 24), and we are sure that the Master formed some close human ties in the course of His ministry, and that only one of His twelve associates proved a traitor. Would that we knew something more definite about Jeremiah's friendships! But we can at least fill up our mental image of them by conjecture; and if we not only venerate but are interested in this great prophet, how can we refrain from doing so? It seems to me, then, not out of place to recollect here the words of Roger Ascham in "The Scholemaster," respecting our own boy-king. "If kyng Edward," he says, "had liued a litle longer, his onely example had breed soch a rase of worthie learned ientlemen, as this Realme neuer yet did affourde." Surely it is probable enough that the person of the Jewish boy-king formed in like manner the centre of a little society of kindred spirits, for we know that Jewish kings were not idolized as divine like the Egyptian Pharaohs—a society of which Jeremiah was a youthful member, and the two Hilkiahs[2] (one the High Priest, the other also a priest, and the father of Jeremiah) were among the recognized leaders. The probability amounts almost to certainty in the

[1] "The Prophecies of Isaiah," 3rd ed ii. 195 (comp. p 26).

[2] It has been conjectured that Hilkiah, the father of Jeremiah, is identical with "Hilkiah the priest," in 2 Kings xxii. (*e g*, by Clement of Alexandria, "Strom." i. p 328, comp Jerome, "Quæstt. Hebr ad 1 Chron. ix. 15," and by Joseph Kimchi). This is not indeed impossible. It is true that "Hilkiah the priest" belonged to the line of Eleazar (1 Chron. vi. 13), whereas Abiathar, who as we have seen, had "fields" at Anathoth, was of that of Ithamar. It is a very fantastic criticism which can build any argument at all on this harmless statement, why should not the high priest Hilkiah have had landed property at Anathoth? But I will not on this account be tempted by the conjecture. Hilkiah was not an uncommon name.

case of the High Priest, for it was he who, later on, brought the Book of Law to the notice of the king; it is something less than this in the case of Jeremiah's father, and yet, considering the conditions of education at this period, it is scarcely credible that the religious ideas of the son should not have been largely derived from the father. The name of the latter—be it remarked—means "Jehovah is my portion"—a phrase which was at once a deep confession of faith in the true God, and a silent protest against the heathenish name and character of the late king Amon. He who could utter this phrase in the sense which it bears in Psa. xvi. 5 (comp. Jer. x. 16, li. 19), cannot have been ill-qualified for leadership in the noble army of religious reformers.

But would Jeremiah himself, previously to the eighteenth year of Josiah, have called himself a reformer? I do not see why he should not have done so. It is possible indeed that he only aspired to carry out the plans of his leaders in a modest, unobtrusive way; but if even the pots in Jerusalem and Judah might, by a consistent religious thinker, be called holy to Jehovah (Zech. xiv. 20, 21), much more might a humble-minded young priest be called—I need not say a reformer—but, in Biblical language, an amender of the ways of Israel. At any rate, the inner experiences related in chap. i. are not psychologically intelligible, if he had not brooded deeply over the defects of the national religion, and longed to be made use of in removing them. That no action was taken for several years of Josiah's reign, proves how carefully the friends of reform considered the position of affairs, and how anxiously they waited for some indication of the Divine will. The seniors would naturally be the most averse to a hasty movement. They would caution the juniors against compromising Jehovah's cause by a "zeal not according unto knowledge." They would point out how few and at present inactive were the higher as compared with the lower prophets, and how the princes, or elders of the people, who had a constitutional share in the government, were still attached to the fascinating local superstitions. Nothing, they would in effect say, but a visible sign of the Divine displeasure will break up this unnatural calm, and at once add a new practicalness to the preaching of the higher prophets, and predispose both princes and people to listen to it.

CHAPTER III.

HOPES AND FEARS QUICKLY REALIZED.

Jeremiah's early discourses, and the historical inferences warranted by them—The quiescence of the reforming party—The sign granted at length—The threatened Scythian invasion.

WE have seen that after a spiritual training, which, though but dimly discernible, is none the less certain, Jeremiah was called to be a prophet in the thirteenth year of King Josiah. By birth, as the heading tells us (1. 1), he was connected with Anathoth in Benjamin.[1] Dreary enough the place ('Anâta) looks now—a wretched little village, which forces from us, in a slightly different sense, the old prophet's exclamation, *O thou poor Anathoth* (Isa. x. 30, R.V.). Anciently, no doubt, it was a fortified town, and some of the stones built into one and another of its few poor houses present the appearance of great age. It stood, in fact, on the great northern road, as Isaiah intimates in the passage from which I have quoted. One great advantage it had for Jeremiah's training—it was not far from Jerusalem, which he could easily reach in a little more than an hour's walk. But in itself it was not adapted to form a cheerful or a poetic mind. Cut off from the thrilling sight (to a devout beholder) of the Holy City, its inhabitants look down eastward and south-eastward on the Dead Sea and the Lower Jordan—striking elements in a landscape, no doubt, but requiring to be

---

[1] I cannot here enter into the question of the antiquity of the arrangement of the Levitical cities, the list of which in Josh. xxi. (see *v.* 18) includes Anathoth.

varied, and deficient in happy associations. There, however, Jeremiah was tied, by inheriting a piece of land (comp. xxxii. 6–12, xxxvii. 12)—a point in which he reminds us of Abiathar, the well-known high priest of David, who lost his office on the accession of Solomon and retired to "his own fields" at Anathoth (1 Kings ii. 26). Since Jeremiah's call to be a prophet, however, he naturally resided chiefly at Jerusalem, though there is a striking episode in his career of which Anathoth is the scene. The capital was the true home of prophecy—the *valley of vision*, as Isaiah calls it (Isa. xxii. 5, if Delitzsch be right). Would that we could have heard the young and once timid prophet after the great transformation wrought within him by his call! But alas! neither of his first discourses nor of any succeeding one have we an exact report; and it is only with much qualification that one can assent to Ewald, who regards chap. ii. as Jeremiah's earliest public address. No doubt the opening words, *Go and cry thus in the ears of Jerusalem* (ii. 1), may seem to indicate that all the following words were actually spoken not long after the prophet's call, but when we observe the generality of much of the contents, and the strong appearance of condensation, we see that Jeremiah must have composed chap. ii. some time after he began his ministry on the basis of notes or general recollections of a number of discourses. It is therefore not so much a discourse as the quintessence of several discourses. Four leading considerations are developed in it :—
I. Israel's infidelity contrasted with the fidelity of Jehovah to Israel and of the other nations to their gods (*vv.* 4–13). II. Israel's punishment and its cause (*vv.* 14–19). III. Israel's inveterate and unblushing idolatry, and its practical inutility (*vv.* 20–28). IV. Israel's sole guiltiness (Jehovah having performed His own part of the covenant) and its magnitude.

There is much that is striking in the chapter, from Jehovah's loving address with which it opens, to the mixture of earnestness and irony in the concluding description of Israel's guilt. There is also much that might well startle us. Take verse 1, for instance—I venture to quote it in Reuss's version, which is at once graceful and scholarly—

Je te garde le souvenir de la tendresse de ton jeune âge, de l'amour de ton temps de fiancée, quand tu me suivais à travers le désert, par une terre sans culture.

It is quite certain that the words here ascribed to Jehovah

(with intuitive certitude on the part of the prophet) give an idealizing view of the Israel of antiquity, and that the popular religion of Israel, even after Moses had spoken, was very different from that spiritual religion to serve which Jeremiah consecrated his life.

Then take verse 13, doubly beautiful to those who can realize the preciousness of water in the East—

For two evils hath my people committed; me have they forsaken, the fountain of living water, to hew out for themselves cisterns, broken cisterns, that hold no water.

It is not less certain that the contemporaries of Jeremiah were not conscious of having forsaken Jehovah, though, as we shall see, their Jehovah was very different from the Jehovah of the prophet. In proof of this, see *v.* 23 of this very chapter, where the Israelites are represented as meeting the charge of going over to Baal-worship by a direct denial of the offence. A fair-minded student is bound to say that Jeremiah and his opponents were both right. Jeremiah was right, in that the moral and spiritual elements of early Israelitish religion had been nearly extinguished through the influence of the impure religions of Israel's neighbours ; his opponents were right, in that Israel in its worst days never ceased to worship Jehovah as the national God. The Baalim of the different cities and villages to which Jeremiah seems to refer in ii. 28 (=xi. 31) were not necessarily, in the mind of the worshippers, "other gods beside Jehovah," and even when they were, their worship did not exclude that of Jehovah.

The fault of the Jews was not, strictly speaking, in throwing off the service of Jehovah, or, as Jeremiah says, changing their gods, but in refusing to rise, at the call of the nobler prophets, to a higher stage of religion, in not even standing still, but sinking to a lower level.

Again, take *v.* 18—

Well then, what hast thou to do with a journey to Egypt to drink the water of the Nile? or what with a journey to Assyria to drink the water of the Euphrates?

To this the Jews might very well have replied, that their experienced politicians did but adapt themselves to circumstances ; that Israel's imperial position under David and Solomon was due to the temporary depression of both Assyria and Egypt, between which its territory was situated ; that, even were Israel to be reunited, its only chance for safety would lie in attaching itself to the stronger of those two powers; that a policy of isolation would be fatal at once to the little country of Judah, and that the only question could be whether a philo-Assyrian or a philo-Egyptian policy were the more expedient. The right rejoinder, in the spirit though not in the words of Jeremiah, would be this—that God had committed to Israel the deposit, not indeed of a perfect religion, but of one which, by wonderfully varied means of the Divine selection, both could and would be developed into a religion adapted for all nations; that, as long as political independence was necessary for this object, Jehovah would preserve His people without its having to condescend to statecraft ("perverseness and crookedness," as it is called in Isa. xxx. 12 [1]), and that when it ceased to be required, God would still preserve the moral and spiritual independence of Israel as He preserved its forefathers in Egypt, and consequently that Israel's true interest lay in dutifully co-operating with its Divine Guide.

The rejoinder would be, I repeat, a true one; and yet we must not be unjust to the politicians, who thoroughly acted out their own idea of patriotism, and who were in their own sense religious men. Was not Hezekiah himself at one time tempted to rely too much on a human alliance (Isa. xxxix.), and was not a king (Azariah or Uzziah), who is only less commended by the historian than Hezekiah, the prime mover in a Syrian coalition against Tiglath-Pileser II.?[2] Certainly the temptation to rely on the arts of the politician was not less at this part of Josiah's reign than under his great ancestors. Decay had begun in the blood-cemented empire of Assyria even before the death of Assurbanipal, and this cannot have been unknown to the "intelligence department" of the Jewish court. It was owing to this that, as the second chapter of Jeremiah shows us, the philo-Egyptian party (comp. Isa. xxx 2, xxxi. 1) had supplanted the philo-Assyrian one in the councils of the sovereign. We see from this that, whatever the personal inclinations of Josiah and his nearest friends might be, he was not as yet sufficiently independent to strike out a line for himself; and we may observe

[1] See the "Variorum Bible" on the passage.

[2] This is at any rate accepted by Schrader, and regarded as probable by the cautious Tiele in his "Babylonisch-Assyrische Geschichte," part 1 (Gotha, 1886), pp. 230, 231.

HOPES AND FEARS QUICKLY REALIZED.

in this connection that already in the narrative of his call Jeremiah speaks of the *kings of Judah* (i. 18), *i.e.* perhaps the large and influential royal family which seems to have shared the important governmental function of judgment with the reigning king (xvii. 20, comp. xxi. 11, 12.

Thus the facts implied in Jeremiah's second chapter cast a bright light on the quiescent attitude of the reforming party at this period. It is evident that the " sign," for which, as we saw in chap. ii., the reformers must have been looking, had not yet been given, and that people were generally prosperous, and went on with their quaint medley of religious rites, trusting that Jehovah, at any rate, had no longer any complaint against them. As Jeremiah puts it—

Thou saidst, I am innocent; surely his anger hath turned from me (ii. 35).

Some, I am aware, have found a precisely opposite statement in *vv.* 14–17, where the past tenses retained in the Revised Version are no doubt substantially correct. But though these verses may be a later interpolation, as Ewald holds, due, perhaps, to a disciple of the prophet's, it seems to me perfectly possible to explain them as a vivid, dramatic description of the almost inevitable calamity which hung over Judah. " Prophetic perfects " (see Driver, "Hebrew Tenses," pp. 21–25) are common enough, and passages like iv. 14, vi. 8, warn the reader not to take the description too prosaically (for chaps. iv.–vi. form a group of prophecies).

I will not linger further on this chapter, and only remark that it opens a welcome view of the Biblical training of the youthful Jeremiah. The great prophets of the eighth and following centuries were no "untaught geniuses." Hence, Jeremiah, like his fellows, is fond of borrowing ideas and phrases from older writers; this very chapter presents numerous points of contact with that fine song (Deut. xxxii.) of unknown authorship, enshrined, by a singular good fortune, in the Book of Deuteronomy. It formed no part of that Book of the Law which one of the Hilkiahs, as we shall see, brought to light, but is an independent Scripture, though for centuries covered over, as it were, by Deuteronomy, very much as that book itself is said to have been found by Hilkiah covered over in a corner of the temple. I think, however, that Jeremiah is, in one respect, the superior of his nameless predecessor; he treats his countrymen more tenderly, more sympathetically. Not tenderly enough, perhaps, as we should think, and yet with a wonderful amount of sympathy, if we compare his first prophecy (if chap. ii may be called such) with the Song attached to Deuteronomy, and indeed with the works of any of the prophets who went before him, except Hosea. It was the gospel which opened wide the floodgates of truly *humane* sympathy; but Jeremiah, in spite of the relics of antique sternness which still cling to him, has a tender fellow-feeling with his people, which may be compared to the first delicate streaks of advancing dawn. Surely God chose him out precisely because he was cast in this softer mould, even as He chose out Hosea to be the prophet of the decline and fall of the kingdom of Israel. And why? Because there is no chance of an audience for the prophet of woe, if no sound of a stifled sob strikes the ear; would our own Carlyle have influenced the last generation as he did, if men had not felt that underneath that rough exterior there beat the warmest and most sympathetic of hearts?

That Jeremiah was fond of Hosea's book is certain; the touching words which open chap. ii. are closely parallel to a passage in Hosea (ii. 15). A happy instinct guided him; he felt himself allied in genius to the elder prophet; and he must have noticed how similar his own circumstances were to those of Hosea. I will not, however, exaggerate this similarity. Jeremiah had a harder fate than Hosea in this respect, that whereas Hosea was always able to look with some degree of hope to Judah, in Jeremiah's days the last remnant of Jehovah's people seemed swiftly nearing destruction.[1]

It is true that Providence still has an eye upon Judah; both the guilty sisters shall yet dwell together as favoured children of Jehovah (iii. 18); but we may be sure that to the increased severity of the judgment upon Judah, there corresponds a deeper gloom in the mind of its prophet; Hosea was not tried as severely as Jeremiah.

Altogether this third chapter deserves an attentive and sympathetic study. There seems to me no reason why criticalness and sympathy should not be combined in the same reader. Let me then point out some phenomena which might escape an uncritical reader. The chapter begins (as the margin of the Revised Version rightly states) with the word *saying*—evidently

---

[1] Ewald, "The Prophets of the Old Testament," iii. 68.

a mere fragment of a superscription. Those who know anything about manuscripts (and even the unlearned can easily imagine what I am describing) are aware how apt words, and even sentences, are to get dropped out of the text in the process of transcription; sometimes, too, words and phrases will become illegible, and the scribe who makes his copy from such a manuscript will forget to indicate that there is a gap in his text. Sometimes, moreover, words will get copied into the wrong line, and this seems to have been the case here, the first part of the heading of *v.* 1 having been transposed to *v.* 6. Let us then read *v.* 1 thus,—

And the word of Jehovah came unto me in the days of Josiah the king, saying, &c.

To those who read their Bible as attentively as their Shakespeare or their Virgil, this critical remark will not, I hope, seem trifling. It requires however to be supplemented. Is it possible that verses 4 and 5 were meant to close a section of this, in general, well-arranged group of prophecies? This is how they run in Reuss's version, from which I again quote because of its simple dignity and essential fidelity—

Maintenant, n'est-ce pas ? tu me cries; Mon père ! toi, le fiancé de ma jeunesse ! s'en souviendra-t-il donc toujours ? me gardera-t-il rancune à jamais ? Voilà comme tu parles, tout en faisant le mal, et en y persistant.

I am only considering the passage now in its literary aspect; the facts of history which explain it will come before us later. Notice then from this point of view that such deeply-felt expressions can hardly stand at the end of a prophecy. The divine speaker is wrought to a high pitch of feeling; he is touched by the tender expressions of the personified people of Judah, which indeed correspond to the sweet appeal of Jehovah (quoted, from Reuss's version, in page 22), but knows only too well that they are but unmeaning sounds. And so he begins to expostulate in the style of Isaiah (i. 12), "Why spread out your hands before me. I hate such prayers when coupled with evil practices. With unchanged minds you return home and calmly repeat all the old abominations." Some further development of these ideas is clearly wanted; Jeremiah is not without the instincts of an artist, and does not leave his finest *motifs* only half worked out. What we seem to want here is a contrasted picture of Jehovah's lovingkindness to Judah ; then, a renewed expression of horror at Judah's infidelity ; and then, a picture either of the almost inevitable judgment, or (for Jeremiah has in him a strong dash of the emotionalism of Hosea) of the final conversion of heart which God's people must and will in His own good time experience. This is the close which verses like iii. 1–5 lead us to expect, and there actually is a passage which exactly meets our requirements ; only it is separated from verses 1–5 by another passage which the editor (a disciple of Jeremiah's ?) seems to have inserted here to illustrate the hopes held out in verses 21 and 22, and so give a more complete answer to the question, *Will he keep (anger) for ever (v. 5)?*[1]

Observe first of all the contrast,—

Moi, j'avais dit : Comme je te mettrai parmi mes enfants ! Je te donnerai un pays de délices, un patrimoine magnifique, le plus excellent qu'ait un peuple ! Je disais : Vous m'appellerez père, et vous ne vous détournerez pas de moi (iii. 19).

Next, the horror at Judah's surprising infidelity (does not *house of Israel* here include Judah? comp. ii. 4, 26)—

Eh oui ! Comme une femme devient infidèle à son amant, ainsi vous l'avez été a moi, maison d'Israel, parole de l'Eternel (iii. 20).

See how deeply the Divine speaker has been hurt ! He refuses the word used by Judah in *v.* 4 (comp. Prov. ii. 17), which expresses the intimate friendship between husband and wife, and substitutes another, already used by Hosea (iii. 1), and indeed by himself in verse 1, to describe a superficial and illegitimate attachment. Of course *house of Israel* in this verse must be taken to *include* Judah.

Lastly, the graphic description of the genuine heart-conversion in the days to come, which reminds us of the picturesque *tableau* in chap. xxxi. Here, however, I must desert Reuss's version, and venture on an English rendering—

Hark ! there is a sound upon the heights, tears and entreaties of the children of Israel, because they have perverted their way, have forgotten Jehovah their God. " Return, backsliding children ; I will heal your backslidings." " Behold, we are come unto thee ; for thou art Jehovah our God" (iii. 21, 22).

---

[1] In this view I mainly follow Stade, "Zeitschrift für die alttestamentliche Wissenschaft," 1884, p. 151, &c.

But gloomy indeed did the immediate prospect of Judah appear to the young prophet—so much so that in the prophecy which extends from iii. 6 to iii. 18 he announces on the part of Jehovah—

Backsliding Israel hath shewn herself more righteous than treacherous Judah (iii. 11),

and, more astonishingly still, invites the backslider to return with the tender assurance—

I will not knit my brow at you, for I am full of lovingkindness, saith Jehovah, I will not keep (anger) for ever . . . . Return, backsliding children, saith Jehovah, for I am a husband unto you: and I will take you one of a city and two of a family and will bring you to Zion [1] (iii. 12, 14).

As I have already said, I regard the prophecy from which these quotations are taken as distinct from iii. 1-5 and 19-25. It may have been written at the same period as the latter, but it has some noteworthy differences, *e.g.*, that the future is described in still more attractive terms, and with a singular spirituality; also that the phrase *backsliding children*, which in verse 22 refers to Judah (*v.* 21 compared with *v.* 2 proves this—note the phrase *the heights* in both), in verse 14 evidently refers to the northern Israel. We must remember that "backsliding" (both adjective and substantive) is a favourite word of Jeremiah's (see ii. 19; iii. 6, 8, 11, 12, 14, 22; v. 6; viii. 5; xiv. 7; xxxi. 22; xlix. 4) the different use of such a phrase need not therefore surprise us. I may remark too that the word forms another link between Jeremiah and Hosea. And so we get an answer to a question which may have troubled some readers, viz., Had Jeremiah really such grave cause for complaint against Judah? I mean that the idea of "backsliding" occurred naturally to idealistic teachers like the prophets—to Hosea not less than Jeremiah, and to Jeremiah before as well as after the year of the great reformation. I think, however, that both the prophecies which together make up chap. iii. received a heightened colouring, if indeed they were not altogether put into shape,

---

[1] For "knit my brow" the Hebrew has "cause my countenance to fall" —if we cannot translate a figure, we must substitute a corresponding one for it. "Kind" is, more fully, "rich in lovingkindness" (*khésed*—the bond of the covenant-relation between Jehovah and Israel).

subsequently to the eighteenth year of Josiah, though based on Jeremiah's notes or recollections of his pre-reformation activity.

I must now pass on to another portion of the first great group of prophecies, viz., chapters iv. and vi., from which we may, I think, infer that the looked-for "sign" from heaven came at last, encouraging the reformers to take up their task in earnest. Who has not heard of Attila and the Huns, and the horror excited by these fierce barbarians among the civilized peoples of the Roman Empire?[1] A close parallel to this is furnished by the Scythian invasion of Assyria and Babylonia, not to add Palestine, in the early part of the reign of Josiah. Who the Scythians were, what was the order of their desolating inroads and how far they extended, belongs rather to the historian of the ancient East than to the biographer of Jeremiah to discuss. Our knowledge of these subjects depends primarily on the narrative of Herodotus (i. 74, 103-106, iv. 1), the Hebrew historical records being here, as so often, imperfect, and the cuneiform tablets being as yet not fully transcribed and not in all respects satisfactorily explained. That the Scythians, like the Cimmerians, whom, according to Herodotus, they displaced, were originally nomads, is clear; but it is possible that, after having passed the Caucasus, they settled themselves permanently in a province of northern Armenia called Sacasene (from Sacœ the Persian name of the Scythians, Herod. vii. 64), and made this their headquarters during their later ravages. Gugu, a chief of "the land of Saḫi," captured by Assurbanipal,[2] may, as some think, have been a Scythian prince; and it is an attractive view which connects *Gog, the prince of Magog* (Ezek. xxxviii. 2, 3) with this Gugu. At any rate, there is no doubt as to the vast and general subversion which they produced. The powerful kingdom of Urartu (comp. Ararat) henceforth disappeared from history. The Moschi and the Tabali, Assyria's gallant foes, were reduced to a small remnant which took refuge on the mountains by the Euxine Sea,[3] and it is of this apparently that Ezekiel speaks in the following graphic passage, so important for the delineation of the popular view of the underworld—

---

[1] See Gibbon, "Decline and Fall of the Roman Empire," chap. xxxiv., and notice his parallel of the Mongols.

[2] "Annals of Assurbanipal," cyl B, "Records of the past," ix 46

[3] See Lenormant, "Les origines de l'histoire," ii 1, pp 458-461, cf Schrader, "Keilinschriften und Geschichtsforschung," p 159.

HOPES AND FEARS QUICKLY REALIZED. 31

There is Meshech, Tubal, and all its multitude round about its grave; all of them unclad, slain by the sword, who caused terror in the land of the living. And they lie not with heroes, giants of the olden time, who went down to Sheól in full armour, with their swords put under their heads, and their shields upon their bones, for there was terror at their prowess while they lived (Ezek. xxxii. 26, 27).[1]

Province after province of the civilized and semi-civilized East was visited by this *crashing storm* (Ezek. xxxviii. 9). The incredibly fertile plains of Mesopotamia were laid waste. Towns and villages which had not the protection of walls were pillaged and destroyed (comp. Ezek. xxxviii. 11); only well-defended cities could defy the attacks of the bold Scythian *archers* (Ezek. xxxviii. 15, comp. Herod. iv. 46). The wave of ruin swept along Palestine by the coast-road to the borders of Egypt. That most ancient temple of Aphrodite at Ashkelon, of which the lately-discovered temple at Cythera was a copy, was plundered (Herod. 1 105). Psamitik (Psammetichus) only averted an invasion of Egypt by "gifts and prayers." Did the little country of Judah remain unscathed? If Hitzig and Ewald are right in finding allusions to the Scythians in the Psalter (the former refers Psalms xiv. and lv., the latter Psa. lix., to this period), we must answer in the negative. This view, however, is not a good specimen of the critical tact of these eminent scholars, and Knobel has very naturally included this in a too bitter indictment of this faulty though never-to-be-forgotten leader of thought (See *Expositor*, 3rd series, vol. iv., p. 263). The obvious inference from the narrative of Herodotus is that Judah was in the main exempt from injury. The highlands of Judah were protected by nature, besides which the Scythians knew well enough where to make the most productive conquests. It is probable however that straggling parties turned aside inland. The fertile plain of Sharon, studded with villages on their little *tels* or eminences, must surely have suffered, especially as the road swerved from the coast-line at some distance to the north of Joppa. Here the straight way was barred by a thick forest called Assur,[2] well known as late as crusading times, for it was

[1] I follow Cornill's corrected text.

[2] See Maspero in the "Album" of Egyptological papers published in honour of Dr. Leemans.

at this point that Cœur-de-Lion overcame Saladın in a great battle on Sept. 7, 1191, under the walls of Arsuf, the ancient Apollonia. Some (after Pliny and Syncellus) have found a trace of their presence in the name Scythopolis (= Beth-shean, a finely-situated town, now Beisan, on the edge of the cliffs which descend from the Wady Jalûd to the Ghor). Even if this be not a corruption of Sıkytopolis (city of Siccuth), we surely cannot venture to connect it with *these* Scythians.[1]

One thing at least is more than probable—that two faithful servants of the *true* Jehovah were called to be prophets when the danger from the Scythians began to loom in the horizon. One was Zephaniah, whose short book seems based on the prophet's notes of his discourses during the terrible crisis. We cannot help turning over its pages, for they illustrate passages of Jeremiah; for us at least, Zephaniah is not a "minor prophet." This, then, is what he says, *Be still*, for the judgment is irrevocably fixed; *yea, Jehovah hath already prepared the sacrifice, hath consecrated his invited ones* (Zeph. i. 7; comp. Isa. xiii. 3; Jer. li. 27, 28, where *prepared* in the Revised Version should be *consecrated*, as in Isa. *l.c.*; see also Isa. xxxiv. 6, Jer. xlvi. 10). *The great day of Jehovah*, he adds, *is near; it is near and hasteth greatly* (Zeph. i. 14)—a passage which to us has a special interest, because this and the following verse partly suggested the famous hymn of Thomas of Celano, beginning *Dies iræ, dies illa*. There are those in Judah, our prophet tells us, who have hitherto known neither shame nor fear; surely these cannot but tremble now at the imminent recompence of their heathen wickedness. False Israelites! No better are they than their neighbours; nay, their obduracy makes them still more deserving of punishment. On the other hand, true seekers after Jehovah should go quietly on in the path of obedience, *if perhaps ye may hide yourselves in the day of Jehovah's anger. For Gaza,* he continues, *shall become a desert tract, and Ashkelon a desolation; they shall drive out Ashdod at noonday, and Ekron shall be rooted out* (Zeph. ii. 3, 4). Such was the prophet's anticipation, when the Scythians began their southward march. All the peoples with which they came into contact should have to rue their wickedness; the barbarian

[1] Its population was predominantly a non-Jewish one (2 Macc xii. 30 ' Jos. "De Bello Jud," ii 18, and "Vit." 6). "Scythian" may mean "barbarian" (comp. 3 Macc. vii. 5; Col. iii. 11).

HOPES AND FEARS QUICKLY REALIZED.

horde was, like Attila, the "Scourge of God." That the prophecy, thus explained, was not fulfilled to the very letter, is no argument against this view; the Book of Jonah is a warning to us not to be surprised if God's dealings with man are gentler sometimes than His threatenings.

Let us notice, before we pass on, Zephaniah's unusually clear perception of the greatness of God's world; in his judicial survey of the peoples known to him, the space allotted to Judah is not more than agrees with its real position among the nations. Also that no measures of reform had as yet been introduced—no plan of action had as yet commended itself to that little band of friends which included (probably) Josiah, the two Hilkiahs, Jeremiah, and to which we may now add the name of Zephaniah. But each member of this upward and forward looking company was being gradually ripened for his own share in the work. Zephaniah's own importance would be doubtless enhanced, if he belonged to one of the branches of the royal family. Is there any ground for such a supposition? Ibn Ezra thinks that there is, and the reader will perhaps agree with him, on looking at the first verse of the Book, in which, contrary to the usual practice, the genealogy is carried up to the fourth generation, and if he observes the name last mentioned—Hizkiah, or, as the Revised Version more consistently gives it, Hezekiah. Truly, *the wind bloweth where it listeth, and thou hearest the sound thereof, but canst not tell whence it cometh nor whither it goeth.* The Spirit of revelation chooses the most unlikely instruments, calls Elisha from the plough, Amos from the herd, Zephaniah (it may be) from the steps of the throne.

And who was the second of the prophets called forth by the danger from the Scythians? The reader will have guessed his name already; it was Jeremiah. Among the minor motives which overcame this prophet's hesitation, one must have been his people's urgent need of an interpreter of the signs of the times. In Judah, as in England now, people were only too ready for external and non-moral views of political questions; this was the constant trouble of Isaiah, it became that of Jeremiah. Against the "opportunism" of the statesmen he directs the weapons of his sarcasm. *Why gaddest thou about so much*, he says, *to change thy way* (thy policy, as we should say)? *Thou shalt be ashamed of Egypt also, as thou wast ashamed of Assyria* (Jer ii. 36). Not from Egypt, not from Assyria,—unable soon to help themselves—shall the great wind come which shall smite the four corners of the house, so that it falls[1] (Job. i. 19). From another and a more energetic race, *ever replenished* (in Jeremiah' language—see v. 15) from a secret store of vitality, the new dangers will arise. Like some mighty perennial stream, or (to quote again from the opening vision) like the contents of a caldron (Jer. 1 14), will "the evil" come. *For lo, I will call all the families of the kingdoms of the north, said Jehovah, and they shall come* (Jer. i. 14, 15; comp. iv. 6, vi. 1). We see, however dimly, that, as the punishment of accumulated sins, some new and more awful enemies are threatened, and when we consult the pages of history, we cannot doubt that these are, first the Scythians, and next the Chaldæans. The phrase (if I am not mistaken) was selected *after* the course of history had sharpened the prophet's eye to understand his remembered vision better—selected in order to include both the Scythians and the Chaldæans. "The north" had long since been marked out as the great arsenal from which God drew forth first one weapon of vengeance and then another. To Isaiah it suggested the Assyrians (Isa. xiv. 31); to Jeremiah the not less destructive nations who continued their work.[2] First, however, the Scythians. Surely it is of these dread ministers of judgment that our prophet speaks with emotional exaggeration in language such as the last man might employ, on the morning of the great doomsday,—

"*I saw the earth—it was a waste Chaos; and heavenwards—the light thereof was gone, I saw the mountains—they trembled, and all the hills moved to and fro; I saw—mankind had disappeared, and all the birds of the heaven had flown. I saw—the garden-land (had become) desert, all the cities thereof had been broken down,[3] because of Jehovah, because of his hot anger.*

[1] That Job is a "parable" was early seen (see "Job and Solomon," p. 61). The great sufferer may be poetically individualized, but he is more than a common man—he is a symbol, not merely of afflicted humanity, but of Israel.

[2] How elastic the symbol was, appears from Jer. xlvii. 1, where a clause inserted by the editor (*before Pharaoh smote Gaza*) suggests that he understood the *waters from the north* (v. 2) to mean the army of Neco on its southward journey to Egypt.

[3] I do not say that this feature of the description applies to the Scythians. Jeremiah adapted his prophesies respecting the Scythians to the later Chaldæan crisis, just as he adapted to it the older prophecy against Moab, preserved in Isa. xv, xvi, and the old poem in Num. xxi. 27-30 (see Jer. xlviii.) See pp 40, 41.

... *At the noise of horsemen and bowmen the whole land fleeth; they go into thickets, and climb up upon rocks, every city is forsaken, and not a man dwelleth therein* (Jer. iv. 23-26, 29).

But I must not linger on this interesting theme. Suffice it to add here a sentence which has struck me in reading (since the above was written) the posthumous revised edition of vol. iv. of Lenormant's " Histoire de l'Orient," published in 1885 with the friendly aid of a disciple of the lamented Assyriologist (M. Babelon),—

" Quand on lit, dans les premiers chapitres de Jérémie, une description de ces hordes de barbares qui se ruèrent sur la Palestine comme sur la Mésopotamie, on croirait assister à une invasion des soldats de Gengis ou de Tamerlan, dont les Cimmériens sont d'ailleurs les ancêtres " (p. 379).

There is nothing arbitrary, then, in what the preceding pages have offered as a reconstruction of a half-forgotten chapter in the history of Judah. From every point of view, it is clear that we have arrived at a new epoch, and if Zephaniah can claim the distinction of being its earliest prophet, Jeremiah has still the superiority in the richness and variety of his subject-matter. The transformation of the timid, sensitive Jeremiah evidently began at once. A marvellous maturity strikes us even in the opening chapters of his book, and though these, in their present form, may reflect a later stage of his experience, yet the maturity visible may in part be attributed to his Spirit-led meditations before his call came. Jeremiah, then, was a reformer even before Josiah's great reformation.

What a hope it gives us both for ourselves and others when we see how much the Spirit of revelation made of Jeremiah! I spoke of some of the unlikely agents of that Spirit among the prophets who preceded him. But who can have seemed more unlikely than Jeremiah? Who of Josiah's little band could have expected to see his timid friend occupying any prominent position? He at least, it might have been said, was of too soft a nature to lead, and too sympathetic by far to endure the strain of prophesying in an age which was growing tired of prophets. He *was* perhaps too soft to take the lead in action, and perhaps without the example of Zephaniah that sensitive shrinking from the acknowledged call of duty might have even more resembled the agony of Gethsemane. Mysterious are the ways of the Spirit ; an electric spark often seems to pass from one to another in a company of young men, and so perhaps it was with Zephaniah and Jeremiah. *And there appeared unto them tongues parting asunder, like as of fire; and it sat upon each of them* (Acts ii. 2).

To those who have followed me thus far, the form and bearing of the man underneath the prophet's mantle have, I hope, become somewhat more real than before. He has none of the so-called apathy of the Stoic; he may use bold words at the risk of life, but he does so with quivering lips. Even in the solemn hour of his consecration, he has had sore misgivings, and would gladly have made way for a stronger man. But one of his chief qualifications is precisely his sense of weakness; he needs no *thorn in the flesh* to make him pray to be clothed upon with Divine strength. He is not a hero by nature, but by grace; and in his sometimes strange confessions we clearly read that grace never expelled nature. His life is at once the most natural and the most supernatural in the Old Testament. Let us then be patient even with ourselves; God is better than our fears, and more generous than our highest hopes, if in base cowardice we do not shrink back from His call.

CHAPTER IV.

MORNING-CLOUD GOODNESS.

The crisis and its effects—Religious reaction.

WE have seen in the preceding chapter that in the early part of the reign of Josiah a great migration of peoples took place ; first of all the Cimmerians, and then the Scythians (who in the Babylonian inscriptions are called Gimirrai[1]—a name more properly belonging to the Cimmerians) spread ruin and desolation through the fairest countries of Asia. The latter of these two barbarian hordes even violated the sacred land of Jehovah. Can we doubt that the prophets on their watch-towers were keenly alive to the danger? Nothing but a dread of admitting unfulfilled predictions can have prevented some critics of the last and the present generation from recognizing the light which these facts of history throw upon the language of the two contemporary prophets—Zephaniah and Jeremiah. The limits of this volume prevent me from entering into the question of the relation of prediction to fulfilment. Again and again, however, the expositor is obliged by the force of truth to state facts which conclusively demonstrate that "it is not fate that presides over prophecy, nor does fatality follow it."[2] Prophecy is simply the declaration and illustration of the principles of the divine government sometimes in the past, sometimes in the present, sometimes in the future. The illustrations, however, are always inferior in strict accuracy to the principles, and among the

---

[1] Schrader, "Keilinschriften und Geschichtsforschung," p. 150 ; Lenormant, "Les origines de l'histoire," ii. 1, p. 547.

[2] Edersheim, "Prophecy and History in Relation to the Messiah," p. 153.

illustrations those which have to do with the circumstances of the hour are more implicitly to be trusted than those which have to do with the past and with the future. Zephaniah and Jeremiah were prophets in the sense which I have described, and their expositor is not to be tied down by the mistaken theories of dull and unsympathetic theologians.

So far, then, as we know for certain, the only one of the nations of Palestine upon which the threats of Zephaniah were at all fulfilled was Philistia (Herod. i. 105); and it is but a probable guess that Judah, so earnestly warned both by Zephaniah and by Jeremiah, suffered somewhat from the returning Scythians. God, who had stretched out His hand over His guilty land as if to annihilate it, withdrew it, as it seems, after (at most) a very mild chastisement. That Zephaniah and Jeremiah did not foresee this, does not detract from their prophetic character. God meant them to make the utmost use of a very real danger to Judah in teaching and admonishing their people. It was certain to both that the national sins must be followed by an awful national judgment, and Jeremiah especially went on, like Evangelist in the "Pilgrim's Progress," urging his countrymen to flee from the wrath to come. Like the wise men to whom we owe the canonical proverbs, like the Rabbis their successors, and above all like "the Master" Himself, he did not disdain the homeliest illustrations. It is a condensed parable, borrowed from his favourite Hosea (Hos. x. 12), with which he begins the prophecy of the northern invasion in chap. iv.[1],—

For thus saith Jehovah to the men of Judah and to Jerusalem,
Plough for yourselves fallow ground, and sow not among thorns.

It is needless to explain this illustration; one might take it for a scene from our Lord's Parable of the Sower. Doubtless it is but a condensed note of a more elaborate and pointed discourse, like that with which Isaiah concludes one of *his* great warning prophecies (Isa. xxviii. 23-29). Both regard agriculture, in the spirit of primitive times, as derived from the manifold wisdom of God, who *doth instruct him* (the husbandman) *aright, and doth teach him* (Isa. xxviii. 26 R.V.). *Sow not among the thorns*, says the prophet, implying that his hearers

---

[1] This chapter ought to begin at verse 3, verses 1 and 2 belong to the preceding prophecy.

were doing so at the time. He had at length joined Zephaniah in announcing the approach of the instrument of God's wrath. The preaching based on the terrors of judgment seems to have produced some result. In iii. 4 (see p. 27) Judah personified is represented as *from this time* addressing Jehovah by the most endearing of titles. We may be sure that the little band of highminded and likeminded friends to which Jeremiah himself belonged had tried, each in his own circle, to call forth a fitting spirit of contrition and amendment. Could the efforts of these good men be absolutely and entirely resultless? Consider for a moment the great spiritual forces laid up at the outset in the people of Israel, to which, through Jehovah's lovingkindness, was due a long succession of inspired men taken from the ranks of the people. Could these forces be entirely spent? No; the good spiritual elements inherited from far-off ancestors had doubtless been impaired by the adverse influences of Canaan, Assyria, and Egypt—endangered, but not entirely destroyed. And so a certain amount of moral reformation must have been produced, and, we infer from Jeremiah, was actually produced through the efforts of God's servants at this period. But it was too much like the reformation of which Hosea speaks in northern Israel,—*your goodness is as a morning cloud, and as the dew that goeth early away* (Hos. vi. 4).

Upon shallow and superficial natures, already "choked" with the "thorns" of noxious habits, the most diligent cultivation was thrown away. So Jeremiah came to think; and yet may not the scantiness of the result have been partly due to the style of the prophet's teaching? He had not entirely got beyond the imperfect moral conceptions of Isaiah, who says in effect in his opening discourse (Isa. i. 15-17), "Wash you, make you clean, and then God will hearken to your prayers," implying that the sinner himself can nip his evil inclinations in the bud—can, by his native strength, "cease to do evil" and "learn to do well." Jeremiah in iv. 3, 4 speaks like Isaiah. In other passages indeed he approaches the point of view of the Fifty-first Psalm. In ii. 22 he says, *Though thou wash thee with lye, and take thee much soap, yet thine iniquity is marked* (*i.e.*, deeply ingrained) *before me, saith the Lord Jehovah;* and in xiii. 23, *Can the Ethiopian change his skin, and the leopard his spots? then may ye also do good, that are trained to do evil.*

But he does not get so far as *Purge me with hyssop, and I shall be clean; wash me, and I shall be whiter than snow* (Psa. li. 7); he even says, not as it would seem ironically, in iv. 14, *O Jerusalem, wash thine heart from wickedness, that thou mayest be saved* (compare the striking language of iv. 4).[1] The reason of this inconsistency is that he has no knowledge as yet of the indwelling of the Spirit of God, which is surely the second half of the Gospel, and which is almost revealed in one of the prophecies attached to the original Book of Isaiah (Isa. lxiii. 11) and in the Fifty-first Psalm (*v.* 11), both written, as I at least must believe, later than the time of Jeremiah.

The results, then, of this earnest but onesided preaching were a bitter disappointment to the prophet. What indeed was the good of a few isolated good actions, as long as the moral bent remained unchanged? Or, to speak parabolically with Jeremiah, How could even a single sheaf of ripe wheat be harvested in a field choked by thorns? And so the prophet, in reproducing the discourses of this period, gives but one verse to (I suppose) the exhortations of many days, and at once passes on to give a most graphic and deeply felt description of the advance of the swarming barbarians, reminding us of a similar picture of the expected advance of the Assyrians in Isa. x. It is possible that at a later stage the prophet of woe became the bearer of the glad tidings of deliverance. To Jeremiah's deeply religious mind, the retirement of the Scythians would appear Jehovah's merciful recognition that there were at least "ten righteous" in the city (Gen. xviii. 32) for whose sakes a brief space was granted for a fuller repentance. Not having a complete collection of Jeremiah's discourses, we are at liberty to guess this. But certain it is, that in finally editing the prophecies which make up chaps. iv. and vi., Jeremiah introduced some new features, and otherwise heightened the colouring of some descriptions, to make them suit later and in reality more dreadful foes—the Chaldæans (see p. 34, note 3). This is in harmony with the manner

---

[1] *Circumcise yourselves to Jehovah*, &c. Is this phrase (with which comp. vi. 10) suggested by Deut x. 16? If so, we must, it would seem, include it among the features (see below) added by the prophet to his earliest discourse some years afterwards. That Jeremiah should adopt the less advanced expression (as compared with the language of Deut xxx. 6), would be in harmony with the acknowledged result of criticism that Deut. xxx. is one of the later additions to the original Deuteronomy.

of the prophets, and indeed of the Jewish writers in general. Jeremiah deals with his own earlier predictions as the authors of the ancient versions, to whom the Bible, as Geiger says, was "no dead book," deal with the Scriptures in general; he works them up anew, or rather "works over" them, to adapt them to later circumstances. That difficulties might arise to readers in remote centuries, did not of course occur to him; Providence has given to each fragment from the pen of prophets and apostles an importance which the writers could not have anticipated. But let us not interpret these in many respects peculiar works as if they were indited yesterday, and as if we had them in their first draft. Let us frankly recognize that they may be susceptible of two interpretations with equal claims on our attention. They are in fact a fusion of kindred historical scenes, to some extent analogous to the fusion of details from two national catastrophes in Psa. lxxix.

It will perhaps make it easier to understand this fusion of prophecies if we remember that, however sharp the agony of this crisis may have been, it cannot have lasted long. The whole period of the Scythian successes must have been much shorter than is stated by Herodotus, if he is right in dating it from the defeat of Cyaxares.[1] At any rate there can have been but a brief interval between Jeremiah's first gloomy forebodings and the withdrawal of Jehovah's chastening hand. It is surely not a misplaced comment that God is at once more loving and more just than finite mortals can be. He "seeth not as man seeth" (Job x. 4), and recognized elements of good which Jeremiah, with his tear-bedimmed eyes, could scarcely notice. He was ready to make allowances ($\epsilon\pi\iota\epsilon\iota\kappa\eta\varsigma$,[2] as the Septuagint of Psa. lxxxvi. 5 has it) for shallow and superficial natures and for inconsistent characters,—for the plants which "forthwith sprung up," but "had no root," or (to quote a feature more parallel to Jeremiah's own words in iv. 3) to those which were "choked" by "the thorns" (Matt. xiii. 5–7). In His lovingkindness He spared Judah and Jerusalem for this time; but in His justice He made use of the Scythians to prepare the chosen instrument for carrying out that bitter purpose of which He

[1] Comp. Meyer, "Geschichte des Alterthums," 1 557, Maspero, "Histoire ancienne des peuples de l'Orient," ed 4, p. 514.

[2] Finely adapted to the $\ddot{a}\pi a\xi$ $\lambda\epsilon\gamma\acute{o}\mu\epsilon\nu o\nu$ *sallākh* (A.V. and R.V. "ready to forgive").

had said, *I have not repented, neither will I turn back from it* (iv. 28)

Assyria and Chaldæa, those two great peoples of the basin of the Euphrates and the Tigris, had long since filled a large place in the minds of the Jews. The former looked upon herself as the queen of nations, but her power had been seriously impaired by her ceaseless wars; the energetic warrior caste, to which its conquests were due, not being replenished (as was the case in Turkey formerly) from outside, declined more and more, and even in Judah her fall had long since been foreseen by the illuminated eye of the prophet Nahum. With no acquired moral justification, and no principle of cohesiveness, the great Assyrian empire could not but fall, not gradually like that of Rome, but with a sudden and terrific crash. To her at least might be applied the prophetic words first uttered at this crisis respecting Jerusalem, *Evil impends from the north and a great ruin* (iv. 1).

But all this is still in the future. At present, to quote an earlier prophet, *behold, joy and gladness, slaying oxen and killing sheep, eating flesh and drinking wine* (Isa. xxii. 13), in the exuberant festivity, not (as in Isaiah's prophecy) of despairing sensualists, but of a people "rejoicing before Jehovah" for all the benefits that He had done unto them. Earnest no doubt were the thanksgivings offered both in the temple at Jerusalem and at the various local sanctuaries. Yes, at the "high places" as well as at the house where Jehovah was "enthroned upon the cherubim"; for in all good faith the Jews must have believed that their moral and religious practices had just received a Divine sanction of the most positive kind. As long as the Scythians were near, the Jews would seem to have listened to Jeremiah, and prompted by alarm to have made certain promises of amendment. *Truly from this time,* says the Divine oracle, *thou criest unto me, My father, (and,) Thou art the bridegroom of my youth* (Jer. iii. 4). Then in terrified accents the Jews inquire, *Will he retain anger for ever ? will he keep it perpetually ? Verily,* the prophet adds from his experience of what actually took place, when the danger was removed, *thou hast spoken (such things), but hast done those evil things effectually* (Jer. iii. 4).

That Jeremiah, in spite of his proneness to take dark views, was disappointed at the heathenish reaction which now set in may be inferred from the extreme bitterness, the *sæva inaignatio*, of the opening words of chap. v.,—*Roam ye through the streets of Jerusalem; look well, take notice, and seek in the broad places thereof, if ye can find a man, if there be any that doeth justice, that seeketh faithfulness; and I will pardon her* (Jer. v. 1). May we not safely regard this as one of those exaggerations to which from his temperament this prophet was peculiarly liable? for surely, if the prophets really warned the Jews of the approach of a judgment, it follows from the withdrawal of the "outstretched hand" that there must have been a few righteous men within the city. God knew better than His servant, and in the course of His providence contradicted the extreme expressions of that passage, which may be compared to the overstatements of Elijah in the wilds of Arabia, and those of the Florentine Elijah—Savonarola, in the earliest period of his reforming activity. Still, we need not hesitate to accept Jeremiah's authority for the less favourable aspect which the popular religion once more assumed. This is how the prophet continues to unburden his mind in chap. v. The first passage testifies to a loosening of the moral bands of society; the second, to the increased opposition offered to the nobler class of prophets. *Jehovah, do not thine eyes look for faithfulness? if thou smitest them, they feel nothing; if thou consumest them, they will not receive correction; they make their face harder than rock, they will not turn* (v. 3).

They have denied Jehovah, and said, "*Not he*[1]; *upon us shall no calamity come, sword and famine we shall not see"; and* "*Those prophets shall become wind; speaker, there is none in them; it shall be done thus unto themselves"* (v. 12).

In fact, it is from this point that we may date the beginning of Jeremiah's long martyrdom. Priests and prophets were now to a great extent united against him and his friends, and *my people*, he sadly says, assuming the person of Jehovah, *love to have it so* (v. 31). The king, however, is not mentioned in this dark chapter, some of the details in which we hesitate to take too literally, although to resolve them into mere allegories

[1] The speakers mean to deny, not the metaphysical existence of Jehovah, but rather His moral government of the world, like the ungodly described in Psa xiv and similar passages. *Not he* means "Not he is the true lord of the world," "Not he is the avenger of the innocent " (cf. the commentators on Psa x. 11, 13, xii. 5, xiv 1)

would destroy half their force.[1] All classes except the highest being described and condemned, one naturally asks, What was Josiah doing? What were his feelings, and what his course of action, on this large accession of strength to the heathenish party?

Surely we cannot doubt that Josiah would gladly have interposed, *had he been able*, and that his feelings were those of alarm and shame. It is true that he had hitherto deliberately tolerated the old religious customs ("high places" and all that they involved), which, in so far as they merely indicated deficient religious insight, may not have seemed to him as unmitigatedly evil as they did to the later historian. Let us remember that to the student of religions the customs which would be odiously repulsive if reintroduced become full of meaning, and therefore relatively excusable in the light of antiquity. Josiah was not a critical student, but he may well have understood the traditions of his people better than the vehement Jeremiah, and have known or believed that certain of them were still to some extent the manifestations of a naive and sincere piety. On the other hand, there were other customs which must have appeared to him as pernicious morally as they did to Jeremiah, especially those which, like the custom of child-sacrifice, had but recently been introduced into the popular religion. This expression may perhaps be criticised. Readers of Dr. Kuenen's "Religion of Israel" must well remember the powerful passage in which he sums up the evidence for the survival of human sacrifices among the Israelites (vol. i, p. 237). But the utmost that this great critic can prove is the possibility that sporadic cases of human sacrifice occurred in early times. In the same connexion he quotes Mic. vi. 7,—

> *Shall I give my firstborn for my transgression,*
> *The fruit of my body for my personal sin?*

The author of Mic. vi., vii., however, is, regarded from a religious point of view, one of the precursors of Deuteronomy (comp. Mic. vi. 8 with Deut. x. 12), and, from a historical one,

---

[1] It is certain that the customs which were bound up with the reactionary Baal-worship were profoundly immoral (see my notes on Hos iv 11-14 in the "Cambridge Bible") But *v* 7, according to the best reading, runs—... *though I made them to swear (allegiance to me), yet they committed adultery*, (comp. Psa lxxiii. 27), which favours at least a partial reference to a relapse into heathenish religion.

contemporary with an influx of idolatry and a bitter persecution such as only occurred in the reign of Manasseh (see my "Micah," p. 14). Child-sacrifice was, as I have said, a recent importation, and surely it is even more shocking to natural feelings of humanity than the hewing of Agag in pieces before Jehovah which was permitted in the rude age of Samuel. Is there any evidence that child-sacrifice was ever a distinctively Israelitish practice? Phœnician, Arabian, and Babylonian, it undoubtedly was;[1] but we must not too hastily assume that it was known to all the Semitic tribes before their separation. The influence of Babylonia and Assyria upon the Semitic East was vast long after that prehistoric event. As the Babylonians borrowed this cruel rite from the "Accadians," so did the Phœnicians and (if I am not mistaken) the Arabians from the Babylonians. Remember too that I am now speaking of the comparatively pure religion brought by the tribes of Israel from the desert of the wanderings; what their more distant ancestors may conceivably have practised is not germane to my subject. It is with good reason that a late chronicler says of Ahaz that he *made his son* (or, as the Septuagint in Lucian's recension gives, *his sons*, τοὺς υἱοὺς αὐτοῦ, comp. 2 Chron. xxviii. 3) *pass through the fire, according to the abominations of the nations whom Jehovah had expelled before the children of Israel*[2] (2 Kings xvi. 3). That

[1] Sayce, "Hibbert Lectures" (1887), p 78, Wellhausen, "Skizzen und Vorarbeiten," Heft iii (1887), pp. 112, 113, Baudissin, art. "Moloch," in Herzog's "Encyclopädie," ed. 2, x. 174, 175. Notice the doubtless synonymous Phœnician names, Rešpuyathon and Malikyathon, in which Rešper is the name of the heavenly Fire-god and Malik=Moloch, *i e*, "king of heaven" It may be observed in passing that it is doubtful whether Malik, Melech, Molech, or Moloch (we may adopt which form we please) can strictly be called a *proper* name of the great heaven-god For the horror at child-sacrifices felt in a humane age, see the end of Plutarch's treatise on Superstition.

[2] Baudissin, in the article already referred to, thinks that the custom of appeasing the god Molech (Sept, Moloch) by sacrifices of children probably began before Ahaz, though from some unknown cause the cult of Moloch became specially prevalent in and after the time of that king This view he supports by the virtual identification of Molech or Moloch with Baal in Jer. xix. 5, xxxii. 35. He rightly denies that the phrase "to cause to pass through the fire" can be used of mere fiery lustrations. Doubtless, however, the children were *slain* before the fire-rite was performed upon them (see Ezek. xvi. 20, 21, xxiii. 39, and comp. Isa lvii. 5, Psa cvi. 37, 38).

very narrative and that very law to which reference has been made conclusively show that when they were written, or rather when the traditional story in the one and the custom which lies at the root of the other became current (this takes us back to a still earlier period), these horrible child-sacrifices were not approved by the general consciousness of Israel; the ram in Gen. xxii. is a *substitute* for Isaac, and the firstborn of man in a well-known law (Ex. xiii. 13) was to be *redeemed* In contradistinction to Ahaz, it is recorded of Josiah that he *walked in all the way of David his father* (2 Kings xxii. 2), and the primitive simplicity of David's religion (see 1 and 2 Samuel) must not blind us to its comparative refinement.[1] I think, then, that I have not claimed too much for Josiah. If his friend Jeremiah has a "fear and love of God's holy name" which contrasts so "amazingly" with the low type of religion prevalent in Israel, and by this contrast, as Colenso has said,[2] convince us of his inspiration, can we doubt that Josiah, true son of David as he was, and even in youth a "seeker after the God of David" (2 Chron. xxxiv. 3), felt as truly, though not quite as warmly, as Jeremiah, and that he cast many a look of horror on what the prophet calls the *way of Israel in the valley* (Jer. viii. 23)? If even for us the picturesque scenery of the glen of Hinnom ("moaning" is a suggestive even if not an undoubtedly correct rendering) is spoiled by the awful memories of Moloch's religion, how much keener must have been the feelings of one who lived in the midst of the still uncertain struggle against its abominations! I admit the difficulty which arises. If these were really Josiah's sentiments, why did he lose a moment in extinguishing the horrid rites of "the Topheth"?[3] So we may naturally ask, but, as I suggested above, it is doubtful whether he had the power to do so. If the present ruler of Egypt could

[1] Can we fairly say, with Kuenen, that "David, at the instigation of the Gibeonites, seeks to avert Yahveh's anger by the death of seven of Saul's progeny" ("Religion of Israel," i. 237)? Doubtless he is not shocked by the impalement of Saul's descendants as we should have been, but, believing that the guilt of bloodshed lay upon his people, could he have acted otherwise than he did? It was not a sacrifice but an act of vengeance which the Gibeonites performed.

[2] Colenso, "On the Pentateuch," part v, p 300.

[3] See Jer xix. 13, *the place of the Topheth* (i e, according to a common but doubtful etymology, "the abomination," *lit*, "the object of spitting," comp. Job xvii 6).

with difficulty be persuaded that it was safe to venture on a somewhat similar step,[1] how can a king of Judah, who was by no means an absolute sovereign, be blamed for his backwardness?

So much, at least, is certain, that Josiah and his friends must have had a sad life. Disappointed once already, they had nothing to expect from the future but still more bitter disappointments, if they attempted the smallest reform in their own strength. Meantime the good old Israelitish character was in danger of a sad transformation. Must not the frenzy of nature-worship in course of time intoxicate the unhappy devotees, and assimilate them to the impure and cruel character of their Phœnician neighbours? Yes, it must do so; Judah has sinned worse than Israel (Jer. iii.), and must be punished, both inwardly and outwardly—inwardly, by being given over to moral degeneracy, and outwardly by being cast off from the land which she has defiled. But in a strange and unlooked for way one more chance is to be offered her; for the sake of "ten righteous men" the city is to be spared for a while, if so be the covenant between Jehovah and Israel can on man's side be renewed.

[1] The abolition of the *dôseh*, or trampling upon a human causeway, which Tewfik always abhorred as "an inhuman rite" (see Butler, "Court Life in Egypt") Comp Miss Edwards, "A Thousand Miles up the Nile," p 707, and (for the same usage at Beirut) Thomson, "The Land and the Book," p 156.

CHAPTER V.

"HE THAT SEEKETH, FINDETH."

The finding of the book of Divine instruction—The national covenant—
Jeremiah, a preacher of Deuteronomy.

LET us now transport ourselves in imagination to the year 622 (or 621) B C.—the eighteenth year of the reign of Josiah, and try to realize the religious condition of the people of Judah. Beyond question, they were " servants of Jehovah," but their Jehovah (I speak of the mass of the people) was simply the supreme deity in a Pantheon, and had insensibly adopted the characteristics of the Canaanitish Baal. All through these eighteen years no forward movement had been made, in spite of the genial atmosphere of peace which, since the retreat of the Scythians, seemed to invite a closer attention to religious culture. How much there was that needed reform ! The most honoured sanctuary of Jehovah was still polluted by idolatrous polytheistic emblems. Altars still smoked both to Him and to other divinities " under every green tree and upon every high hill." Children were still sacrificed to the cruel Fire-god in the torrent-valleys like that of Hinnom " under the clefts of the rocks." Worship was still offered to the host of heaven upon the housetops, while at every street-corner in the larger towns there were shrines of Jehovah or Baal or the " queen of heaven."[1]

[1] See Jer. ii. 20, 28, iii. 6, 13, vii. 17, 18, xi 13, xix. 13, and comp. 2 Kings xxiii. 4-15 For the child-sacrifices, see Jer. ii. 23, vii 31, xix 5, xxxii 35, and comp Isa lvii. 5. Of the prophecy to which the latter passage belongs, Ewald very justifiably asserts that it (like Mic vi , vii.) transports us into the times of Manasseh, or those immediately following his death, and adds that the piece bears the closest resemblance to the earlier pieces of Jeremiah (" Prophets of the Old Testament," iv. 321).

"HE THAT SEEKETH, FINDETH." 49

Josiah and those who sympathized with him had still to endure these painful sights and sounds, for no plan of reform had, according to our chronological notices, as yet commended itself to the practical mind of the king. Such was the state of affairs, when a lightning-flash all at once illuminated the scene. A messenger had been sent by Josiah to the temple on business connected with the repairs of the building. Nearly two and a half centuries ago the sacred building had been efficiently restored by Joash, the account of whose work is placed in designed parallelism (compare the two descriptions[1]) to that of Josiah. We are not told what the circumstances were which led to the new restoration; but we must conjecture that they bore a close relation to the gradually progressing though not publicly recognized reform-movement. The messenger himself was Shaphan, the scribe or chancellor, also known as the father of Jeremiah's patron Gemariah (Jer. xxxiv. 10, 19, 25), and grandfather of the equally friendly Micaiah (Jer. xxxvi 11-13). We shall have to refer to him again; he was evidently one of the adherents of a progressive or spiritual religion. At present we must accompany him to his royal master, and watch the effect of the tidings which he bears from the temple, where a discovery has just been made by Hilkiah the priest. It is a book which has been found, containing directions on religious and moral points which cut at the root of many popular customs and practices. The name which Hilkiah gives to it is "the book of *tōrāh*" (*i.e*, of Divine direction or instruction); the narrator himself calls it "the covenant book" (2 Kings xxiii. 2). The Chronicler, however, gives it a fuller title—"the book of Jehovah's *tōrāh* given by Moses" (2 Chron. xxxiv. 14), which probably expresses the meaning of the earlier narrator. For certainly it *was* as a Mosaic production that "the book of *tōrāh*" effected such a rapid success, though not (even according to the compiler of Kings) the whole of what is now called the Pentateuch. There can be no longer any doubt that the book found in the temple was substantially the same as our Book of Deuteronomy. Does the narrative in Kings describe the book as "the book of *tōrāh*" and its stipulations collectively as "the covenant" (2 Kings xxii. 8, xxiii. 3)? These are also phrases of the expanded Book of Deuteronomy (Deut. xxix. 1, 21, xxx. 10, xxxi. 26, &c). Do the king and the

[1] Comp. 2 Kings xii. 4-16, xxii. 3-7.

people pledge themselves *to walk after Jehovah, and to keep his commandments and his precepts and his statutes with all their heart and with all their soul, performing the words of this covenant that are written in this book* (2 Kings xxiii. 3)? The same phrases occur over and over again in Deuteronomy (see Deut. viii. 6, 11, vi. 5, x. 12, 13, iv. 13, xxix. 9). Does Josiah devote himself to the suppression of the local sanctuaries and the centralization of worship? This is also one of the principal aims of the Book of Deuteronomy.

Whenever, therefore, the Old Testament is rearranged for English Bible-students, we may expect that the chapter on the Reformation of Josiah will contain something like the following section :—

And Hilkiah the high priest said to Shaphan the chancellor, I have found the lawbook in the house of Jehovah. And Hilkiah gave the book to Shaphan, and he read it, and came to the king, and told him, Hilkiah the priest hath given me a book. And Shaphan read it before the king.—And among the commandments of the lawbook that Shaphan read before the king were found these words: Hear, O Israel: Jehovah is our God, Jehovah is one; and thou shalt love Jehovah thy God with all thine heart, and with all thy soul, and with all thy might.—Ye shall destroy all the places, wherein the nations which ye dispossess served their gods, upon the high mountains, and upon the hills, and under every green tree; and ye shall tear down their altars, and dash in pieces their standing stones, and burn their Ashérahs (or *emblems of Ashérah*) *with fire; and the graven images of their gods ye shall break down, and shall destroy their name out of that place. Not thus shall ye worship Jehovah your God. But unto the place which Jehovah your God chooseth out of your tribes to put his name there to inhabit it, shall ye seek, and thither shalt thou come; and ye shall bring thither your burnt-offerings and your sacrifices. Thou shalt not plant an emblem of Ashérah, of any kind of tree, beside the altar of Jehovah thy God which thou shalt make thee. Neither shalt thou set thee up a pillar which Jehovah thy God hateth.*

When thou art come into the land which Jehovah thy God giveth thee, thou shalt not learn to do after the abominations of the nations which were before thee. There shalt not be found in thee any that maketh his son or his daughter to pass through the fire, any that useth divination, or an enchanter, or a sorcerer, or a charmer. For these nations which thou dispossessest do hearken unto sorcerers; but for thee Jehovah hath not so ordained. Jehovah thy God shall (continually) raise up for thee a prophet from the midst of thee, of thy brethren, like unto me; unto him shall ye hearken.[1]

I pause here for a moment in the interests of my reader. The future ("shall Jehovah raise") has here a frequentative sense, as in Isa. x. 5, *Against an impious nation am I wont to send him* (not, "will I send him," as A.V. and R.V.). It means "shall from time to time raise," and the verse contains a promise that a prophet in the highest sense (as opposed to the soothsayers just before mentioned) shall never be wanting, and a direction to pay unconditional obedience to such a prophet. It is therefore a grand glorification of the inspired Hebrew (or, shall I say? Mosaic) prophethood which we have before us; not a Messianic prediction, except so far as it indicates that a victorious king was not adequate to God's gracious purposes for Israel and the world, that not only a "Messiah" was requisite but a prophetic mediator to interpret the Divine counsel to man. (It is no objection to this view that xxxiv. 10-12 denies that a prophet ever arose "like unto Moses"; for this passage is not the work of the author of Deuteronomy (see chapter vii.).

And if thou wilt hearken unto the voice of Jehovah thy God, he will set thee on high above all the nations of the earth; but if thou wilt not hearken, then will all these curses come upon thee and overtake thee, until Jehovah have consumed thee from off the land, whither thou goest in to possess it. And when the king heard the words of the lawbook, he rent his clothes.[2]

Such is the only setting in which a Biblical scholar, who, if I may model my phrase on that of Dante,[3]

> . . . 'twixt reverent and free,
> I know not which is more . . .

---

[1] This rearrangement has been judiciously made already for American readers. The title of the book is, "Scriptures Hebrew and Christian, Arranged and Edited for Young Readers as an Introduction to the Study of the Bible." By E T. Bartlett, A M., Dean of the Protestant Episcopal Divinity School in Philadephia, and Ja P. Peters, Ph D, Professor of the Old Test. Languages and Literature in the same school. Vol. I. London, James Clarke & Co, 1886.

[2] 2 Kings xxii. 8-10; Deut. vi. 4, 5, xii. 2-6, xvi 21, 22, xviii. 9-15, xxviii. 15-21.   [3] "Purgatorio," xxiv. 13, 14 Longfellow).

is permitted to place the kernel at least of Deuteronomy (if this somewhat misleading name is still to be used [1]), but not more than this, for the fifth of the so-called "Books of Moses" has most certainly *grown* like the other four. It is too soon to inquire what this "kernel" was; too soon to set forth the probable origin of this earliest part of the book. To our regret, though not to our surprise, the narrator is silent on much which we modern students would like to know. Conversations on this mysterious lawbook must have taken place between the king and his friend the high priest, but they have found no record in history. The narrator only mentions the profound impression which the book at once made upon the king. Was the latter afraid of the curses pronounced upon a persistently disobedient people? So the narrator appears to think. I would rather suppose that a spirit of great hopefulness came upon him, now that the wished-for "sign" from heaven had come, and that his only remaining desire was to ascertain, not whether the pen of Moses wrote, but whether the successors of Moses in the prophetic office guaranteed it to be according to the will of God. He sent therefore to one of those who were specially called to "interpret" that will (Isa. xliii. 27, R.V.). The circumstances of the visit are noteworthy. When a prophecy of woe has to be delivered to Hezekiah, it is Isaiah who visits the king (Isa. xxxix. 3); prophetism and royalty are still almost equal powers in the state. But since Isaiah's death the relation of these two powers has changed. In the present instance, it is a prophetic personage to whom the king sends his ambassadors. It is an interesting but not very important fact [2] that this personage is a woman. Possibly she was selected as being at once of advanced age and high in repute as well with the king as with the people (this qualification would exclude Jeremiah). There were doubtless, as in Ezekiel's time (Ezek. xiii. 17-23), many prophetesses, but not many

---

[1] The name means "repetition of the law"; it is founded on a philological mistake, and assumes a critical view which very many believe to be equally erroneous. The philological mistake referred to is the rendering of Deut. xvii 18, where the Septuagint has "this deuteronomy" (instead of "a copy of this law"). The doubtful critical view is that "Deuteronomy" is later than the rest of the legislation in the Pentateuch.

[2] The later Jews judged otherwise, however, if we may argue from the so called Tomb of Huldah on Mount Olivet.

Huldahs; the rarity of them would with some add to her personal reputation. The prophecy ascribed to Huldah[1] by the later compiler has, for different reasons, been a stumbling-block to students. The moderns have remarked that Josiah went through life in perfect unconsciousness of any dark fate brooding over his people, and that the phraseology is that of later prophecy; the ancients were more puzzled by the statement that Josiah should die *in peace* (some copies of the Septuagint gave *in Jerusalem*—in Salem). The king's next step suggests that he really wished the reforms called for by the lawbook to be the result of a national movement (comp. Isa. xxvii. 9, xxx. 22). The wish was too languid, to judge from the king's subsequent methods, but may he not really have wished to see Isaiah's prophecy fulfilled? At any rate, he summoned an assembly in which the whole nation was duly and fully represented, and which accepted the newly "found" lawbook, as soon as it was read to them, in a form probably shorter than that in which we have received it. Finally all present joined the king in a solemn "covenant," binding themselves to carry out faithfully "the words of this book." The narrative runs thus:

And the king sent, and there were gathered unto him all the elders of Judah and of Jerusalem. And the king went up to the house of Jehovah, and all the men of Judah and all the inhabitants of Jerusalem with him, and the priests, and the prophets,[2] and all the people, both small and great; and he read in their ears all the words of the book of covenant[3] which was found in the house of Jehovah. And the king stood on the platform,[4] And he made the covenant before Jehovah, to walk after Jehovah [i.e., to serve no other god], *and to keep his commandments and his testimonies and his statutes, with all his heart and all*

[1] There are coins with the name of Huldah, a Nabatæan queen, the consort of King Aretas Philodemos, a contemporary of Pompeius ("Zeitschr. der d. morgenland. Gesellschaft," xiv. 370, &c.)

[2] Jeremiah, therefore, was present, as we may presume.

[3] That "the book of covenant" is different from that mentioned in Exod. xxiv. 7, needs no showing. Observe that Deuteronomy is entirely silent respecting that covenant-book and its acceptance.

[4] So R V. margin rightly. Some conspicuous place, specially reserved for the king, seems to be meant (comp 2 Kings xi 14) The Hebrew '*ammud* means anything which stands firmly—usually (but not necessarily) a pillar. Josephus has, στὰς ἐπὶ τοῦ βήματος.

his soul, to perform the words of this covenant that are written in this book. And all the people entered into the covenant. And the king commanded all the people, saying, Keep the passover unto Jehovah your God, as it is written in this book of covenant[1] (2 Kings xxiii. 1–3, 21).

But what is meant, the reader will ask, by this word "covenant" (*berith*)? It would take too long to discuss it philologically and exegetically. It means, however, when used in connexion with God, a law to the observance of which certain promises are attached. Looking at the history of Israel from the vantage-ground of Christianity, we may say that it is a history of "covenants." From time to time God has revealed His will to chosen persons, telling them how He would be worshipped, how men should behave themselves to be like their God, and how He would reward them for their faithful obedience. Such a revelation is, in Hebrew phrase, a "covenant." There was a "covenant" with Abraham, with Moses, and, we might analogically say, with each of those prophets who had something really new to declare, such as Hosea and Isaiah and Jeremiah. And now the religious stagnation or retrogression which has prevailed since the time of Micah is all at once interrupted by the ratification of a fresh covenant. Not that either "new" or "fresh" is to be taken literally; there is but one "covenant" between Jehovah and Israel—that of Sinai, and all other covenants are but developments of its meaning. In other words, that "prophet like unto Moses" and his faithful priestly coadjutor of whom I have spoken were favoured with a fuller intuition of that which was involved in the old Mosaic covenant. They were not great men; they could not take the intellectual initiative like Hosea and Jeremiah; but the peculiar combination of prophecy and law which they produced was something which had not yet been seen, and from which even the Christian student need not disdain to learn. It was a "covenant"—that is, God vouchsafed to make Himself authoritatively known to the Jews in the way best suited to their actual stage of development. And (if I may glide from an academic into a popular religious phraseology) just as we through our parents at the font thankfully accepted God's covenant in Christ, and responded to it by a promise before God

---

[1] Klostermann has pointed out that 2 Kings xxiii 21 must originally have stood after *v.* 3

and the Church to make His commandments, promises, and threatenings the rule of our lives, so did the men of Judah through their representatives at this memorable assembly.

This in itself is a sufficiently unexpected result. Could we have believed that those who till now had not only exercised boundless freedom in the choice of a sanctuary, but associated Jehovah with a number of other "divinities," including even the cruel Moloch,[1] would at the call of Josiah and on the reading of a hitherto unknown book permit their moral and religious life to be revolutionized? It is a riddle which at first sight baffles our comprehension. For an Israelitish king was not an absolute sovereign, and could not (like German princes in the 16th century) convert his people by force, nor had Josiah the assistance of a prophet with that wonderworking power and unique popular authority which according to tradition belonged to Elijah.

Let me now quote a portion of the 11th chapter of Jeremiah's book. It will perhaps assist us in solving this psychological problem, and suggest the reflexion that, if Josiah had no Elijah to help him, he had a friend and fellow-worker who was better adapted to the altered times.

The word which came to Jeremiah from Jehovah, as follows:—

. . . And thou shalt speak[2] unto the men of Judah and unto the inhabitants of Jerusalem in these terms, Thus said Jehovah, the God of Israel, Cursed be the man that heareth not the words of this covenant, which I commanded your fathers when I brought them out of the land of Egypt—the iron furnace, saying, Hearken to my voice, and carry them out [*i.e.*, these words] *in the fullest measure, so shall ye become to me a people and I shall become to you a God, that I may maintain the oath which I swore unto your fathers that I would give a land*

---

[1] I retain the received way of denominating the heavenly Fire-god. But, as I have already pointed out, it is at least very doubtful whether Malik = Moloch ("king") ought to be regarded as a proper name.

[2] I follow the Septuagint in reading the 2nd person singular. The received Hebrew text has the 2nd pers. plur., and prefixes, *Hear ye the words of this covenant.* This is evidently wrong. The original reading may have been, *Publish thou the words*, &c., or else the whole of the opening clause may have become illegible in the standard manuscript upon which our text ultimately depends, and the words which now supply its place may have been inserted by guess from verse 6.

flowing with milk and honey, as it is this day. And I answered and said, Amen, Jehovah.

Thus spake Jehovah unto me, Recite all these words in the cities of Judah and in the streets of Jerusalem, saying, Hear ye the words of this covenant, and carry them out. For solemnly have I warned your fathers, when I brought them up out of the land of Egypt (and) unto this day, from earliest dawn, Obey my voice. But they have not obeyed, nor bent their ear, but have walked every one in the stubbornness of his evil heart, so I brought upon them all the words of this covenant which I commanded them to carry out, but they carried not out (Jer. xi. 1–8).

I do not know how to understand this prophecy (the importance of which is shown by the double form in which it has been handed down,[1] and which is clearly isolated from the context), except by supposing that Jeremiah undertook an itinerating mission to the people of Judah, beginning with the capital, in order to set forth the main objects of Deuteronomy, and to persuade men to live in accordance with its precepts.[2] The ideas and phraseology of the section are in some respects so akin to those of the kernel of Deuteronomy,[3] and the reference to the curses threatened for disobedience reminds us so strongly of Josiah's reference (2 Kings xxii. 13) to *the wrath that is kindled against us, because our fathers have not hearkened unto the words of this book*,[4] that the supposition

---

[1] Verses 2–5 give one form of it, and verses 6–8 another. R V. has rightly altered A.V's., "Then the LORD said" (*v.* 6) into "And the LORD said "

[2] It is now seventeen years since I consulted Dahler's French work on Jeremiah (2 vols., 1825, 1830), but I well remember the forcible way in which the above hypothesis is presented.

[3] By the word "kernel" I mean the earliest and most original part of the Book of Deuteronomy. Comp. Jer. xi. 3 with Deut. xxviii 15–19; ver. 4 with Deut iv. 20 ("iron furnace"), xxvi. 17, 18, xxvii. 9, xxix. 12 (Israel a people to Jehovah and Jehovah a God to Israel) ver. 5 with Deut. vi 3 ("a land flowing," &c), ver. 8 with Deut xxviii 15 ("words," in "all the words,"=" things spoken of," *i e* , in this context, curses such as those in Deut. xxviii 16–68 , see 2 Chron. xxxiv. 24, "all the curses "). Comp. also Jer. vii 23–26

[4] I am well aware of the critical uncertainty of this part of the narrative in Kings But it does not seem to me sufficient to compel me to pass over this very obvious comparison. Kuenen and Dillmann, at any rate, accept Deut. xxviii , which contains the blessings and curses, as the work

cannot be evaded or dispensed with. It is just possible that there is a faint recollection of this mission of Jeremiah in the not very accurate account of the reign of Jehoshaphat preserved in that recast of historical traditions and pious fancies made, long after the return from the Captivity, in what we call the Books of Chronicles. There we read—what is entirely opposed to the earlier account in Kings—that Jehoshaphat took away the "high places," and sent nine Levites and two priests throughout all the cities of Judah to teach "the book of Jehovah's *tōrāh*" (2 Chron. xvii. 6–9). It is possible that the compiler of Chronicles (a man of fervent piety from whom we have much to learn, but most inaccurate as a historian) antedated the mission of the preachers of the law, just as he antedated the full development of the musical service in the temple. At any rate, if Jeremiah's words mean anything at all, they cannot mean less than this—that he went about in Jerusalem and the provincial cities (possibly as far as Shiloh, vii. 12) explaining a book which closely resembled our Deuteronomy, and persuading the Jews to live according to it. Put this fact side by side with that of the great national assembly which seems to have passed off so smoothly, although the object to be obtained was so contrary to the wishes of the majority of the Jews. Does not the one fact illustrate the other? Jeremiah, I know, is reluctant to admit that his preaching met with the least success: but that is because he put his notes and impressions into shape at so late a period in his ministry. That which he knew had been all along his great object, he did fail for the most part to obtain. But this is quite consistent with his having had those temporary successes which still relieve the gloom of ministerial disappointment. One such he probably had, as we have seen, on the first news of the approach of the Scythians; may he not have had another when, in the enthusiasm of youth and the strength of a Divine call, he carried with him as the textbook of his missionary addresses the first complete account of Israel's holy religion?

The reader will recall that, according to the view which I endeavoured to make plausible, Jeremiah was a reformer in

---

of the Deuteronomist, and if it be such, I have a right, on the authority of 2 Kings xxii. 13 (comp. *v.* 11) to assume that Josiah read it and was much affected by it spirit before he was called to be a prophet, and bel.nged to a band of religious friends who clustered around the pious boy-king Josiah. He will remember how long the friends waited in suspense for some sign from heaven or some practical scheme of reform. The sign from heaven had come, and both Zephaniah and Jeremiah had sought in vain to get the people to see its meaning. The Jews did indeed see their danger, and, as a kind of life-insurance, made some hasty promises of amendment, but no radical change followed (Jer. iii. 4, 5) And now, full of renewed zeal, Jeremiah goes forth with a practical scheme of reform, of which he may or may not know the authors, but which he has recognized as an inspired interpretation of the fundamental ideas of the covenant of Sinai. He has felt its full power himself, and has from the heart said 'Amen' to its varied contents. But the principle to which, as it would seem, he makes his first appeal in addressing his countrymen is that of fear. He doubtless knew the coarseness of their moral fibre, and hoped against hope that those who began with fear would end with love, and that the promises would seem all the sweeter when the threatenings had been realized in their awful seriousness. It is not Christ's way; but then Christ addressed a prepared people, and without concealing the dark side of heavenly truth, He trusted far more to the attractive power of the promises than to the deterrent efficacy of the threatenings of the Gospel. Jeremiah tried the opposite plan and failed. In the world of grace as well as in that of nature, it sometimes seems as if God made experiments, before the best and final plan were adopted. Not that God is finite, but that in this as in other respects His works are adapted to the faculties of those who are to study them. Nature without evolution, and revelation without historical progress, would both of them lose half their charms.

Jeremiah is not as yet to any great extent a type of Christ; he will become more so later on, when his personal training is more complete, and he has received the crowning revelation of his life. At present he is but continuing the work of Elijah on Mount Carmel; or rather, the second Elijah is the iconoclast Josiah, and Jeremiah in his missionary circuit prepares the way for that series of violent measures which is described in 2 Kings xxiii. I cannot see that the part played by Josiah was as noble as that of Jeremiah; in the roll of honour the royal iconoclast must stand below the preacher. It was a confession of weakness, however, that both Hilkiah and Jeremiah allowed Josiah (who would surely have respected their opposition) to commit these arbitrary and in some cases cruel acts. At any rate, if the latter trusted the results of his mission, why did he not bid Josiah wait for a spontaneous iconoclastic movement of his (Jeremiah's) converts (comp. Isa. xxx. 22)? Or why did he not throw himself at the king's feet, and beg and implore what he might not venture, like Elijah, to command? Had even he learned no lesson from the transitoriness[1] of Hezekiah's violent reforms? Yes; but not all that he might have learned. He knew that nothing but a fresh revelation could induce the people either to initiate or to accept at the king's hand the much needed reforms, but he did not yet see that without a true spiritual motive, without conversion of heart, the moral standard and the ideal of life must remain low, and the new law of worship simply issue in a fresh idolatry. This was the reason why both he and Hilkiah stood by while Josiah executed judgment on the outward forms of superstition. King, prophet, and priest were alike victims of the delusion that, when the storm of revolution had raged itself out, the Divine law would become the national rule of life, and so a claim would be established to the blessings promised by Jehovah to the righteous nation.

I am not blaming, however much I may pity, these great men; we can but dimly imagine the debasing influence of the worships which Jeremiah preached against and Josiah violently put down; and if the prophet's hearers were not to be trusted to rise of their own accord against these abominations, this does but increase our surprise at the ultimate results of the divine education of this very people. Nowhere is the fact of a Divine Providence so powerfully attested to the religious mind as in the later history of the people of Israel.

[1] It has been suggested that the account of Hezekiah's reforming measures in 2 Kings xviii. 4 contains anachronisms, the writer not being willing to suppose that so pious a king would have left the "high places" untouched. Certainly the Chronicler commits just such an anachronism in his account of Jehoshaphat (2 Chron. xvii. 6) But is it likely that any of the writers concerned in the narrative now before us were quite so devoid of historical sense? This demands a further examination,

CHAPTER VI.

THE ANCIENT LAW TRANSFORMED.

The publication of the first Scripture, its significance—The leading ideas of Deuteronomy—The effects of the recognition of the Lawbook.

IT is not my design in the present chapter to discuss the details of the historical passage which describes the reformation of Josiah Beyond question, it was a rough and vigorous reformation, which could never have been effected but for the "Mosaic" lawbook, and very different from the compromising measures of the newly established Church in the country districts of the Roman empire.[1] Both in the capital and in the provinces, as far even as Bethel and the cities of Samaria (where a new heathenism had joined itself to the old heretical worship, 2 Kings xvii. 29–31), a work of purification by destruction was carried out which is quite unique in the earlier chapters of the ancient history of religion. Where in fact can we find a parallel to the zeal of Josiah in the Semitic East till we come to Mohammed?[2] and if the non-appearance of dolmens and the like in Western Palestine be due (as Conder plausibly holds[3]) to the reformations

---

[1] See Albert Marignan, "Le Triomphe de l'Église au quatrième siècle" (Paris, 1887)

[2] The heretical Egyptian king Khuenaten (Amenhotep iv.) did but erase the name of the old Theban deity whose worship he superseded by that of the solar disk And in spite of Mohammed's zeal against idols, he left not only the "black stone" at Mecca, but numerous dolmens all over Arabia— the *anṣāb* or sacrificial stones (lit "standing stones" = Heb *maççēbōth*, "pillars," Deut xii 3 &c.), against which, however, he warns his followers ("Korán," v 92).

[3] "Syrian Stone-Lore," p. 126, comp. "Heth and Moab," pp. 264–5, Stanley, "Jewish Church," i 59 Mr. Oliphant found four huge prostrate

THE ANCIENT LAW TRANSFORMED.

of Hezekiah (?) and Josiah, these kings of Judah effected a more complete abolition of idols than even Mohammed. Of idols, but not of idolatry. The altar-stones and pillars might be broken, and the chapels destroyed, but the old sanctity still clung to the sites, as Jeremiah found later on to his cost. Did the prophet co-operate with Josiah in his iconoclastic work? So far as the temple was concerned, it is possible enough that he did, but I prefer to think of him, not so much as the iconoclast, but as the persuasive preacher. And what if he did represent Deuteronomy to be the work of Moses? Did not the illusion cover an important truth? Did not the authors of the new lawbook enable men to see into the heart of the Mosaic covenant, by speaking to them as Moses would have spoken had he come to life again as a prophet and a reformer? Other writers had made the same attempt in a more mechanical way; their work had failed however to produce any considerable effect. Collections of primitive laws had been made, based perhaps on Mosaic or early post-Mosaic material (comp. Hos. viii. 12 [1]), among which we may safely include the Decalogue (Exod. xx. 1–17, comp. Deut. v. 6–21), the greater Book of the Covenant (Exod. xx. 22–xxiii.), and the lesser Book of the Covenant (Exod. xxxiv. 11–26), which, as many critics consider, ought properly to be arranged as a second Decalogue.[2] But there is no proof that those collections enjoyed any public, that is, national recognition, and their circulation was probably limited to the priests (if the collection was a ritualistic one), and to the few educated people among the laity (if the collection related to social duties). It is worth noticing that the Deuteronomist (even if two authors are concerned, we may sometimes for variety or convenience use the singular) represents Moses as sending the individual Israelite to "the priests the Levites" (= "the Levitical priests") for an authoritative "direction" (*tōrāh*). He doubtless reflects the customs of his time, and we may assume (a good commentary on Leviticus would amply justify the assump-

---

slabs of stone which, he says, had evidently once formed a dolmen, near the secluded village of Mugheir in the northern Samaritan hill-country ("Haifa," p. 337).

[1] Render, "I *am wont to write* unto him, &c , but they *are counted* as a strange thing " Comp. Smend, "Moses apud Prophetas" (1875), p 13

[2] Comp Briggs, "Old Testament Student" (Chicago), vol. ii. (1882–1883), pp 264–272.

tion) that there were various collections of legal traditions (at first unwritten, and then written) in the possession of priestly families on the basis of which the priests ("those that handle the *tōrāh*," Jer. ii. 8, comp Deut. xxxiii. 10) gave, orally, their *tōrāh* or " directions."

Still, though many may have carried their perplexities to the priests, some—that is, of course, the more educated—would sometimes at least, avail themselves of such written records as were extant. For these, and for the priests themselves, and above all, for the general life of the nation, it was of the utmost importance that the legal traditions of Israel should be revised, harmonized, corrected, reorganized. For it is more than doubtful whether all the pre-Deuteronomic collections of laws subserved the interests of a truly progressive and in some measure spiritual religion. There are indications enough that the religious literature of the Israelites was not entirely confined to those whom we look up to as the inspired writers, and it appears from a passage in Jeremiah that the formalist priests and lying prophets employed the pen to give greater currency to their teaching. *How do ye say* (the question is addressed to the laity), *We are wise, and the law of the* LORD [Jehovah] *is with us ? But, behold* (this is the prophet's answer), *the false pen of the scribes hath wrought falsely* (marg., *hath made of it falsehood*) Jer. viii. 8, R.V. The prophet cannot refer here to Deuteronomy ; he can only mean something analogous to the heretical Gospels of early Christian times—something which, though it pretended to a divine sanction, was really subservient to false religious principles.

It was a truly memorable event this publication of the first Scripture, for henceforth it became possible for the religion of an insignificant Asiatic people to survive a national catastrophe and become the faith of the human race. A poor Bible, some one may say. Yes ; but it was a Bible admirably adapted to those times. And does not the distinctive quality of our Bible consist partly in this—that it contains the comparatively poor religious standards of past ages? Just consider what a difference this makes between a Christian and a Mohammedan Reformation. Moslems, not less than Jews and Christians, are a "people of the Book"[1] ; but their Book only belongs to a

[1] Mohammed uses this phrase of Jews and Christians in "Korán," ii. 56, &c.

THE ANCIENT LAW TRANSFORMED. 63

single period and comes from a single man. To reform Mohammedanism is therefore to go back twelve hundred years and believe as Mohammed believed. But a Christian Reformer is not thus rigidly confined to the standards of a single age or person.[1] By comparing Scripture with Scripture in a critical but religiously sympathetic spirit,[2] he discovers which are really the essential doctrines and the fundamental facts, and exercises the right of restating them to his own generation, just as prophets and reformers did of old to theirs. That inspired prophet and priest (so great in their self-effacing humility) who composed the main part of the Book of Deuteronomy, re-created Moses for their own age. They adapted older laws with the utmost freedom, but in the spirit of Moses and his equally inspired successors, "bringing forth out of their treasury things new and old." And whenever the same need is felt, it should be the Christian's happy faith that the right man will be sent for the task.

Deuteronomy may be a poor Bible, from a modern point of view; but it is rich in significance, if judged by a historic standard. It sought to place the whole moral and spiritual life of Israel upon a new basis. It condenses the essence of the past, and anticipates the future developments of Judaism (in Ezra's form of it) and Christianity. And upon the whole in how effective a style! As Ewald has well said, "A work which transformed the ancient law with such creative power, so emphatically threatened all those who despised it with the severest Divine penalties, and, on the other hand, spoke with such tenderness and human feeling about its observance, was in every respect adapted to make a profound impression on its readers, and to produce the effect for which it was designed."[3] It could not have been composed by a mere priest. The Deuteronomic *tōrāh* is in fact the joint work of at least two of

[1] The Christian religion of the nineteenth century cannot be the same as that of the second or the fourth, it need not be opposed to it, but it cannot be identical with it. Dr Bigg, in his "Bampton Lectures" (1886), has made a similar remark of the Christianity of the fourth century as compared with that of the second.

[2] Some readers will mentally make the comment that this union is inconceivable. But are there then no living persons in whom this union is an accomplished fact? The infinite variety possible in the Christian life is only now beginning to be realized.

[3] "History of Israel," iv. 227.

the noblest members of the prophetic and the priestly orders, each caring for that particular jewel which God in His providence had deposited with him. From the prophetic writer comes the width of view so conspicuous, for example, in x. 12-22, and which contrasts strangely with the exclusiveness imposed by tradition upon his priestly companion (see xxiii. 3-8 ; xxv. 17-19 ; xx. 17). To the priest is due the general conception of a religious organization of the national life, as well as the arrangements of its details. He too is animated, within the sphere of Israelitish interests, by a fine spirit of humanity, which sometimes even leads him to make impracticable requirements (see *e g.* xx. 1-9). A poor Bible? Nay ; such a combination of priestly energy and policy with the idealizing prophetic spirit was the greatest work which the Divine Spirit acting upon the human had yet produced.

Of this remarkable book the following are the four chief ideas. 1. Jehovah is the one God worthy of the name Elohim —" the Elohim," as he is called both by the Deuteronomist and by the disciple who added to his work (iv. 35, 39, vii. 9). It was enough to assert the comparative inability of other gods to help—see iii. 24, iv. 7, and comp. " the God of the gods (Elohim) and the Lord of the lords, the great, strong, and fearful God (El.)," x. 17. So in vi. 4 we read, *Hear, O Israel; Jehovah our God is one Jehovah* (*i.e.*, Jehovah is unique in kind and in nature). We need not be surprised, however, that in some of their moods the writers regard the other gods as mere wood and stone—iv. 28, xxviii. 36, 64, xxix. 17 ; comp. Jer. ii. 27. 2. The life of the community in all its aspects is to be worthy of the servants of a holy God. Israel is to be, as another writer expresses it, "a kingdom of priests and a holy nation " (Exod. xix. 6.) 3. There is to be only one temple ; the many local shrines and stone monuments of a lower worship are to be destroyed. This was on account of the licentious nature-worship which connected itself with the festivals held in the open air around the " high places."[1] 4. One tribe alone (in

[1] Such " chapels " as may have existed must have been for the most part rather rude , the essential thing was the altar. Comp the Homeric τέμενος βωμός τε θυήεις (" Il." viii. 48 , xxiii 148 , "Odyss " vii 363). The later Jewish traditions on the construction of these chapels are put together in Levy's "Neuhebräisches Wörterbuch," art. *bāmāh*. See also Ewald, " History of Israel," iii 306 note.

opposition to the custom of the northern kingdom[1]), is to supply ministers for the sanctuary; they are to be no mere servants of the king (contrast 2 Sam. viii. 17, xx. 25), but to have an inherent authority of their own. Not all Levites, however, are to have the duties and privileges of the priesthood. Those who are not priests may be local teachers and judges, and are commended to the liberality of their fellow-Israelites; and any Levite may remove from the country-districts to Jerusalem, and receive a share of the priestly duties and emoluments. These ideas are inculcated or promoted in two ways—by series of definite laws and by exhortations. Hence there is both a priestly and a prophetic element in Deuteronomy. The charm of the book lies in the sweetly impressive tone of the prophetic passages. But we must not forget the Divine sanction given afresh to the principle of law; the prophetic element does but spiritualize the legal. And, if the trite but natural reflexion may be pardoned, the Redeemer has delivered His followers from the "curse" but not from the obligation of law. Indeed, was it not the leading object of His holy life to make men perform the law of God—"His Father and their Father"—from love? And may we not venture to say that the authors of Deuteronomy have so transformed their hero as to make him a true though imperfect type of Christ? It is true that St. John says, *The law was given through Moses, but lovingkindness and truth came through Jesus Christ* (John i. 17), apparently assuming an antithesis between them; but the word "came" here means "were fulfilled" (see Prov. xiii. 12), and is there not a promise or anticipation of the Divine lovingkindness in the discourses of Deuteronomy? It is indeed a most superficial view which treats this book as a mere legal document. The Moses whom it brings before us really represents noble spirits like Jeremiah (whom we have learned to regard as a type of Christ). He can indeed command, but, like our Lord, he prefers to persuade. He does not refuse to incorporate many very imperative utterances—monuments of an earlier stage—into his so-called recapitulation of the *tōrāh*. There are whole series of laws in Deuteronomy which have quite the short, dictatorial style of the old legislation. But in those prophetic passages of which I spoke, the "stiffness and severity" of the ancient form of

[1] We must remember that part of the northern kingdom had been attached to the dominions of Josiah (see below).

expression disappears. Moses becomes like unto Christ; he "speaks in his own name to the people; he searches out every human reason which could operate on their conscience, and impel them to keep the law; and, moved by the warmth of his love, he speaks to the heart, because the action of this alone can proceed from love."[1]

That the view of Moses and his teaching given in Deuteronomy is a highly idealized one could not escape the attention even of those English scholars who still occupy the antiquated position of Hengstenberg. "His work (*i e*, that of Moses)," remarks one of the youngest and, though still immature, not the least able of the number, "was not for one generation: 'mediator of the Old Covenant,' he stands high above all other prophets and saints; already half glorified, no longer subject to the limitations of time, he surveys the Israel of all ages until the coming of Christ, and accordingly his work assumes (viz. in Deuteronomy) a prospective and ideal character, so striking that unbelieving critics could not but mistake it as the evidence of a much later origin."[2] To "unbelieving," say rather "modern," critics Deuteronomy is conspicuously devoid of the ecstatic element which theory compels this writer to assume; but they will all gladly welcome the admission that the book stands by itself, and has a message and an interest for the Christian as well as for the Jewish Church.

"Love is life's only sign," says the poet of the "Christian Year." This is the very essence of the religious thinking of the Deuteronomist. Israel, like the Church, has been "first loved" by Jehovah; and "the true Israelite is he who loves both his fellow-Israelites and Jehovah of his own accord, just as Jehovah of His own accord loved Israel."[3] This truth is equally set forth in Deuteronomy and in the Deuteronomist's great spiritual predecessor, Hosea The primal love of Jehovah to Israel fills the foreground of each writer's discourse, and all human relationships within the Israelitish community are rooted in this. This love is, however, a moral love: Jehovah

---

[1] Ewald, "History of Israel," iv. 223 (but compare the more nervous and forcible German of the original work).

[2] G Vos, "The Mosaic Origin of the Pentateuchal Codes" (Lond, 1886), p 90 The author is an American of Dutch extraction, and, we may confidently expect, will before ten years are over have changed his opinions.

[3] Cheyne, "Hosea" (Cambridge School and College Bible), p 28 (Introd)

is not more loving than righteous. Moral and spiritual corruption will be—must be punished by ruin and destruction. The abominations old and new which disfigured the national religion in the time of the authors of Deuteronomy, must, as these inspired men felt, bring God's curse upon those who practised them. This is the essential idea of the awful threats hurled throughout this book by the imaginary Moses at the close of his career against the races which would be found in Canaan by the Israelites. As a matter of fact, it cannot be proved on historical grounds (see "Encyclopædia Britannica," art. "Canaanites") that those races were either expelled or destroyed by the invaders. On the contrary, they were gradually amalgamated with the Israelites, who became in the arts of civilization, and too often in the practices of religion, their willing pupils. It was never the policy of the leaders of Israel to lay waste cities and massacre their populations indiscriminately, and even destroy the innocent cattle. "These are only the pictorial mode in which the writers (of Deuteronomy) express their utter abhorrence of the practices which destroyed the sanctity of Israel and insulted the majesty of Israel's Holy One. Strangely do these fierce sentiments read beside the repeated declarations of the divine compassion, the reiterated appeals to the heart of loyalty and trust, which give to these pages such a kindling glow. It is well that we can in part resolve the inconsistency which seems to discredit the value of a piety apparently marred by such bloodthirsty ferocity. The writers present their principles under the limitations of imaginary circumstances that were never real."[1] This will not indeed apply to the case of the Amalekites, for there is no evidence that this race was religiously dangerous to the Israelites. The explanation is given in Deut. xxv. 17, 18 ; comp. Exod. xvii. 14. The Deuteronomist would of course remember the extinction of the remnant of Amalek in the days of Hezekiah (1 Chron. iv. 41–43).

I must leave the reader to compare the reforming measures of Josiah (2 Kings xxiii.) with the directions in the Book of Deuteronomy. Each fact will be found to correspond to some provision in the law, except to some extent the treatment of the country priests. According to Deut. xviii. 6–8, the Levites of

[1] Carpenter, article on the Book of Deuteronomy, "Modern Review," April, 1883, p. 274.

the provinces were to have equal rites with the priests of the temple, if they came up to Jerusalem. But in 2 Kings xxiii. 9 we read that the priests whom Josiah brought up to join in the Passover were not permitted to sacrifice, but *ate unleavened bread among their brethren.*[1] This fact is interesting, because the mention of it seems to contradict the theory that Deuteronomy was a forgery, composed either (if before the 18th year of Josiah) in the interests of the temple-priests, or (if after the Reformation) to justify the course which Josiah and his friends had taken. Would that it were possible to compare the system exhibited in Deuteronomy with the civil and religious condition of Judah some years after the Reformation. Were the laws strictly observed? and above all, did the spiritual teaching of the prophetic passages take hold upon the people? Alas! we lack the material for a satisfactory answer to these questions. The account of Josiah's reign in 2 Kings is tantalizingly fragmentary, and it is impossible to point definitely to any prophecy of Jeremiah's as describing the post-Reformation part of the reign of Josiah. That Jeremiah himself was deeply influenced by Deuteronomy both in his ideas and in his phraseology, is no new proposition to the reader. The phenomena have led some critics to conjecture that he even wrote Deuteronomy.[2] This I see no sufficient reason to believe. It is certain, however, that he was far the greatest of the school of writers formed upon the Book of Deuteronomy—a school which includes historians, poets, and prophets, and without which the Old Testament would be deprived of some of its most valued pages.

[1] I follow Klostermann, who holds that the words, *And he brought up all the priests from the cities of Judah* (2 Kings xxiii. 8), and the whole of ver. 9, are misplaced, and belong properly to a description of the preparations for the Passover which once existed but is not now preserved (see 2 Kings xxiii. 21, 22). This view accounts for the mention of the "unleavened bread." Comp., however, Robertson Smith, "The Old Testament and the Jewish Church," pp. 360-362

[2] Comp. a valuable excursus in Kleinert's "Das Deuteronomium und der Deuteronomiker" (1872) comparing the vocabulary of Deuteronomy with that of other books, which specially notices not only those words and phrases which occur but also those which do not occur in the Book of Jeremiah, and which also distinguishes between Deuteronomy proper and the additions to it.

CHAPTER VII.

FRAUD OR NEEDFUL ILLUSION?

Criticism of the narrative in 2 Kings xxii —The Mosaic authorship of the Lawbook, not tenable—Reasons for this—Notes on the allusions to Egypt in Deuteronomy, and on the finding of the Lawbook.

I HAVE endeavoured in the preceding chapter to give a general sketch of Josiah's great reformation, without diverting the reader's attention to modern disputes whether of a historico-critical or of a purely exegetical character. The latter are doubtless more capable of settlement, but the former raise points of a more wide-reaching significance. I must therefore at least touch upon the former ; a slight treatment of historico-critical questions is painful to me, but it is all that a regard to the proportions of this work will allow me to attempt. A monograph on Deuteronomy would only make incidental reference to Jeremiah ; a monograph on Jeremiah, especially if not written solely for the college student, can only present a short and far from exhaustive account of the controversy of Deuteronomy. There are some points which can be and have been settled, and some upon which a degree of uncertainty cannot be avoided ; it is right to lay most stress upon the former

Let us not then be concerned if we hear it said in some quarters that the narrative in 2 Kings xxii. contains patent improbabilities, and is inconsistent with facts derived from the Book of Jeremiah. There are many other ancient narratives presumably based upon tradition which are in the main accepted in spite of similar difficulties. It is difficult to believe that so elaborate a narrative is purely fictitious. It is not the wont of Hebrew story-tellers to draw exclusively upon their imagination. Even the Chronicler, who is sufficiently biassed by what we may call his ecclesiastical interest, would not have indulged in so flagrant a violation of the truth of facts.[1] And if the narrative were indeed a pure fiction, it would surely not have contained an incidental and perfectly simple-minded admission that Josiah had, in one important respect, not carried out the directions of the lawbook (2 Kings xxiii. 9; comp. Deut. xviii. 6, 7). Two points at least ought, I think, by the most sceptically inclined critic to be accepted as historical, viz. (1) that the "lawbook" was published in Josiah's reign with the view of recommending certain reforms and establishing the national religion on a firmer basis; and (2) that Hilkiah, one of its chief promulgators, asserted that he had found it in the temple. The view implied (probably) in 2 Kings xxii. and expressed in 2 Chron xxxiv., that the "book of *tōrāh*" had the leader of the Exodus for its author, cannot from a critical point of view be maintained, for these among other reasons, that the Deuteronomist (if we may so for convenience refer to the author or joint-authors of the original Deuteronomy) has (1) employed documents manifestly later than Moses, (2) made allusions to circumstances which only existed long after Moses, and (3) expressed ideas which are not such as are, psychologically speaking, possible in the age of Moses.

1. The evidences of the Deuteronomist's dependence on the Yahvistic narrative[2] in the Pentateuch—written, at earliest (Dillmann), in the middle of the seventh century B.C., are embarrassing from their very abundance. Here are a few headings of statements borrowed from the Yahvist, which I quote with but little attempt at selection from the classical treatise

---

[1] It is worth noticing that the Chronicler adopts the narrative of the finding of the lawbook in the temple (2 Chron. xxxiv. 14-33), although its tendency is directly opposed to his own simple-minded view that the Law had been the foundation of Israelitish life since the time of Moses. Considering that he certainly selects and modifies his material with a view to edification, it is singular that he adopts a statement which, on the hypothesis mentioned above, was of comparatively recent origin. He actually does omit another important part of the narrative in Kings, viz , the description of Josiah's violent measures, which implied a previous state of things very inconsistent with Mosaic orthodoxy. He writes as a devout churchman, but he is not without some claim to the character of a historian.

[2] "All are agreed that Deuteronomy is later than the Yahvist," remarks the orthodox theologian, H. L. Strack ("Handbuch der theologischen Wissenschaften," i. 136). To use the non-form "Jehovist" in this connexion would be absurd.

of K. H. Graf.[1] Jacob's going down to Egypt with seventy persons (Deut. x. 22 ; xxvi. 5). The oppression of the Israelites and the Exodus (vi. 12, 21, 22 ; vii. 8, 18, 19 ; and often) The destruction of the Egyptians in the Red Sea (xi. 4). The manna (viii. 3, 16). The water out of the rock (viii. 15), The temptation at Massa (vi. 16, ix. 22). The tables of stone and the golden calf (ix. 7–21). The forty years' wandering (viii. 2, 15, xi. 5). The serpents (viii. 15). Balaam (xxiii. 5, 6). It is true that in the Deuteronomic parallels we sometimes meet with deviations from the Yahvistic narrative, but these are hardly sufficient to outweigh the minute points of agreement which also occur. They only prove that our author derived his material from more than one source, his secondary authority being sometimes popular tradition, sometimes perhaps his own creative imagination. But the case becomes even stronger when we consider the introductory portion of the book (i. 1–iv. 40) by itself. This is a free recapitulation of the account of the wanderings contained in the earlier books, and was evidently intended as a convenient connexion between Deuteronomy proper and the Yahvistic narrative. Let the reader only carry his studies a little farther, and see how a scholar of the Deuteronomist has edited Joshua, and he will not quarrel with any one for asserting that the Yahvistic narrative must have been written first, and that a Deuteronomistic writer composed Deut i –iv. 40 as a link between his own and the earlier work.

2. But these are far from being the only points in which the author of Deuteronomy has betrayed himself. He is full of allusions to circumstances which did not exist till long after Moses. The Israel of his description is separated from the Israel of the Exodus by a complete social revolution. The nomad tribes have grown into a settled and wealthy community (notice the phrase "the elders of the city," xix. 12, &c.), whose organization needs no longer to be constituted, but only to be reformed. I do not say that no directions can be found which bear on their face the stamp of a primitive age. Our author did not hesitate to adopt earlier laws, though he neutralized their possible evil effect either by distinct modifications or by the context in which he placed them. But the elaborate

[1] Graf, "Die geschichtlichen Bucher," u s.w., pp 9–19 ; comp Bp Colenso, "The Pentateuch and Book of Joshua Critically Examined, vi. 34, 35.

character of most of the Deuteronomic arrangements conclusively proves the lateness of their origin. See, for instance, the laws of contracts (chaps. xv., xxiii., xxiv.), of inheritance (chap. xxi.), and, above all, of war (chap. xx) ; and contrast the last-mentioned with the very primitive directions in Numb. xxxi. 25–30. The fact that in Deut. xx. the law-giver distinctly contemplates wars of foreign conquest, brings down the date of the law below the period of David. Or take still more definite allusions. The law regulating the kingship is proved by its contents to be later than the time of Solomon, whose dangerous tendencies are not obscurely alluded to (xvii. 14–20) ; the law confining the right of sacrificing to the tribe of Levi, to be later than the Mosaic age [1] (even in the widest sense of the term), later than the times of David and Solomon,[2] later than Jeroboam,[3] and probably later than Azariah ;[4] the warnings against the lower forms of prophecy (xviii. 10–12), to be not earlier than the first of the great succession of prophetic teachers of a moral and spiritual religion—Amos and Hosea ; the prohibition of star-worship (iv. 19, xvii. 3), to be not earlier than the Assyrian period ;[5] and lastly, the law restricting sacrifices and festival observances to the temple at Jerusalem (xii. 5–27, xvi. 1–17, &c.) to be later certainly than Amos and Hosea,[6] later certainly than Mesha's Moabitish inscription,[7] and later almost certainly than the reign of Hezekiah.[8]

[1] Exod. xx. 24–26, as all critics (see especially Dillmann) agree, is addressed to the whole body of the Israelites, not to a single tribe.

[2] 2 Sam. viii. 18 (see "Variorum Bible"), vi. 13, 14, xxiv. 25 ; 1 Kings viii. 62, 63.

[3] 1 Kings xii. 31 (see "Variorum Bible"). Had the sacerdotal rights of the Levites been generally recognized, Jeroboam would not have ventured on promiscuous ordinations. [4] 2 Chron. xxvi 16–21.

[5] This form of worship being derived immediately from Assyria, Amos prophesies that the Israelitish star-worshippers shall have to carry the images of their star-gods (*to which he gives Assyrian names*) beyond Damascus, a vague but significant expression for Assyria —"Therefore ye shall take up Sakkuth your king, and Kaivân your star-god, even your images, which ye have made unto yourselves" (Amos v. 26, see Schrader, and comp. 2 Kings xxi 5).

[6] Amos and Hosea, though denouncing star-worship, say nothing against the non-idolatrous worship of Jehovah at the local shrines

[7] Mesha states that he took "altars (strictly, altar-hearths) of Yahveh" from the town of Nebo in the trans-Jordanic country (Moabite Inscription, line 18).

[8] According to 2 Kings xviii. 4, Hezekiah abolished the "high places"

3. It will also be clear, on a little reflexion, that there are ideas expressed in Deuteronomy which can only have arisen at an advanced stage of religious development.[1] I will not now appeal to the Deuteronomic idea of the exclusive right of Jehovah to Israel's worship, for that is also expressed in the Decalogue. Nor will I lay any stress on the repeated prohibitions of the use of "similitudes" in the worship of Jehovah (Deut. iv. 12, 15-18, &c.). For this prohibition, too, occurs in the Decalogue. But there are several characteristic ideas of Deuteronomy, to the use of which as evidence of a late date no exception can be taken.

Thus (i.) the thought of giving a religious colour to the whole of the national organization is the logical development of the idea so earnestly inculcated by Isaiah (iv. 3, vi. 13, xi. 1-9, &c.) of the "holy people" (seven times in Deuteronomy). It is the thought of one who was a statesman, as well as an inspired prophet, and who saw that in the coming struggle for the national existence of the Israelites, their only hope lay in the deepening and concentrating of their religious life. Hence those elaborate arrangements which descend even to such minutiæ as the substance of a man's clothing (xxii. 11, 12), but which are all set in a framework of religious precepts and principles. We have before us, in fact, the prelude of the Levitical reformation set on foot by Ezra. The author of Deuteronomy and his friends, with not inferior earnestness though with less rigour than Ezra, attempted the bold experiment (bold, for any but prophets and the disciples of prophets) of converting a nation into a church, and an earthly kingdom into a theocracy. But the fundamental idea of the "holy people" is Isaiah's. It was that great prophet's function to transfer the conception of holiness from the physical to the moral sphere. Others no doubt had laboured in the

or local sanctuaries. It is an open question whether this strong statement is correct Even Josiah, though he insists on the sanctity of Mount Zion never fulminates against "high places" From 2 Kings xxiii. 13 we gather that even very near Jerusalem the reformation was but slight.

[1] Not only are the ideas peculiar, but they are expressed in a phraseology as peculiar—thoroughly unlike that of the rest of the Pentateuch, and presenting many points of contact with Jeremiah Besides, the general character of the style points equally to the silver age of Hebrew literature (comp. Ewald, "History of Israel," i. 127).

same direction, but none was so "clothed with the Spirit" for the work as Isaiah. The notion current among the Israelites of their relation to Jehovah was of a privilege enjoyed by a natural, indefeasible right. Isaiah fought against this illusion. He taught that it was not enough to be outwardly a child of Abraham; the enjoyment of the Divine favour was conditional on the performance, not merely of ceremonies, but of certain primary moral acts. The difference between Isaiah and the author of Deuteronomy is simply that the one looks for the "holy people" to an ideal future; the other seeks, prematurely enough, to realize the conception in the present.

(ii.) The idea of limiting the public worship of Jehovah to a single sanctuary (xii. 5-17, &c) is closely connected with that of the "holy people." If Israel took his stand on his religion, it was necessary for him to distinguish it as sharply as possible from that of his neighbours and antagonists. As long as Jehovah was worshipped at the local sanctuaries called "high places," the forms of worship were liable to become assimilated to those of alien, unspiritual religions. The significant figure of "whoredom" for idolatry (Jer. ii. 20, &c.) sufficiently indicates the danger by which the Israelites of this period were threatened. Yet religion could not be entirely divested of material symbols. Hence even Isaiah, with all his hatred of formalism, insists repeatedly on the sanctity of the temple-mount, though (call it inconsistency, or call it a wise discretion) he refrains from fulminating against the country sanctuaries. A complete measure of religious centralization was reserved for the author of Deuteronomy.

(iii.) Still further to increase the popular reverence for the temple-worship, the Deuteronomic legislator gave a solemn sanction to the exclusive claims of the Levitical priesthood.[1] From the Mosaic age onwards, they ministered the Divine *tōrāh* to the Israelites who came to them (comp. Deut. xxxiii. 9, Jer. ii. 8); but it cannot be shown that they alone "stood before Jehovah to minister unto him," as this legislator commanded that they should do. It is only natural to suppose that this important innovation (so it may be called, even though it may have been based on a growing custom) belongs to a late and somewhat revolutionary age.

[1] Passages friendly to the Levites, Deut xviii 1-5 (comp xii 12, 18, 19, xiv. 27, 29, xvi. 11, 14, xxvi 11-13), xxiv 8, xxxi 9, 25, 26

In the course of the foregoing negative proof I have been compelled to bring forward positive evidence in favour of a very late date for Deuteronomy. David and Solomon, Mesha, king of Moab, the Yahvist, Amos, Hosea, and Isaiah, must have lived prior to the author of the lawbook; and we have just found reason to suppose that its composition belongs to a revolutionary period of Israel's history. Now, Hezekiah's reign being excluded[1] (see above), the reigns of Manasseh and Josiah remain—the only ones of which the Second Book of Kings relates any reformation or revolution. The former is the more plausible from the point of view of the ordinary reader.[2] Assuming this to be the period of the composition of the book, we could make a shrewd guess as to the cause of its being deposited in the temple. Manasseh, it seems, hated the strict religion and morality which Deuteronomy was written to promote, and the true-hearted prophet and priest who composed the book could not venture, we might reasonably assume, to keep it in their own hands. It is no doubt strange that the book should have been lost sight of by its priestly custodians. Possibly, however, the secret of its hiding-place had been confided to but one or two, and the few who knew it had died without handing it on. At any rate, one might say that Providence watched over the roll, and caused it to be brought forth at the right moment. I do not myself hold this view, however, and only develop it here to assist the reader's imagination. If the book were written under Manasseh, it is at least strange that the book should not, either in its exhortations or in its commands, make any allusions ($\phi\omega\nu\tilde{\alpha}\nu\tau\alpha$ $\sigma\upsilon\nu\epsilon\tau o\tilde{\iota}\sigma\iota\nu$) to the fact that Jehovah's central sanctuary had been invaded by idols (2 Kings xxi. 4, &c.). Looking at the lawbook by itself, one can understand it better if written under Josiah. The hopefulness of the writer, which penetrates each page of his book, was justified by the character of the new king, and it seems reasonable to sup-

[1] See, however, Vaihinger in Herzog's "Realencyclopadie," ed. 1, xi. 327-8.

[2] Since writing the above, I find that a young and able German writer, Rudolf Kittel, who began his career with a temperate criticism of Wellhausen's "Geschichte Israels" (now more fitly styled "Prolegomena zur Geschichte Israels") adopts Manasseh's reign as the date of Deuteronomy in his new "Geschichte der Hebraer." I agree with Dillmann that Josiah's reign is rather more probable.

pose that the book was published soon after it was written, while its joint-authors were still alive, because this helps us to account for the rapid success of its ideas. Add to this the fact that the literary influence of Deuteronomy lying (as it would seem) with Jeremiah, and there remains but little excuse for doubting that the authors of Deuteronomy were among the actors in the great reformation of King Josiah.

The one great advantage of referring the lawbook to the reign of Manasseh, is that it permits us to form the highest possible moral estimate of Hilkiah and Shaphan. Rough critics (especially if tinctured with the old-fashioned dogmatic rationalism) are apt to fly off from the one extreme of Bible-hero-worship to the other of Bible-hero-depreciation, and accuse at any rate Hilkiah of complicity in a forgery. We still, in English books especially, meet with statements that our only choice lies between the "good old view" of the Mosaic origin of Deuteronomy and that of its purely fictitious character. I confess that, in spite of these statements, I cannot think that the latter hypothesis merits a long examination. Let the following remarks suffice.

I will admit that the hypothesis of forgery (advocated by Von Bohlen and others) is not to be rejected straightway on the ground of its moral repulsiveness. M. Alexandre, the editor of the Sibylline Oracles, has remarked on the excellent morality of their contents coexisting with the fiction of their authorship. The moral standard of one age is not that of another, and great saints have allowed themselves in practices which would now be disclaimed by all good men. Nor yet may it be scouted on the ground that it is plainly impossible to palm off a modern statute-book as ancient upon a whole nation. Sir Henry Maine has given an instance of such a successful forgery in the history of English law ("Ancient Law," p 82), and what has been done in one country may, the conditions being not essentially different, be effected in another. But the hypothesis is in the highest degree improbable, because Deut. xviii. contains (as we have seen) a law relative to the country Levites which directly clashes with the class interests of the Zadokite priests, from whom, on the hypothesis of forgery, Deuteronomy proceeds. It is also critically unnecessary. O course, it is only the middle part of the book (chaps. v –xxvi.) about which there can be any dispute—that part which in the opening and closing chapters is referred to as "this *tōrāh*," i. 5, iv. 8 (comp. *v.* 44), xxvii. 3, 8, 26, xxviii. 58, xxix. 28, xxx. 10, xxxi. 11, 12, 26, xxxii. 46. This portion is no doubt declared to be Mosaic. There is no possibility of explaining this away. Listen to the Book, —

And Moses called all Israel, and said unto them, Hear, O Israel, the statutes and ordinances which I speak in your ears this day. . . . (Deut v. 1).

And Moses wrote this law [*tōrāh*] (Deut. xxxi. 9).

What did this mean to the mass of those who, in Josiah's eighteenth year, heard the lawbook read? It is self-evident that no human being could recall from oblivion the statement of fundamental laws which Moses (by a sudden concentration of his intellectual powers—for he was primarily a man of action, and neither an orator nor a writer) may possibly have given at the close of his career. It would be difficult[1] to suppose that the men of Judah adopted such an absurd idea, or even that they held a theory most reasonable in the case of Ecclesiastes that the author did but assume the character of a hero of antiquity by a literary fiction.[2] They were not subtle-minded people, and must have drawn the most obvious inference from the facts presented to them, viz., that the lawbook had been lost for centuries, and been recovered only now by the high priest Hilkiah. That the latter (who had his own interpretation of the word "Mosaic," to which I will turn presently) permitted this belief to exist may be stigmatized by some as deceit ; what he practised, however, was not deceit nor *de*lusion, but rather *il*lusion. Need I justify the principle which, unconsciously to himself, lay beneath his action? Novalis may exaggerate

[1] I say "difficult" and not "impossible," for I remember that Fathers of the Church did believe Ezra to have rewritten the Law of Moses under Divine inspiration. But the credulity of theologians, when assisted by a predisposing motive. is greater on some points than that of ordinary men. Besides, the doctrine of verbal inspiration was not as yet developed.

[2] I do not in the text refer to the theory of a *legal fiction*, because I doubt whether, unless we use the pruning-knife very vigorously, the middle part of Deuteronomy can have been understood on this theory or principle. I do not deny the existence of legal conventions generally understood as such by educated Israelites (comp Robertson Smith. "The Old Testament in the Jewish Church," p. 387), but the nucleus of our Deuteronomy seems to me too large and complex to be put on a level with isolated laws such as Numb xxxi. 27.

when he says, "Error is the necessary instrument of truth; with error I make truth." But he is strictly correct in his following words, "All transition begins with illusion."[1] Both historically and educationally it is clear that at certain stages of development men cannot receive the pure truth, which must therefore be enclosed for a time in a husk of harmless error. The history of the prophets shows us that, as a matter of fact, Providence employed much illusion in training its instruments. Jeremiah himself at length became aware of this in his own case, and not without a momentary disappointment at the discovery. "Thou hast deceived me, Jehovah," he exclaims, "and I was deceived" (or, "enticed"; Jer. xx. 7, R.V.); and the New Testament suggests the view that, when the older writers speak of the rewards of Israel's obedience, they sometimes make a large use of illusion —*For if Joshua had given them rest, he* (David) *would not have spoken afterward of another day. There remaineth therefore a sabbath rest for the people of God* (Heb. iv. 8, 9, R.V.). The illusion respecting the authorship of Deuteronomy lasted for centuries, and produced, as we may reverently suppose, no injurious effect upon the Church. But in modern times, and especially now, when the reign of law is recognized not less by the defenders than by the opponents of theology, to ask men to believe that Deuteronomy was written by Moses, or that its substance was spoken though not written by Moses and supernaturally communicated to Hilkiah, would be to impose a burden on the Church which it is not able to bear, and to justify the prejudice against the Church's Biblical scholars which finds frequent utterance in the secular press.

But in what sense did Hilkiah himself call "the book of *tōrāh*" (for 2 Chron. xxxiv. 14 substantially expresses his meaning) "Mosaic"? He means partly that the Deuteronomist absorbed older laws into his code (the full evidence for which must be sought in Dillmann's great critical and exegetical work); partly and more especially that this keen-sighted man wrote as Moses would have written, had he been recalled to life for this purpose. For instance (1), Moses, as the Deuteronomist firmly believed, maintained the claims of Jehovah to an exclusive worship. Hence, even if Moses in his own very early days

[1] "Hymns and Thoughts on Religion by Novalis," translated and edited by W. Hastie (1888), p 90.

permitted or even perhaps encouraged local sanctuaries (Exod xx. 24, comp. xxii. 30), it was clear to the Deuteronomist that, when they had ceased to be useful, Moses would have abolished them. Therefore he, "sitting in the seat of Moses," did abolish them. (2) In Deut. v. 9 the Deuteronomist reverently reproduced the statement of the Decalogue that God " visits the iniquity of the fathers upon the children unto the third and fourth generation," a statement true to the experience of an earlier age, and yet, in his faithfulness to the later leadings of the Divine Spirit, he frankly declared (as he thought that Moses in his place would have declared) in vii. 9, 10, that while mercy is transmitted, wrath is fully worked out on those who have incurred it. Comp. Deut. xxiv 16, the doctrine of which encountered extreme opposition in the post-Josian period (see Jer. xxxi. 29, 20 ; Ezek. xviii. 2–4), many Jews being still incapable of appreciating a truth which the "good old view" absurdly supposes to have been propounded at the Exodus. (3) In Exod. xxi. 7 (a passage belonging to the greater "Book of Covenant," and doubtless regarded by the Deuteronomist as Mosaic) it is enacted that a Hebrew bondwoman shall not be set free at the end of seven years like a bondman; but in Deut. xv. 12–18 the law is made uniform for both sexes. (4) In Exod xxii. 30, firstlings are to be offered to God on the eighth day; but in Deut. xii. 17, 18, xv. 19, 20, they are to be eaten at the sanctuary at the yearly festivals.[1] (5) In Exod. xxii. 31. carrion is to be cast to the dogs ; but in Deut. xiv. 21, social relations having become more developed, the "sojourner" ($g\bar{e}r = \mu\acute{\epsilon}\tau o\iota\kappa o\varsigma$) is allowed to eat it. At other times the author of Deuteronomy simply gives a further development to an ancient law. Thus the law of usury in Exod. xxii. 24 recurs in Deut. xxiii. 19, 20, with a permission to take usury from a stranger ; and the directions as to taking pledges in Exod. xxii. 26, 27, recur in Deut. xxiv. 10–13, with the addition that the choice of the pledge is to be left to the giver of the pledge. Thus the law on the punishment of death for the renegade, which in Exod. xxii. 19 receives the most concise expression possible, is expanded in Deut. xvii 2–8 into the description of a complete judicial procedure. Thus, too, the law of the sab-

[1] Comp. Robertson Smith, "Additional Answer to the Libel" (1878), pp. 17, 18, 55 , and especially the full comparison of the laws in Deuteronomy and in the "Book of Covenant" in Graf, "Die geschichtlichen Bucher," pp. 20–24.

batical year in Exod. xxiii. 10, 11 is condensed into as short a space as possible in Deut. xv. 1, in order to throw into bolder relief an independent ordinance on the mercy to be shown to the debtor during this year.[1] I might, in fact, far exceed my available space in showing how largely older collections of laws have been used.—To sum up briefly: The object of the Deuteronomist was to keep up the historic continuity of the "Mosaic" school of legalists—the orthodox school, one may call it, in opposition to those "lying pens" of which Jeremiah speaks (Jer. viii. 8). The object of Hilkiah was to terminate the painful hesitancy of the believers in a spiritual religion by producing the joint work of some well-trained priest and prophet as the only suitable and divinely appointed law of the state. To abolish polytheism and the dangerous local shrines a new prophecy and a new lawbook, of a more efficacious character than any which had yet been seen, were clearly necessary. These were provided in the original Book of Deuteronomy.

Who was the author, or rather, who were the authors, of the original lawbook? The question reveals, first of all, a want of comprehension of the *ethos* of the inspired writers. No trace can one find in them of the least regard for personal distinction; indeed, the Oriental mind in general is so convinced of the littleness of the individual, that even outside the "household of saints" personal fame is an object of trifling importance. Let us take a lesson from Josiah, whose anxiety was not as to the original author of the lawbook, but as to its agreeableness to the will of God. It argues, next, a defective sense of what it really concerns us to know. What does it matter whether the prophet of Israel's Restoration was, or was not, literally a "second Isaiah"? or whether the author of the prophecy (or of part of the prophecy) attached to Zech. i.–viii. was, or was not, like his predecessor named Zechariah? Whether Hilkiah was or was not a joint-author of Deuteronomy is a point which has much exercised some critics. No doubt "Moses" in Deut. xxxi. 26[2] directs the Levites to *take this lawbook and put it by the side of the ark of the covenant;* this may seem to sup-

[1] Kleinert, "Das Deuteronomium und der Deuteronomiker" (1872), pp 49, 50.
[2] From the point of view of critical analysis, Deut. xxxi. 26 does not belong to the book read by Josiah (see further on).

FRAUD OR NEEDFUL ILLUSION?

port the hypothesis of forgery. And yet can we suppose that Hilkiah was clever enough to justify his (supposed) forgery in so natural a way? Was the art of forgery already so far advanced? It would be interesting biographically could we ascertain that *Jeremiah* was the prophet who (as it seems) assisted the unknown priest in the composition of the book. Could it further be shown that the high priest Hilkiah was Jeremiah's father, one would be strongly tempted to accept Hitzig's view that the "finder" of the lawbook was also its joint-author. But I doubt whether the knowledge of these facts would throw any fresh light on the prophet's character. As a matter of fact, the internal evidence supplied by the Book of Jeremiah is strongly opposed to his having been a Deuteronomist. It is true that the Book is full of phraseological points of contact with Deuteronomy. That great scholar Zunz (whom George Eliot has made known to many unlearned readers) has pointed out sixty-six passages of Deuteronomy, echoes of which occur, as it seems, in eighty-six passages of Jeremiah.[1] We must remember, however, (1) that Jeremiah is imitative; (2) that not all these passages are undoubtedly Deuteronomic and Jeremian respectively;[2] (3) that the influence of Deuteronomy can be traced in many pages of the Old Testament, which there is no ground whatever for assigning to the Deuteronomist; and (4) that while the mood of Jeremiah alternates between despondency and indignation, the Deuteronomist's is that of majestic calm and trust. There are also remarkable differences

[1] "Gesammelte Schriften," 1. 219-222. Bishop Colenso's list in the Appendix to Part vii of his work on the Pentateuch includes too much Kleinert's excursus on the phraseology and vocabulary of the Deuteronomist is more truly critical In his sixth dissertation he sums up the linguistic differences of the two books König's list in his "Alttestamentliche Studien," Heft ii (1839), pp 23-98, requires sifting.

[2] In the original Book of Deuteronomy (if the whole of chaps. v.–xxvi. may be regarded as such) there occur twenty-four passages which are echoed in prophecies of undoubted Jeremian origin. Taking these latter together, there are (according to Zunz's list) only seven chapters or sections (i, iv, x 17-25, xviii, xxxi, xlv, xlvii.) which do not present phraseological points of contact with *our* Book of Deuteronomy These calculations will give the reader some idea of the state of the case To be strictly accurate several tables would be necessary. No "echo" of Deuteronomy is detected by Zunz in Jer. iv. and xxxi. But does not the prophet allude (though in a perfectly free manner) to Deut x. 16, xxx 6 in Jer. iv. 4, and to Deut xxvi. 19, xxviii 1 in Jer xxxi 7?

both in the choice of words and expressions, and in the linguistic type of the two books. The Deuteronomic exhortation to "love God," and the Deuteronomic titles of God and of Israel respectively, "a consuming fire," "a jealous, a merciful, a faithful, a terrible God," "a special people," "a holy people," "thine inheritance," are wanting in Jeremiah; on the other hand, there is nothing in Deuteronomy corresponding to those descriptions of God's attributes in the style of the Psalms in which Jeremiah takes so much delight, *e.g*, "O Jehovah, my strength, and my fortress, and my refuge," Jer. xvi. 19, cf ix. 23, x. 7, 10, xi. 20. Still more remarkable, perhaps, are the linguistic phenomena. Aramaism abounds in Jeremiah; it is hardly to be traced in Deuteronomy. Any student approaching the subject with a fresh mind will, I think, agree with me on the general superiority of the style of the Deuteronomist.

Consider this point, too—that, however akin Jeremiah's conception of religion may be to that of the Deuteronomist, he shows no sign of interest in the cultus or of any special regard for the Levitical priesthood. He denies that the regulation of sacrifices formed any part of the Sinaitic law (Jer vii. 22), and continually denounces the conduct of the priests (Jer. i. 18, ii. 8-26, iv. 9, v. 31, viii. 1, xiii. 13, xxxii. 32). The number and vehemence of the passages referred to are not outweighed by such sporadic instances of a milder view as xvii. 26, xxxi. 14, xxxiii. 11, and 17-24. Indeed, this last passage (xxxiii. 17-24) is very possibly not Jeremiah's work. The whose section in which it occurs (*vv*. 14-26) is omitted in the Septuagint. I may now safely leave this question. It was worth discussing, because the reader may now see less arbitrariness in my future treatment of Jeremiah's course as a preacher.

It only remains to explain the phrase "the original Book of Deuteronomy." We can scarcely claim to restore with precision the very book which made such an impression on Josiah. It is undoubtedly contained in the middle part of Deuteronomy; the only question is whether the whole of this part belongs to the original book. I think that, allowing for some *few* later insertions[1] and glosses, we may regard chaps. v.-xxvi. as the original

[1] As such Dillmann regards ix. 25-x. 11, and xi. 29-33. In my critical analysis I mainly follow Kuenen's new edition of Vol. 1 of his "Onderzock," translated as a separate work by Mr Wicksteed (1886), compare (with this Wellhausen's reprinted in his "Skizzen und Vorarbeiten," Heft ii. 1885), and Horst's in "Revue de l'histoire des religions," 1888, p. 1, &c.

"book of (Divine) instruction." It is probable that i. 1–iv. 44, and iv. 45–49 are two distinct introductions, composed independently by two different writers, close students of the original "book of *tōrāh*" in that which is most distinctive of it, the former of whom may perhaps have had some really Deuteronomic material to work upon. The book itself begins with the "Ten *Words*" (not, Commandments), of the first of which (Deut. v. 6, 7) chaps. vi. 4–xiii. 18, and, in a less strict sense, chaps. xiv. 1–xvi. 17, may be considered as an exposition. The author then "passes (though not without re-crossing the line occasionally) from that which concerns religion in the narrower sense of the word to the outward realm and its arrangement" (xvi. 18–xxvi. 15). And here comes in that appeal, couched in the liveliest prophetic style, to the instinct of self-preservation, which seems to have made so deep an impression on Josiah and his contemporaries :—it was for them indeed that it was specially written. As the Book of Deuteronomy now stands, this appeal is interrupted at the very outset (as any one may see by reading xxvi. 16–19, xxvii. 9, 10, and xxviii. 1, &c. consecutively) by directions (not by the Deuteronomist) about some great stones or στῆλαι on which "the words of this *tōrāh*" were at a later time to be inscribed. They are further interrupted by certain formulæ of benediction and malediction to be recited in the ears of the people on mounts Gerizim and Ebal respectively. "Interrupted" may seem to imply blame; but it is not the passage itself, which in the light of travel is one of the most striking in the Bible, but its unfortunate position which one criticises. Chaps. xxvii. 9, 10 and xxviii. form the true conclusion of the original Deuteronomy; to which, as an epilogue, the writer added xxxi. 9–13, containing the directions of Moses on the writing of the orally-delivered *tōrāh*, on its safe custody, and on its public recitation every seven years.[1] Chaps. xxix , xxx. are by a student of the Deuteronomist, who takes for granted the fulfilment of the curse (comp. Lev. xxvi. 44), and makes it the point of departure for his hopes of Israel's conversion and prosperity in the future. Possibly he had Deuteronomic material to work upon; this point cannot be dogmatized upon. But at any rate he was a noble writer; the holy affectionateness of Moses, as he is

[1] How clearly this is an imaginary Mosaic word. Comp. Deut xvii 18, where every king is directed to *write him a copy of this law (tōrāh) in a book.*

here represented, is most affecting. The Song of Moses (xxxii. 1–43), together with xxxi. 14–23 and xxxii. 44, not improbably once belonged to a different work on the life of Moses. Chaps. xxxi. 24–30 and xxxii. 45–47, which are in the Deuteronomic manner, may have been inserted by a writer of the school of the Deuteronomist when he fitted the Song and the accompanying passages into their present place. The Song is a fine work of the best type of prophetic religion, and has many points with Jeremiah. The writer of the book from which it was taken thought it worthy to be ascribed to Moses. There are linguistic affinities between it and the ninetieth psalm to which early Jewish students gave the same origin. The collection of rhythmical sayings on the tribes in chap. xxxiii is certainly an early work,[1] and of great historical interest.[1] But neither this nor the few remaining passages of the book need detain us now. Let me only add, that, in spite of the critical dissection of Deuteronomy which in honesty I have been obliged to give, I can enjoy the book as a whole as much as any one, and can admire the skill with which the different parts have been put together. It is a fine imaginative account of the latter days of Moses, and I glow with pleasure as I read the concluding words, *There hath not arisen a prophet since in Israel like unto Moses* (Deut. xxiv. 10). Yes, truly; for in *this* Moses I detect the germ of Jeremiah—the forerunner of Christ.

NOTE ON THE "FINDING" OF THE LAWBOOK IN THE TEMPLE.

It would perhaps have startled the reader, if, in the preceding note, I had mentioned the statement of Hilkiah in 2 Kings xxii. 8 as due to the imitation of an Egyptian custom, and urged that this created a presumption in favour of the view that the philo-Egyptian circle from which this statement proceeded was also the circle within which the original Deuteronomy was composed. And yet there would have been some plausibility in this. It was a suggestion of M. Maspero's in the "Revue critique" (I think, in 1878) which first drew my attention to the subject, and it has often struck me, as from an Egyptological point of view, a not unreasonable one. Every year, in fact, reveals fresh points of contact between the culture of Egypt and that of the neighbouring countries, and it requires a firm hold on the peculiarity of Hebraism not to exaggerate the *rôle* of teacher which in many respects

---

[1] As early, certainly, as the reign of Jeroboam II., the "saviour" given to Israel (2 Kings xiii. 5); see Graf's very cogent argument, "Der Segen Mose's," p. 81.

FRAUD OR NEEDFUL ILLUSION?

belongs to the people of the Nile-valley. The facts on which M Maspero's suggestion is based are these It was a common practice of Egyptian scribes to insert in their transcripts of great religious or scientific works a statement that the writing in question had been "found" in a temple. For example, chap. lxiv. of the "Book of the Dead" (an authority for some important religious doctrines) was declared in certain documents to have been found by an Egyptian prince, in the reign of Mencheres, beneath the feet of the god Thoth.[1] Again, a chapter in the medical papyrus preserved in the British Museum bears the following rubric: "This cure was discovered at night by the hand of a minister of the temple of the goddess who happened to go into the Hall in the temple of the city of Tebmut in the secret places of that goddess. The land at the time was in darkness, but the moon shone on that book all over it. It was brought as a valuable treasure to His Majesty King Kheops."[2] And one of the medical treatises in the Berlin papyrus edited by Brugsch "was found, in ancient writing, in a coffer of books at the feet of the god Anup of Sekhem, in the days of the holiness of the king of the two Egypts, the Veracious"[3] Now it is too much to believe that the priests and learned men of Egypt were so ignorant of their own literature as to discover these important works by a pure accident. It is much more probable that it was a conventional fiction of the priestly class to say that a book had been "found" in a temple, when it was wished to affirm and inculcate its sacred and authoritative character with special emphasis May there not then (considering the other traces of an acquaintance with Egypt in the book) be an imitation of this custom when Deut xxxi 26 makes "Moses" say, *Take this book of tôrāh, and put it by the side of the ark of the covenant?* The position assigned to the lawbook beside the ark (in a box of some kind, we must suppose) corresponds to that of the "coffer of books at the feet of (the Egyptian god) Anup." Deuteronomy does not indeed bear the title "found in a coffer beside the ark", but Hilkiah in the narrative of 2 Kings says that he found the book in the temple. Is it not possible that the book was—not lost by accident, nor yet placed in the sanctuary with the intention to deceive—but simply taken to the temple and formally placed there as authoritative Scripture, and then communicated to Josiah with the view of its promulgation? My answer is that the lawbook as known to Hilkiah did not (as we have seen) contain Deut. xxxi. 24-30, that Hilkiah represents a party opposed to foreign influences (comp Jer. ii. 18), and that the authors of none of the other religious classics of Israel (however Egyptian their colouring, as in the case of the Joseph-story) imitate this custom of the Egyptian *literati*. It is only in Phœnician literature than we can perhaps find a parallel to it, Philo of Byblus (second cent. A.D.) asserts that the Phœnician history of Sanchoniathon had been concealed and brought back to light by himself.

---

[1] Brugsch, "Geschichte Ægyptens," ed. 1, p. 84; Maspero, "Histoire ancienne de l'Orient," ed. 1, p. 73.

[2] Buch, "Egyptische Zeitschrift" (1871), p 63.

[3] Brugsch, as above, p. 60, Maspero, as above, p. 57.

NOTE ON THE ALLUSIONS TO EGYPT IN DEUTERONOMY.

One of the principal arguments for the Mosaic authorship of Deuteronomy is based on its allusions to Egypt and to Egyptian customs, combined with the absence of allusions to Assyria. Dr Bissell, one of those young American scholars from whom so much may be hoped, goes so far as to represent this as fatal to the theory of the late origin of the lawbook [1] Such allusions to Egypt doubtless exist, though the list requires sifting. Among the best attested are the references to the ox treading out the corn unmuzzled (Deut xxv 4), cf Wilkinson, "Ancient Egyptians," ii 46, and to the practice of irrigating the soil "with the foot" (Deut xi 10), i.e., in Mr. Espin's words, "by means of tread-wheels working sets of pumps, and by means of artificial channels connected with reservoirs, and opened, turned, or closed with the feet." The frequent references to the servitude of the Israelites in Egypt (Deut v. 15, vi 21, &c) are also remarkable. We might have expected that the writer would show a horror of the Egyptians, but no ; he represents Moses as deprecating such a feeling, and permitting an Egyptian to be admitted to religious privileges in the third generation (Deut xxiii. 7, 8). Lastly, I must mention a very singular passage in the law for the king (Deut xvii 14-20) "But he shall not multiply horses to himself, nor cause the people to return to Egypt, to the end that he should multiply horses forasmuch as Yahveh hath said unto you, Ye shall henceforth return no more that way" (v. 16). No thoroughly satisfactory explanation of this prohibition has, perhaps, yet been given. We may, however, at least, infer from it that in the time of the writer an attachment to Egypt prevailed among the highest classes of the Israelites. Possibly we may illustrate this by the name of Josiah's father—Amon, which is identical with that of the Egyptian Sun-god (cf. No-Amon, No of Amon, or rather Amen, the name of the Egyptian Thebes in Nahum iii. 8) But at any rate there is no necessity from these Egyptian allusions to argue the Mosaic authorship of Deuteronomy In fact, the communication between Palestine and Egypt was so easy, that the wonder is, not that there should be some allusions to Egypt in the Old Testament, or in any book of it, but rather that there should be so few Allusions to Assyria were of course not to be expected in a summary of "Mosaic" laws and discourses I do not venture to assume that the form of the literary fiction in Deuteronomy is borrowed from Egypt, though the assumption would have some plausibility. It would of course cut away the ground for the theory of Mosaic authorship.

---

[1] "The Pentateuch : its Origin and Structure" (1885), p. 278, &c.

CHAPTER VIII.

"HIS REMEMBRANCE IS LIKE MUSIC" (ECCLUS. XLIX. 1).

David's "last words" fulfilled in Josiah—His thirteen golden years after the great covenant—Jeremiah's comparative happiness—His friends among the wise men—Pharaoh Neco profits by the weakness of Assyria—Josiah's defeat at Megiddo, his death—The national mourning—The tragedy of his life, and of Israel's history.

"And these are David's last words:
David, son of Jesse, saith,
The man whom God exalted saith,
The anointed of the God of Jacob,
And the darling of the songs of Israel,
Jehovah's spirit spake by me,
And his word was on my tongue;

The God of Israel said,
To me the Rock of Israel spake:
Who ruleth justly over men,
Who ruleth in the fear of God,
Is like the morning light at sunrise,
A morning without rain.
Through sunshine, through rain,
grass springeth from the earth."
(2 Sam. xxiii. 1-4)

THESE are the words dramatically put into the mouth of David by one of those nameless writers who flourished in the period of the greater prophets—themselves filled to overflowing with the spirit of prophetic religion. Just as several great inspired prose-writers and poets busied themselves in the Book of Deuteronomy (see end of Chapter VII.) with reproducing what must have been the last words of Moses, or what would have been his last words if he had lived in their own time, so several great inspired poets endeavoured, so to speak, to think themselves back into the soul of David, and complete the scanty number of the songs of the founder of psalmody. One of these poets is the author of the eighteenth psalm; another composed that beautiful poem the first part of which is the motto of this chapter. This latter writer may well have lived in the time of Hezekiah or Josiah,[1] and the second part of his poem may reflect the vigorous measures of one or the other of these great reformers. But whichever king suggested this idealization of his remote ancestor, it is in Josiah alone that the opening words of the poem are fully realized. Of him, more than of any other king, may it be said that he was the darling both of Jehovah and of Israel ; and the words of the poem do but express in ornate language the idea of Jeremiah's noble epitaph (as I have called it) on his friend : *Did not thy father eat and drink, and do judgment and justice, and then it was well with him ? He judged the cause of the poor and needy; then it was well with him; was not this to know me, saith Jehovah ?* (Jer. xxii. 15, 16).

For thirteen years after the publication of the first Scripture, Josiah continued to occupy the throne of David, of whose ideal he seemed the living embodiment. David fell far short of his ideal, because he had no Scripture as the compass of his life ; whereas the mingled sentiments of fear, love, and hope, awakened in Josiah by the reading of Deuteronomy, could at any time be kindled again to a white heat by meditation upon that inspired volume. The words, *Then said I, Lo, I am come; in the roll of the book is my duty written; my delight, O my God, is to do thy will; yea, thy law (tōrāh) is within my heart* (Psa. xl. 7, 8), even if written later, must represent the state of mind of the good Josiah. I can well believe that he fulfilled the direction in Deut. xvii. 18, and *wrote him a copy of this law, and read therein all the days of his life.* And I think we may safely conjecture that these last thirteen years of his reign were among the happiest of the long period of the monarchy. Certainly they must have been so if the Deuteronomic code was approximately carried out. Even where its provisions seem to us unpractical, their spirit is so exquisitely humane, that a modern reader may well sigh at the slow pace of our improvements. Here is a lawbook, made in the interests not of any class or caste, but of the whole people ; or, if it does display a

---

[1] The song must be taken in connexion with the prophecy put into the mouth of Nathan (see especially 2 Sam vii. 11–16) by a writer who lived when prophecy had long assumed a literary garb, and, in all probability, at the time assigned above to the author of our song, who "thought himself into the soul" of David, just as the author of 2 Sam. vii. 5, &c. "thought himself into the soul" of David's prophet.

preference for any part of the community, it is for the poor and weak. Where is the Christian nation which recognized this even as a standard to be aimed at, until that great awakening of the moral and religious conscience—or, in Bible language, that great Day of the LORD (Jehovah)—which filled up the close of the eighteenth century? Well said the author of Deuteronomy, in the introduction[1] which (after perhaps a few years' experience of the benefits to the nation at large of the system introduced through him) he prefixed to his original work, *What great nation is there, that hath statutes and judgments so righteous as all this law (tōrāh), which I set before you this day?* (Deut. iv. 8). He speaks, no doubt, in the assumed character of Moses; but by the three times repeated expression *great nation* (see *vv.* 6-8) he reveals the fact that the people of Israel had, either through God's longsuffering mercy (Rom. ii. 4) or through His blessing upon its obedience, attained a high degree of temporal prosperity.

It is remarkable that not one of the prophecies of Jeremiah can be referred to these years. Either he still devoted himself to the exposition of the Deuteronomic law, or, if he delivered original prophecies of his own, he did not afterwards care to reproduce them, except of course so far as their contents reappeared in prophecies of later reigns. At any rate, in spite of his melancholy statements at an earlier and a later period, I make no doubt that these thirteen years were a time of comparative happiness to the prophet, that, like Isaiah, he enjoyed the society of friends and disciples, and that to these among others he refers in a subsequent discourse respecting those captives in Babylon on whom Jehovah graciously promised to set His eyes for good (Jer. xxiv. 2-7). Among these friends may have been the nameless author of the first nine chapters of the Book of Proverbs, which were not written to fill their present place, but once formed an independent work in praise of true Wisdom.[2] In its genial, persuasive tone and sunny spirit, this book reminds us not so much of Jeremiah as of the exhortations in the Book of Deuteronomy, like which it inculcates the doctrine, so well adapted to young pupils and primitive nations, that the fear of God is the one source of earthly happiness.

[1] On the critical analysis of the book, see end of Chapter VII.

[2] "Job and Solomon" (1887), p. 156, &c., comp. Stanley, "Jewish Church," ii. 170, &c.

My readers will admit that there is nothing violent or far-fetched in the view which I have put forward, and which fits itself admirably into a harmonious and well-proportioned historical picture of the times. There were three orders of God's ministers in what by anticipation I may venture to call the Jewish Church—priests, wise men or moral teachers, and prophets. Their respective functions are well indicated in a popular saying reported by Jeremiah (xviii. 18), *Religious direction shall not be lost from the priest, nor counsel from the wise man, nor revelation from the prophet.* There is no doubt that other prophets of the nobler type were on friendly terms with the best of the wise men, whose very language they sometimes borrow,[1] and how can Jeremiah have been unacquainted with so eminent a wise man as the author of this lovely treatise, so closely akin to his own favourite book, Deuteronomy? The value of such conjectures (which, when supported by all the attainable evidence, approach indefinitely near to facts) is that they help to make the Bible story live again to us, and I hope never to cease repeating that this is one of the greatest tasks of the Christian teachers of our day, and closely connected with the future of Christianity among the educated classes.

The wise men or moral teachers flourished most in periods of tranquillity. It was in such a period—that of Solomon—that we can first confidently trace them, and a not less golden opportunity was furnished for their work by these last thirteen years of Josiah. Alas that the "fine gold" so soon "became dim" (Lam. iv. 1)! Alas that the teachers so soon had to become learners again in the stern school of calamity! The inspired poet to whom I owe my motto spoke of a summer sky, with its sweet vicissitudes of sun and shower, causing the grass to spring up, and all homely, common blessings. Suddenly and without a warning, that smiling heaven became black with clouds. Do not let us despise the elementary lesson which this supports, and which it took God's ancient people so long to learn. Trust not the future; fierce are the storms of spring, but those of summer can be as wild, God is not bound to make the years resemble each other in the cloying sweetness of perpetual ease. Midway in life[2] to each of the two best kings of Judah

---

[1] "The Prophecies of Isaiah," note on Isa xxviii 23. In Jer. viii. 9, our prophet refers perhaps to the less religious class of wise men.

[2] Hitzig would render, in the opening line of Hezekiah's psalm (Isa.

came a sore calamity; Hezekiah became sick unto death, but the Lord's hand held him back;[1] Josiah, at the same age of 39,[2] was overmatched by a too powerful opponent, and died in battle. This is how it came about, and why we should regard this event as one of the greatest tragedies of the sacred story.

Let us now go back in imagination about twenty years to the time when the Scythian hordes overran Assyria and Babylonia. Both countries, as we remember, suffered cruelly, but the Assyrians, up to this time the more aggressive and warlike race, had at length been overtaken by a lassitude which had destroyed their physical power of recovering from injury. They had added conquest to conquest, but taken no pains to weld their dominions into a durable empire, and so revolt followed upon revolt, and the reign of Assurbanipal was like the last fine day in autumn—the too brilliant forerunner of a period of trouble and disaster. The death of Assurbanipal (was it 626 B.C. ?) certainly fell in the first part of the reign of Josiah, and the dangerous position of that great king's successor may have encouraged Josiah to extend his own sway over part of the former kingdom of Ephraim, for we find him continuing his iconoclastic progress to Bethel and "the cities of Samaria[3] (2 Kings xxiii. 15-19; comp. 2 Chron. xxxiv. 6). At any rate, Neco II., the reigning Pharaoh, an enterprising monarch (as we know from Herodotus),[4] and strong in all military resources, resolved to

---

xxxviii. 10), "In the middle of my days must I go," &c.; comp. the extreme limit of the age of man in Psa. xc. 10. A suggestive even if wrong rendering !

[1] Isa. xxxviii 17, *thou hast held back my soul from the pit of destruction.* R V.'s rendering is barely possible, but the text only says, "thou hast loved my soul out of," &c. I prefer to follow the reading of the Septuagint and the Vulgate, with most recent critics.

[2] With most, I assume the correctness of the revised text of 2 Kings xxii. 1.

[3] Is it possible to account for Jeremiah's special kindness and courtesy towards northern Israel in chaps. iii and xxxi. by a desire to make up for the judicial severity of his royal patron (2 Kings xxiii 19 20), which must have deeply wounded the feelings of the remnant of Ephraim?

[4] In v 21, two words need correction from 3 Esdras i 25—"house" becomes "Euphrates", "disguised himself" becomes "firmly resolved"—the latter correction is also confirmed by the Septuagint; lastly, where the received text reads "to make haste," I follow Klostermann in reading "in a dream."

profit by the manifest weakness of Assyria. In the spring of 608, he began a series of campaigns, designing to conquer one by one the provinces of feudatory states of the Nineveh empire. Of these feudatory states Judah had formerly been one. I think it probable that Josiah had for some time past, like Hezekiah (2 Kings xviii. 7), refused tribute to the Assyrian suzerain; at least, it would be unreasonable to suppose that Josiah took the field against Neco, as he presently did, in the character of a vassal of Nineveh. This is all that the earlier of the two Hebrew narrators says on the intervention of Josiah,—

In his days Pharaoh Neco king of Egypt went up against the king of Assyria to the river Euphrates: and king Josiah went against him, and he slew him at Megiddo when he had seen him (2 Kings xxiii. 29).

The Chronicler is rather more full. He feels the fragmentary character of his preceding record, and connects this record with the sad story which follows in a purely mechanical manner.

After all this—that Josiah had prepared the temple, Neco king of Egypt went up to fight by Carchemish on the Euphrates; and Josiah went out against him. And Neco sent messengers to him, saying, What have I to do with thee, king of Judah? Not against thee am I come this day; for upon Euphrates is my war. And Elohim hath commanded me in a dream; keep thee away from Elohim, who is with me, that he destroy thee not. But Josiah turned not his face from him, for he had firmly resolved to fight with him, and hearkened not unto the words of Neco from the mouth of Elohim; and he came to fight with him in the valley of Megiddo (2 Chron. xxxv. 20–22).[1]

We may perhaps regard it as a historical fact that Neco sent an embassy to Josiah; the Chronicler certainly preserves some

---

[1] This delightful writer becomes our chief authority for this period, as Brugsch in an eloquent, melancholy sentence tells us ("Geschichte Ægyptens," ed. 1, p. 737). From Herod. ii 152, iv. 42, we learn to respect in Neco (Νεκῶς) the predecessor of Lesseps (for the Egyptian king fully deserved to succeed in cutting through the isthmus of Suez) and of Diaz and Vasco de Gama (in the circumnavigation of Africa). If Neco and his imitator, the Corinthian tyrant Periander, had but succeeded in their enterprising schemes, how profoundly they would have affected the course of history! The true cause of Neco's abandonment of the canal was probably, not the supposed oracle in Herodotus, but the necessity of increasing his forces for the defence of the Egyptian frontier after his defeat in Asia. On the canal, comp. Ebers, "Durch Gosen zum Sinai," p. 471, &c.

historic traditions omitted in Kings. Even the contents of the message are in themselves probable enough. Like the bold statement of the Rabshakeh in Isa. xxxvi 10, they may be fitly illustrated by the striking description of a dream-oracle in the Annals of Assurbanipal.[1] Neco had his own prophets who could doubtless interpret dreams. If, however, we decline the conjectural reading "in a dream" (see below), we may, if we will, follow 3 Esdras 1. 28, when *the words of Neco* become *the words of Jeremiah*. Certainly, it is probable enough that Jeremiah's person had a supernatural sanctity in the eyes of Egyptian as well as of Assyrian generals. But we know nothing from the Book of Jeremiah of any advice which he gave to Josiah, and the point of the narrative seems to be that even Neco had a true presentiment, while Josiah, the darling of God and man, rushed blindly to his fate. But what was the cause of his aggressive conduct? It is quite impossible that he should have been affected by considerations of statecraft, not merely because he was the friend of Jeremiah, and must have accepted as Divine the early fulminations of the prophet (chap. ii.), but also from the very nature of the case. For policy would have suggested to him either to help Neco, or at any rate not to oppose him. What harm could the Pharaoh possibly do to the Jews? Supposing that he defeated the Assyrians, would he not soon have more formidable opponents in the Medes and Babylonians,[2] a rumour of whose warlike movements must by this time have reached Palestine, and be only too glad to return within his own borders?

I think that a comprehensive study of the history of revealed religion suggests the true explanation. God sometimes sacrifices the individual for the sake of the community—allows him to become the victim of dangerous illusions, in order that they may be seen to be illusions. Josiah—if I have described him rightly—made the Scripture of Deuteronomy the rule of his life. It was not merely a formal but a spiritual obedience that

[1] "Records of the Past," ix. 52 It was Assurbanipal's prophet who had the dream. Probably, like the Egyptian priests, when they sought for oracles, he slept, like Samuel, near the holy place, and regarded his "thoughts from visions of the night" (Job iv 13) as necessarily Divine

[2] Josephus ("Ant " x 5, 1) actually says that Neco's object was to war with the Medes and Babylonians, " who had overthrown the empire of the Assyrians."

he gave to it; he performed God's law from love. I do not in this equalize him with our Lord or even with His saintly followers; but upon the whole we must believe him to have assimilated that great idea, first clearly announced, though not in such few words, by Hosea, and incorporated into the prophetic portion of the Book of Deuteronomy—that "God is love." Josiah cannot have known his countrymen as Jeremiah knew them; he was of too exalted a rank to gauge their spiritual attainments. The idea that his reformation was half a failure could never have occurred to him, and if suggested by another, it would have been against nature for him to admit it. This, then, was one of the illusions to which he became a victim—the illusion that his countrymen knew and served Jehovah, and were consequently the objects of His loving favour, in the same sense or degree as himself. The other was one to which in all probability even Jeremiah was still subject, in common with such a noble and inspired religious thinker as the author of the little book on Divine Wisdom in Prov. i.–ix. It was this—that in the long run righteousness is rewarded in this world by prosperity, and unrighteousness punished by adversity. Josiah would certainly have called himself a righteous man, not in the sense of that Chinese who said that he had never committed a single "sin" (he added that neither had his father nor his grandfather ever done so), but in the sense that he had given his heart to God, and that his chief desire was to perform that law which he so much loved. He must have argued therefore (comp. the argument which Assurbanipal pleads to Istar) [1] that Jehovah would meet love with love, and reward him openly for his faithful obedience. It would have been quite intelligible had Josiah aspired to revive the glorious days of David. Dr. Oort of Leyden and Mr. F. W. Newman have indeed too boldly conjectured that Psa. lxxii. expresses such anticipations on the part of one of Josiah's subjects, and Deut. xx., xxi. might conceivably have stimulated warlike feelings in the monarch. But at any rate, when, at the head of warriors not less righteous (as he fondly supposed), Josiah took the field against a heathen invader, he must, one imagines, have been full of a David-like boldness and faith. Nor, sympathetic as he must have been towards pious psalmists, can he have failed to recall those words which a recent poet had put into the mouth of David,—

[1] See "Records of the Past," ix 51.

> *Jehovah dealt with me according to my righteousness,*
> *According to the cleanness of my hands he recompensed me,*
> *Because I kept the ways of Jehovah,*
> *And did not wickedly depart from my God:*
> *For all his ordinances were before me,*
> *And I did not put away his statutes from me;*
> *I was also perfect towards him,*
> *And I kept myself from guiltiness.*
> *So thou gavest me thy shield of victory;*
> *Thy right hand held me up,*
> *And thy condescension made me great.*
> *I pursued mine enemies and overtook them;*
> *And turned not again till I had consumed them,*
> *I dashed them to pieces that they could not rise,*
> *But fell under my feet* (Psa. xviii. 20-23, 35-38).

But still more must he have thought of those glowing benedictions at the end of Deuteronomy which are expressly attached to the faithful observance of the book of the covenant,—

And it shall come to pass . . . that Jehovah thy God will set thee on high above all nations of the earth. Blessed shalt thou be in the city, and blessed in the field. Blessed shall be thy basket and thy store. Blessed shalt thou be when thou comest in, and blessed when thou goest out. Jehovah shall cause thine enemies that rise up against thee to be smitten before thy face; they shall come out against thee one way, and flee before thee seven ways (Deut. xxviii. 1-8).

For it was not a war of conquest in which Josiah was engaging, but a holy war. The south or the land of Israel had, it is true, been spared; but both in his reforming progress, and, we may now add, even in his final choice of a battlefield, Josiah declared himself to be the rightful king both of north and of south —the legal representative of David and Solomon.[1] If the Assyrians had withdrawn their heavy hand from the territory of Ephraim, was it to be endured that another unbelieving foe should pitch his tents in the very heart of the sacred land? And so no doubt costly sacrifices were offered in the temple before the army set forth, and the twentieth psalm was sung, containing the words,—

> *Now am I sure that Jehovah saveth his anointed,*
> *He will answer him from his holy heaven*
> *With the mighty saving acts of his right hand* (Psa. xx. 6).

[1] See above, p. 60.

The two armies met in the strategically important valley or, to use the more accurately descriptive term, plain (Heb., *bik'āh*, a broad plain between mountains) of Jezreel or Esdraelon.[1] The name of the place was confounded by Herodotus informant with that of a town on the north-east frontier of Egypt, which I shall have to mention again later, it was really Megiddo, not Magdol, where the fatal clash of arms took place (2 Kings xxiii. 29). By what route did the Egyptians arrive? Just before his reference to Neco's defeat of the "Syrians" at "Magdolos," Herodotus speaks of the docks where the ships were built which that king "employed wherever he had occasion."[2] It is not impossible that, to avoid hostilities with Josiah, Neco took his troops by sea to some landing-place north of Judah proper—say, to Dōr, an ancient and famous port,[3] which probably remained Phœnician, even after Nāfath (or Nāfōth) Dōr was conquered by the Israelites (Josh. xi. 2, xii. 23, Judges i. 27, 1 Kings iv. 11). Its Phœnician inhabitants were doubtless as politic as Josiah was the reverse. From Dōr (slightly to the north of the modern village Ṭanṭura) to Megiddo in the great plain of Jezreel was no great distance; Duru (Dōr) and Magidu or Magadu (Megiddo) are in fact mentioned together in the Assyrian inscriptions. The alternative is to suppose that Neco took the same route as Thothmes III. (B.C. 1600?), in whose reign, as the inscriptions tell, "Egypt placed its frontier where it pleased," and who led his invading forces by land to "Maketa" or Megiddo, where he routed the combined forces of Syria and Mesopotamia.[4] At any rate, it was on the battlefield of Megiddo,[5] famous already in the poetry of Israel by the defeat of Jabin and Sisera, and not less celebrated in apocalyptic vision (Rev. xvi. 16), that the unequal struggle

---

[1] Herod. ii. 158.

[2] For the historical associations connected with this "battlefield of Syria," ranging from Thothmes III. and Rameses II. to Bonaparte and Kleber, see Lias's note on Judg. vi. 33 (Cambridge Bible).

[3] See Schurer, "The Jewish People in the Time of Jesus Christ," E. T. Div. ii., Vol 1, p 88.

[4] "Records of the Past," ii 37–39 (Birch); comp. Brugsch, "Geschichte Ægyptens," ed. 1, pp 295–6.

[5] On a low promontory thrown out from the Samaritan hills towards the recess between the Nazarene range and Jebel Daḥy ("Little Hermon") stood the Roman *Legio*, whence the modern *Lejûn*. Here, too, probably, in the most peaceful of landscapes, stood Megiddo.

between Neco and Josiah took place. Alas! the men of Israel fled at the very beginning of the battle;[1] it was as if (applying a well-known Hebrew figure[2]) the aspect of the angry Egyptian king had scattered his enemies. The fate of Ahab became that of Josiah. "a certain man drew a bow at a venture, and smote the king of Israel" (1 Kings xxii. 34, comp. 2 Chron. xxxv. 23). He was brought to Jerusalem to die. What were his last thoughts? Did he still trust God? None can answer that question; but that the faith of many of his subjects was shaken, we may be certain. The problem of a perfect and upright man given into the hand of "the Satan" became from this time forth the problem of Jewish wisdom—the problem of which there is but a faintly hinted solution in the noblest monument of that wisdom, the Book of Job.

That blessed results accrued in the long run to the Jewish Church from this great calamity, could easily be shown. From Megiddo the eye turns instinctively to the hillside on which, twelve miles distant, lovely Nazareth stands. But who thought of looking beyond the sad sights of the immediate present? Faith was paralyzed; the heart of the nation seemed to stand still. Unmixed sadness and consternation spread through all classes. The more recent of our two narrators makes this statement, to which I shall have to return later,—

And all Judah and Jerusalem mourned for Josiah. And Jeremiah lamented for Josiah: and all the singing men and the singing women spake of Josiah in their lamentations unto this day; and they were made an ordinance (i.e., institution) *in Israel* (2 Chron. xxxv. 24, 25).

Such a national mourning was doubtless very different from the prescribed lamentations at an ordinary king's death; one thinks of the mourning after the field of Flodden in Scottish history. The whole land mourned; every family felt bereaved (Zech. xii. 11, 12). But some may in a special sense be called

---

[1] So we must explain the words, *when he had seen him.* It is not stated in the Old Testament that the men of Israel fled; but we may safely presume that the presence of the king was still as all-important to the army as in Ahab's time. So Josephus understood the Biblical passages. He says that Josiah was setting his army in array when one of the Egyptians shot him, and put a stop to his eagerness for the fray; on which he commanded a retreat to be sounded.

[2] See *e g.* Lam. iv. 16.

"chief mourners." First of all, the poor and weak, to whom it had been Josiah's delight to do justice ; and next, the friends of spiritual religion with whom from his earliest youth he had been so closely allied. Let us sympathize, then, most deeply with Jeremiah, whose hopes have once more been dashed to the ground. For the result of the defeat and death of Josiah was, not merely the reduction of Judah to the rank of a subject-state, but above all, the revival of idolatry and the sore discouragement of the little band of reformers. Jeremiah, the most illustrious mourner, must indeed have felt the blow. Henceforth his life is a true martyrdom, only relieved by his rock-like constancy, and by that wondrous revelation to which I have already alluded, and which represents the high-water mark of Jewish religion before the Captivity.

The story of Israel is a succession of tragedies ; but perhaps there is none more touching than the tragedy of the death of Josiah. And for this reason—that he is so entirely innocent. His case was not that of so many of the later Jews, who fell back into an illusion which revelation ought to have dissipated. No ; he could not have believed otherwise than he did. What an enigma his fate would remain, if Jesus Christ had not ratified the presentiments of the noblest Jews since Jeremiah, and proved that the way to the crown lies by the cross. Can we doubt that even this defeated king has received a crown—the crown of one who has lived by the light of God's word, and ventured all rather than distrust His promises? And in the spirit of Josiah's life shall not we, my readers, follow him ? Say not that the standard is too high, that such passionate earnestness is not in our character, that such devotion to conscience is Quixotic. It is the glory of the Gospel that, by using its resources, the common man or woman may exceed the standard of the highest Old Testament saint (Matt. xi. 11). Our heart may be an unsteady thing; but, as the psalmist says, Jehovah is not only the believer's portion in eternity, but his rock in time. With God's "light" and God's "truth" (that is, "faithfulness") for guides (Psa. xliii. 3), the weakest character and the strongest gain alike a supernatural depth and seriousness. They will go with us into battle, like the ark of Jehovah, and ensure us the victory, even though, as in Josiah's case, the victory may not be manifest even to ourselves till we reach the other side—I will not say, of death, but of life. With these heavenly guides, we need fear no shocks whether to our outward or to our inward being. Riches may take to themselves wings and flee away; friends may pass before us into the "silent land"; forms of doctrine may, as with Josiah's contemporaries, prove to be not free from educational illusion; but "Israel's Rock" (Isa. xxx. 29, R.V.) remains. *My flesh and my heart faileth, but God is the rock of my heart, and my portion for ever* (Psa. lxxiii. 26).

I spoke of Josiah's death as one of the greatest of religious tragedies. Alas that in Israel's history there should be one still greater, which, if we felt it aright, would make our hearts bleed. It is a perennial tragedy—that of the veiled face set forth in sculpture on the lovely door of the Chapter-room of my own cathedral. The mourning of the people of Judah for Josiah is taken in the Book of Zechariah (xii. 10-14) as an emblem of a mourning yet future, when God's "ancient people"[1] (Isa. xliv. 7) shall *look on him*[2] *whom they pierced, and shall mourn for him as one mourneth for an only son, and as the mourning for Hadad-rimmon*[3] *in the plain of Megiddo.* The tragedy lies in the well-nigh two thousand years' wanderings of Israel through a labyrinth of slowly brightening

[1] It is often impossible to determine with certitude between different interpretations, and one may sometimes believe that, like other Oriental writers, the prophets and psalmists meant to be enigmatical (comp. Delitzsch's note on Psa. lxxii. 15). Delitzsch explains this phrase of the people of the antediluvian world; Bredenkamp (the latest commentator, who doubtless *ought* to be the wisest), of the people of Israel, called to be God's people since the earliest times.

[2] The received text has "unto me," but the last letter (י) representing the pronoun "me," is probably the first letter, or a fragment of the first letter, of some lost word, the middle part of which has dropped out, and the last part is represented (or misrepresented) by the letters את. The reading "unto him" is, probably, only a conjectural emendation, the acceptance of which does not modify the syntactic peculiarity of the phrase. I have adopted it above, simply from ignorance of the true reading, which may either have been a proper name or a term descriptive of character or office. Who was the person alluded to? Was it the same martyr who seems to be referred to in the ancient prophecy adopted and modified in Isa. lii 13-liii.? If so, Jehovah sympathized with His martyr, and regarded the "insult" as offered to Himself (cf. Psa lxix 9).

[3] Jerome says, "Adadremmon is a city near Jerusalem, now called Maximianopolis, in the field of Mageddon, where the righteous king Josiah was wounded by the Pharaoh called Nechao." At a short distance from

darkness. The clue is missing; when shall the wanderer find it? Sad, beyond expression sad; but is it not a *fascinating* tragedy? Why do so few of us know this? *Is it nothing to you, all ye that pass by*, whose eyes are never satisfied with seeing, nor whose ears with hearing, for whom no poetry is too sensuous, no romance too strange? Ye who have been nourished on the story of the Israel of Scripture—has it so fully satisfied your curiosity that you have not a thought for the second part of that wondrous tale? Has no one told you of the manifold interest of Jewish history in the middle ages, and of Jewish life at the present time? Some of you, who think scorn of poetry and romance, find your pleasure perhaps in the records of missionary work in heathen lands. Is there no pleasure to be won from the records of missions (not merely English missions) to the Jews—a pleasure mingled (I must sadly confess) with pain at the faulty methods which have too often been adopted, but one which brings you very near the heart of Jesus? There may be others among you who fear even this chastened pleasure, and who promote Christian missions simply from a sense of duty. Does not the thought of five thousand poor Jewish refugees added to the population of East London suggest to you the idea of a duty—the duty of bringing them to the great Teacher if you can, but at any rate of helping them, and especially of sympathizing with them, of giving some thought to their past history and present condition. *God hath not cast away his people*,[1] says St. Paul, with the passionate earnestness which is the keynote of his character. Nay, a part of the prophecy is being fulfilled. A "spirit of supplication" has been "poured out" upon many of those who are still in the fullest and truest sense Israelites. No people on the face of the earth weeps so much for its sins and their punishment as the eastern Jews. Those who have once heard them in their synagogues cry in Hebrew, "Forgive us now, forgive us now," confess that they can never forget it. It is almost as touching to see the Jews, as Sir Richard Temple truly remarks, come singly and quietly, without any form or

Lejjûn there is still a place called Rummâne, in which the second part of the name Hadad-rimmon may perhaps survive. It ought to be mentioned that there is another explanation of Zech. xii. 11, but to do it justice, would carry us too far into criticism.

[1] Rom. xi. 1; comp. Jer. xxxi. 38.

ceremony, to weep over the beloved stones at the accustomed "Wailing-place."[1] When shall the other part of the prophecy be fulfilled? When shall they look with desire on Him whom by their ignorant unbelief they have so long pierced?[2]

This is the tragedy of Israel—a people, than which there is none more ancient[3] nor more noble, but neglectful of its highest honour and grandest privilege. To understand the causes of this tragedy, will be the reward of him who ponders the later pages of the romantic story of God's people.

[1] "Palestine Illustrated" (1883), p. 40.

[2] In a few sentences, one can hardly express a point of view, much less give conclusions. May I therefore refer to the article entitled "The Jews and the Gospel" in "The Expositor," 1885 (1), pp. 405-418, which seeks to be just to all who "turn upwards" (Hos. vii. 16) in Israel, whether in a manner congenial to ourselves or not.

[3] I do not forget the constancy of the old Egyptian ethnic type, which permits you, as M E. M. de Vogüé remarks, to confound the fellah who guides you in the Bûlak museum with the statues against which he jostles. But can the motley population of Egypt be called a nation?

PART II.

THE CLOSE OF JUDAH'S TRAGEDY.

CHAPTER I.

THE CLOUDS RETURN AFTER THE RAIN.

Consequences of Josiah's death—Jeremiah's changed attitude towards Deuteronomy—His visit to Anathoth.

IN a volume of poetic reproductions of sacred stories by the late Dr. Neale there is one entitled "Josiah," which suggests a modification of an image employed in the last chapter. At the opening of Josiah's reign it might indeed be natural to compare it to a bright summer sky, but we who know its sad termination must feel with the poet that the pensive beauty of an autumnal day is a more appropriate figure, especially when we remember how, even in England, the glories of autumn sometimes pass away in the tempest of a single night. Yes ; and it was not an English but an Eastern winter, such as we find described by the world-weary Preacher (Eccles. xii. 2) which followed Josiah's death. The religious results of that great calamity were twofold. First, the revival, to some extent at least, of idolatrous practices. This is what Jeremiah himself says (xvii. 2),—*The sin of Judah is written with a pen of iron and with the point of a diamond; it is graven upon the tablet of their heart, and upon the horns of their altars; inasmuch as their children* (*still*) *bethink them of their altars and their Ashérahs under the leafy trees upon the high hills* (the conical hills of Judah which so well adapt themselves to such forms of worship). We cannot wonder at such a natural though inopportune revival. Deep in the heart of primitive man lies the instinct of sacred places and of polytheism. It would be absurd to connect Moslem saint-worship as a whole with the polytheism of the ancient Israelites, but who can doubt that those little white cupolas (Arabic, *qubba*) which continually meet the eye in Palestine, each on its eminence, and often (see the Palestine Fund's photographic view of Tell Hazur near Banias) with its sacred tree or trees, are the direct successors of those "altars upon the high hills under the leafy trees" of which Jeremiah speaks? If, after the lapse of centuries, and in spite of the levelling hand of the conqueror and the sweeping torrent of invasion, the fellâheen are still drawn to the old consecrated spots, and gaily dressed groups can still be seen going up hill and down dale to " visit " some saint or prophet (*i e*, his reputed tomb), is it wonderful that the same fascinating beliefs should have reasserted their sway over the half-converts of Josiah? Why, even Mohammed's early converts longed after the old Semitic sacred trees. One of the oldest Arabic historical works[1] contains this interesting tradition,—" The Qurashites and other heathen Arabs accounted holy a large green tree, and every year had a festival in its honour, at which they sacrificed and hung their arms upon it. On the way to Hunain we called to God's Messenger [Mohammed] that he should appoint for us such trees. But he was terrified and said, 'Lord God, Lord God ! ye speak even as the Israelites did to Moses, Make us such a god as the others have; ye are still in ignorance ; those are heathen customs.'" Mohammed could talk thus, for fortune was on his side ; but Jeremiah had a harder task to reconvert his contemporaries, for it must have seemed to them as if the old beliefs were not merely pleasant but efficacious. We may perhaps express their thoughts thus :—" All the early days of Josiah we had prosperity ; why ? Surely because we not only appeased the god of our own nation but also the old divinities of the land, and besides these, the gods of the powerful nations around us who need to be propitiated even more (comp. Jer. xliv. 17). We believe that it was the jealousy of these supernatural powers, so seriously injured by Josiah, which led to the defeat and death of that wrong-headed king." The details of this recrudescence of the old wounds are not given us, but the general statement in 2 Kings that the four successors of Josiah *did evil in the*

[1] " Vakidi's Book of the Campaigns of God's Messenger," by Wellhausen, p. 356.

sight of Jehovah according to all that their fathers had done, and that of Josephus respecting Jehoahaz in particular that he was "an impious man and impure in his course of life," permits us to form but a low estimate of the national religion. The case of Judah under its kings was not like that of England under the second Charles. If the "head" was "sick," we may be sure that the "heart" was "faint." A formal revocation of Josiah's covenant was unnecessary; it is always simpler to allow laws to fall into desuetude than to repeal them. Those who liked to obey it, might do so; those who did not, might equally follow their inclination. In short, we can hardly doubt that the wise and beautiful Deuteronomic law became at this time, in the vivid language of another contemporary prophet, benumbed or paralyzed (Hab. i. 4).

In one point, at any rate, it may be reasonably held that the work of Josiah was not undone, viz., the abolition of the cruelties of " the Topheth." Although the nineteenth chapter of Jeremiah forms part of a section which principally relates to the reign of Jehoiakim, yet I cannot draw from it the inference that the worship of Moloch had been restored after the death of Josiah. In fact, *v.* 13, where *the houses of the kings of Judah* are threatened with a defilement comparable to that of *the place of the Topheth*, sufficiently shows that "the Topheth" had been disgraced ever since the Reformation;[1] the sins which are rebuked must therefore be the inexpiable abominations of Manasseh's reign (comp. Jer. xv. 4). But with this and perhaps a few other exceptions, we may fairly assume that the old cults came to life again, or rather, were brought back to the light of day. For in fact it is doubtful whether any really popular cult can be put down by main force. Neither Islam nor the Roman Catholic Church has succeeded in doing this. Not to mention the survivals of paganism in both, it is enough to refer to the communities of crypto-Jews which so long existed both in Christian and Mohammedan countries, and one of which in Arabia still exists.[2]

---

[1] How strong an abhorrence of Hinnom was felt by the later Israelites is shown by the use of Geenna in the New Testament for the abode of condemned spirits. (Geenna = *Gê-ben-hinnôm*.)

[2] See an interesting article on Crypto-Jews in the *St James's Gazette*, May 24, 1888, and compare a letter by George Eliot in her "Life and Letters" (by Cross).

A passage in Psa. lxxxv. has lately been explained as referring to this period.[1] We read in *v.* 8, according to A.V. and R.V.,—

> *I will hear what God the Lord* [Jehovah] *will speak:*
> *For he will speak peace unto his people, and to his saints:*
> *But let them not turn again to folly.*

Prof. Cornill thinks that the psalm reflects a definite historical situation, the heavy affliction referred to in *v.* 4 being the tragic death of Josiah. The psalmist doubts the permanence of the good king's work. In *vv.* 9-13 he gives an ideal picture of Josiah's reign, which will also be true of the time to come (*that glory may dwell* = "that glory may continue to dwell") if Israel is faithful to its God. He seems to hear Jehovah whisper this to him—an oracle of peace, coupled with one condition, viz., that the people does not fall back into idolatry And Prof. Cornill thinks that this psalm follows Psa. lxxxiv. with chronological accuracy, for that lovely poem, according to him, was composed in the latter part of the reign of Josiah. It is a very suggestive and plausible view—more so, I think, than Ewald's conjecture that Psa. l. expresses the mind of a prophetic writer (who agrees with Jer. vii. 22, 23) when troubles began to close round Josiah and his people. Neither view can I discuss here; the historical occasions of the psalms are not to be determined by a dictatorial assertion. Neither view, I may add, do I myself hold, but I would rather that my readers adopted one or the other than that they rejected all attempts to find historical situations for the sacred lyrics. Without reconstructing the porticoes, we shall not be in a position to do full justice to the inner glories of the palaces of the Psalter.

Folly it might most truly be called—this falling back into a purely nationalistic view of Jehovah, as a supernatural Power not able or willing at present to protect his people, as not even the chief god of a crowded Pantheon. To such another prophet exclaims, with cutting irony, in the name of the true God, "Of whom wast thou in fear that thou wast thus faithless, and forgattest Me? But thy works shall not profit thee; let thy rabble of idols, when thou criest to them, deliver thee, if they

[1] See essay by Dr. Cornill in the *Homiletic Magazine*, July, 1882. The original is in Luthardt's "Zeitschrift," 1881, p 337, &c.

can!"[1] But there was also a class of persons, not belonging to the lowest ranks, who were differently and not less injuriously affected by the recent catastrophe. These men could not even yet shake off the illusion that righteousness is always rewarded in the present life by prosperity, and wickedness punished by adversity. They had never been able to assimilate the prophetic element in the Deuteronomic fusion of legal and evangelical religion. They were now more than ever bent on reducing religion to a system of rules which might be "learned by rote" (Isa. xxix. 13, R.V. margin). But they were not satisfied with the scanty prominence given to sacrifices in the Deuteronomic *torâh*, and if we may understand Jer. vi 20 as well as Jer. vii. 4 as referring to this period, they attempted to bind Jehovah to them and to their interests by lavish sacrifices, while sadly neglecting those "weighty matters of the law," "judgment, mercy, and faith."

These two classes of persons would naturally give different explanations of the recent calamity. How the former set must have argued we have seen. With it the latter will have agreed in viewing Josiah's death as a sign of the Divine anger. "But the sole divinity," they would say, "whom Judah has offended is Jehovah. We lost our king because we did not as a nation observe the law strictly enough; because idolatrous customs still lingered in our midst More sacrifices are wanted to bring back the sunshine of prosperity. But at least we need not be afraid of a severer punishment. *The temple of Jehovah; the temple of Jehovah; the temple of Jehovah are these, i e.*, these buildings (Jer. vii. 4). Thus did these men faithfully hand on the teaching of those prophets of a former generation, who, as Micah tells us (iii. 11), were wont to *lean upon Jehovah, and say, Is not Jehovah among us? no evil can come upon us.*

Such is the obstinacy of old illusions, even when Providence attempts, as one might say, to dissipate them, even when they have become dangerous errors. Let us not be hard upon the Jews; how uncommon it is for the actors of history to be fully able to read its lessons! *We* know that Josiah's death was "the beginning of sorrows"—the first scene in the last act of

---

[1] In these words Prof. Driver ("Isaiah His Life and Times," p 158) condenses Isa. lvii 11–13 (first part) I have myself long since adopted the critical theory of Ewald relative to Isa. lvi 9–lvii 11a (see "Encyclopædia Britannica," art. "Isaiah").

the tragedy (not indeed of that national tragedy which is still in progress, but of the tragedy of Israel before the Captivity). *We* know that God had decreed to send His people into captivity. *We* know His merciful object in doing so—viz, first, to cure the nation of idolatry, and next, to lead individuals to "serve God for nought," and after conceiving the idea of "saving others," to form the magnificent conception of a perfect Israelite—Israel's and the world's Saviour. *We* know all this; but how could the Jews? Unless those are right who date the Book of Job in this period, there was but one clear-sighted Jew—Jeremiah, and even he could not see to the end of God's ways. One step however we are sure that he took now, if he did not take it before. He cannot any longer have been an itinerant expounder of Deuteronomy. Nothing which could be colourably represented as favouring mechanical religion was a fit text-book for a progressive teacher. It is perhaps a significant fact in this connexion that, in Jeremiah's epitaph (if I may call it so) upon Josiah, he praises the king, not for introducing the *tōrāh*, but for doing justice to the poor, and thus proving that he "knew" Jehovah (Jer. xxii 16). Later on he even becomes the prophet of a "*new* covenant" which is to supersede all previous *tōrāh* (Jer. xxxi. 31). Clearly, then, Jeremiah must before this have begun to be disappointed with Deuteronomy. He may have read it privately—this perhaps we may argue from his continued allusions to it, but in public he confined himself to reproducing its more spiritual, more prophetic portions. As a whole, Deuteronomy must be regarded as thrust somewhat into the background, until at length the problem which it sought to solve was resumed at the close of the Exile, and a fresh combination of elements, partly historical, partly sacerdotal, partly prophetic, was published as our present Pentateuch by the great reformer Ezra.

But though a kind of travel-weariness, to be accounted for on moral rather than on physical grounds, may have attacked the prophet, there was one place not far from the capital which a natural feeling still prompted him to visit. This was his native town, Anathoth in Benjamin, which had been inhabited for centuries by many priestly families. Jeremiah's own family was not one of the poorest, so that his movements, whenever he went there, could not fail to draw public attention. In fact had he been less known, he might have been more honoured—

according to that saying of our Lord, *A prophet is not without honour save in his own country, and among his own kin, and in his own house* (Mark i. 28). Doubtless he had often experienced this on previous visits, but now—after the death of Josiah—he found the neglect of contempt deepening into hatred. He had gone to his native town, absorbed in his message, and as unsuspicious of evil (see the Revised Version of Jer. xi. 19) *as a gentle lamb that is led to the slaughter*, when an unprovoked attempt was made upon his life. With fair speeches (see Jer. xii. 6), unworthy kinsmen of his own sought to draw him into an ambush, and but for a "special providence" his career would have been prematurely cut short. *And Jehovah gave me knowledge of it and I knew it; then thou shewedst me their doings* (Jer. xi. 18, R.V.). "Then" means "when I was in utter unconsciousness." No one can think of excusing such dastardly conduct, only worthy of the Bedouin robbers on the other side of Jerusalem (Luke x. 30, comp. Jer. iii. 2); but can we throw any light upon its motives?

History requires that we should do equal justice to men who in the heat of conflict may have misunderstood each other—that we should remember the complexity and the almost tyrannical power of circumstances, and try and think ourselves back into the position of both parties. In our present study, it may help us to bear in mind that the word of a true prophet was universally believed to have a supernatural efficacy. Balak, for instance, sought to force Balaam to curse the Israelites, and Esau was mortally offended with Jacob for coming "with subtilty" and "taking away his blessing" (Gen. xxvii. 35). Jeremiah himself held the same view, which is of course only a primitive thinker's inference from the Divine origin of prophecy. But who *is* the true prophet and which word of prophecy has a Divine origin? There were always many competing prophets at Jerusalem, and till the value of their oracles had been tested by history, it did not seem possible to say which of them were true prophets. This view of prophecy is not obscurely expressed in Deut. xviii. 22,—

And if thou say in thine heart, How shall we know the word which Jehovah hath not spoken? When a prophet speaketh in the name of Jehovah, if the thing follow not, nor come to pass, that is the thing which Jehovah hath not spoken.

It is not by any means a complete theory of prophecy (it is

in fact qualified by Deut. xiii. 1-3), or even of the relation of predictive prophecy to fulfilment ; but it is one which naturally commended itself to the people, and which prior to his own sad experience our prophet himself probably held.[1] Jeremiah himself cannot have had a high place as yet in popular esteem. For the people appear to have been sceptical as to the claims of a prophet of woe to Divine inspiration, and Jeremiah had delivered most emphatic predictions of national disaster which moreover had not as yet been fulfilled. During the panic caused by the Scythians, he probably was for a time encircled by a halo of sanctity ; this we may infer from the fact that a brief repentance followed upon his impassioned exhortations. But the Scythians returned at last without molesting Judah, and the respect for Jeremiah's prophesying appears to have vanished. Whenever he went abroad, he had to listen to the mocking inquiry, *Where is the word of Jehovah? pray, let it come to pass*[2] (Jer. xvii. 15). And so the wheel of fortune went round ; the prophets who shouted "Peace, peace" (Jer. vi. 14) caught the popular ear, and Jeremiah had either to keep silence or to take up the new vocation of expounder of the law. But now it must have seemed to the Jews as if those old predictions of disaster, which had hitherto, so to speak, floated in the air (comp. Isa. ix. 8), had come down charged with a first instalment of disgrace and ruin. The smile of indifference was exchanged for the scowl of hatred. Men began to fear Jeremiah, and when the priests at Anathoth heard him say these

[1] In Jer. xxviii. 8, 9 the prophet qualifies the older theory thus :—True prophets have, as a rule, for the sins of the people, predicted " war and evil, and pestilence " ; therefore if a prophet falls into the new, sweet strain of peace, he must be regarded with suspicion until the event proves that he has been truly sent. Comp. Jer xiv. 13-15. The popular argument, if I have not been unjust to it, was exactly the opposite Jehovah was Israel's God, and received all due homage from Israel ; consequently Israel (now virtually synonymous with Judah) shall have peace. Once, but once only, Jeremiah seems to ascribe the current prophecies of peace to Jehovah as their author (Jer. iv. 10, comp 1 Kings xxii. 20-23). This may perhaps be due to the as yet imperfect distinction between true and false prophets (contrast Jer. xiv. 13-15, xxiii. 25, Ezek. xiii 1-16). But the passage referred to admits of another explanation (see my commentary)

[2] Some think, however, that this passage refers to the time when Nebuchadnezzar returned in haste to Babylon, after defeating Neco, to secure his crown.

awful words in the name of Jehovah, *What hath my beloved to
do in mine house? will vows and hallowed flesh take thy
wickedness from thee? wilt thou therefore rejoice?* (Jer. xi. 15,
Ewald),—they began to feel towards him as their fathers would
have done to that prophet of Kemósh who said to Mesha, king
of Moab (so the ancient stone records), "Go destroy Israel."
Add to this that the foe, as they deemed him, of the common
weal was a kinsman of their own, and we have a sufficient excuse, not indeed for their treachery, but at least for the bitter
hostility with which the prophet's relations regarded him.

Can we help remarking the parallel between Jeremiah's early
history and that of Jesus Christ? Our Lord, like the prophet,
found His truest home-life—at least, after His ministry had
begun—in Capernaum and Bethany, and not in Nazareth. Of
his neighbours in that village-community it is true in the
fullest sense, that *his own received him not* (John i. 11). They
did not indeed have recourse to cunning and treachery, but *lea
him to the brow of the hill* (well known and dear to Jesus) *on
which their city was built, that they might hurl him down the
cliff* (Luke iv. 29). No wonder that He whose heart was far
more loving even than Jeremiah's lavished the wealth of His
affection on a few, and especially on the one most congenial to
Himself, among His disciples; of this one at least it could not
be said,—

> *It is not an enemy that revileth me, . . .*
> *(But) my companion and familiar friend* (Psa. lv. 12, 14).

Both our Lord and His prophetic predecessor had a longing
for true friendship which was very imperfectly satisfied. In
Jeremiah's case this was so keen as to be oppressive, and, as I
have ventured to point out, some of the psalmists, feeling a
special interest in this prophet, and having formed their ideals
partly upon his life and character, seem to have expressed his
very soul more strikingly even than he has done himself. Especially touching is the new sense which one of these temple-
poets has given to the familiar word "bereavement,"—

> *They render me evil for good,*
> *Bereavement hath come upon my soul* (Psa. xxxv 12, De Witt).

This, as we feel at once, sounds a lower depth of grief than
Jacob's *If I be bereaved of my children, I am bereaved* (Gen.

xliii. 14), or than the following sad words of an imaginative writer of our own day,—

> There's a rival bauld wi' young and auld,
> And it's him that has bereft me;
> For the surest friends are the auldest friends,
> And the maist o' mine hae left me.[1]

The psalmist, I say, who thinks himself back into the soul of Jeremiah, expresses a grief more bitter than that of the patriarch or of the sufferer imagined by the Scotch poet—it is that the oldest friends did not prove the surest—that they left him by no natural compulsion but through treachery. This truly is a grief which can "sap the mind"—which did sap even Jeremiah's mind, not completely indeed, for he knew the *friend which sticketh closer than a kinsman* (Prov. xviii. 24), but enough to breathe into him thoughts which are inconsistent with a perfect inspiration. *But thou, Jehovah, knowest me, thou seest me, and triest my heart toward thee; pull them out like sheep for the slaughter, and consecrate them* (like sacrificial victims) *for the day of slaughter* (Jer. xii. 3). There is the dross of human frailty in this—to be excused as we excuse the bitterness of the prophet-like poet of mediæval Christendom—to be excused, not to be justified. And whenever we read such words even in the Scriptures, whether it be in Jeremiah or in psalms affected only too intimately by Jeremiah, let us mentally correct them in accordance with the words, *Father, forgive them; for they know not what they do.*

In the conjecture which I am now about to hazard I leap over a wide space of time. But Jeremiah's life and character contain the germ of so much that is Christian, that psychologically the conjecture seems admissible that a period came when the flame of resentment died away in the prophet's breast—died away quite naturally, because nothing remained as an object of resentment. Is it not so with ourselves in so far as we have the Spirit of Christ? Does not life bring to each of us in a too often dull and dusty pathway moments of a spiritual quality so rich and rare that our past troubles appear but a *slight bruising* (as St. Paul expresses it), and as working out for us in its initial stage an *eternal weight of glory* (2 Cor. vii. 17)? Such a

[1] Mr. Robert Louis Stevenson ("Underwoods").

moment was given to the Florentine poet when, like St. Paul, he was *caught up to the third heaven* (2 Cor. xii. 2), and "smiled" at the "vile semblance" of earth and its miseries (*Paradiso*, xxii. 133-135). And had not the prophet of the new covenant similar moments, when, like him who in Psa. xvii. has so piercingly complained of his bitter enemies, he could pass into the world of God's light and truth, and say,—

As for me, I shall behold thy face in righteousness;
May I be satisfied, when I awake, with thine image (Psa. xvii. 15).

The Christian proto-martyr himself used language only less bitter than Jeremiah's in his grand final invective (Acts vii. 51-53), but his rough journey to Paradise was brightened by the far holier inspiration, *Lord, lay not this sin to their charge* (*v.* 60). And must not Jeremiah, amid that shower of cruel stones which legend asserts to have crushed his earthly tabernacle, have had the same angelic visitant, and so resembled St. Stephen, not only (as they say) in the form of his martyrdom, but also in his intuition of a Divine fairness which is as far above natural human justice as heaven is above the earth—a fairness which is but one aspect of essential love.

Jeremiah, as idealized by the noblest of his disciples or admirers, was free from any morbid tendency to vindictiveness. Among the psalms of the Passion, as we may call them, for which we are indebted to these nameless writers, there is one which stands out by its complete freedom from the sad legacy of imprecation—it is the twenty-second. This is not to be ascribed to ignorance of Jeremiah's infirmity, for the psalm alludes (or appears to allude) to a verse in the very section which we have been considering. Jeremiah expresses himself thus (Jer. xi. 20),—

But, O Jehovah Sabáoth, that judgest righteously, that triest the reins and the heart, let me see thy vengeance upon them: for upon thee do I roll my cause (*i.e.*, " I disburden myself by commending my cause to thee "); and the words may, I think, be in the psalmist's mind, when he represents the enemies of that ideal Israelite, who is not unlike Jeremiah, but soars above him, being a poetical anticipation of Israel's and the world's Saviour, as uttering this derisive speech,—

He has rolled (his cause) upon Jehovah, let him deliver him;
Let him rescue him, since he delighteth in him (Psa. xxii. 8).

And if you ask me how the disciple could rise above such a master, whose works were to him the oracles of truth, I reply that because his eyes were more fully opened by the lessons of Providence. And this may suggest a comforting thought for ourselves, preceded as we are by so many great teachers that religious truth seems (but only seems) to lie before us full-orbed,—that it may be possible for us to divine what they would say, if placed where we now stand, and reverently to correct and supplement their words, just as the authors of Deuteronomy did to Jeremiah, and the later psalmists to Jeremiah. God's revelations—let me say it again—are never ended; the elements of truth may be as old as the first "covenant" and as changeless as the nature of man, but new combinations of those elements, both in Christian ethics and in Christian theology, have the charm and novelty of fresh communications from the spirit-world. *When he, the Spirit of truth, is come, he will guide you into all the truth.*

CHAPTER II.

ON THE VERGE OF MARTYRDOM.

Jeremiah's sermon in the temple—The fate of Shiloh—The prophet's trial
and acquittal—The martyrdom of Uriah.

IN the process of the Church's education, of which Pentecost
does but begin the second or rather the third part, Jeremiah's
completed life forms one of the chief waymarks. But as yet
one half of it still lies before us. It is a story of bold adventure and of faith; of heroic endeavour persistently maintained,
like Christ's, in spite of failure foreseen; of danger encountered
against heaviest odds in the cause of true religion and, in a
very high sense, of patriotism. Jeremiah's experience at his
native place was the prelude of this part of his career. Henceforth, however, like our Lord at the close of His ministry, he
concentrated his efforts upon Jerusalem. There too he was
sometimes in danger through treachery. This is his own
account of it. *For I have heard the backbiting of many; there
is terror on every side. Inform, say they, and let us inform
against him* (Jer. xx. 10); *i e.*, his enemies, including some
former friends, were not contented with injurious reports respecting him, but encouraged one another to lay an information
against him as a public criminal (comp. Psa. xxxi. 13). And
then Jeremiah continues with the grand but too passionate
outburst,—

*But Jehovah is with me as a fierce warrior; therefore shall
mine enemies stumble and not prevail; they shall be greatly
ashamed, because they have not prospered, with an everlasting
reproach that shall never be forgotten. And thou, Jehovah
Sabáoth, that triest the righteous, that seest the reins and the
heart, let me see my revenge upon them, for upon thee do I roll
my cause* (Jer. xx. 11, 12).

ON THE VERGE OF MARTYRDOM.

The concluding words are repeated with slight variations from Jer. xi. 20, showing that the prophet himself saw the analogy between the two sets of circumstances. He had indeed escaped from persecution at Anathoth, but only to experience a worse renewal of it at Jerusalem. There too he carried on a life and death struggle, though as a rule with less ignoble enemies. Here is a specimen of it. The incident to which I shall refer arose out of a prophetic discourse, which we fortunately possess in two editions (one in chap. vii., and the other in chap. xxvi.). It appears that some great festival or possibly fast had brought together a large number of people from all quarters to the temple, and that Jeremiah was directed to stand between the inner and outer court and address them. One wishes that this among other fine passages of the Bible could be faithfully re-translated in modern English, that the reader might see how forcible the timid, shrinking Jeremiah can become. (Is there any force like his who only bursts out now and then, like a volcano, because the fire within cannot be restrained? Comp. Jer. xx. 9.) But I will at least quote here a few important verses in the best version which suggests itself.

Put not your trust in the lying words, The temple of Jehovah, the temple of Jehovah, the temple of Jehovah, is this[1] (vii. 4).

What? steal and murder and commit adultery and swear falsely, and burn incense to Baal, and go after other gods which ye knew not! and then ye come and stand before me in this house upon which my name has been called, and think, We have escaped—(only) to repeat[2] *all these abominations* (vii. 9, 10).

Do we not seem to hear these self-deluded men (fanatical in the worship of Jehovah in spite of their combination of this with Baal-worship) filling the air with their shrill cries, and calling upon Jehovah to deliver them, because "the temple,

[1] Lit., *are these* (*i.e.*, these buildings). The Hebrew suggests more than we can express in English—viz., that the sanctity of the temple proper communicated itself to all the various buildings connected with it (comp. Matt. xxiv. 1). Similarly in Psa. lxviii. 35 a translator will do well to change "thy (*v.l.*, his) sanctuaries" into "thy (or, his) sanctuary."

[2] The Hebrew has simply "to do" (or "practice"). Comp. Psa. lx. 4, *Thou hast given a banner to them that fear thee, (only) that they may flee from before the bow.* In each passage a striking effect is produced by representing the consequence of an act as something deliberately intended. Some indeed suppose that in the psalm-passage "only" was originally a part of the text.

the temple, the temple is this," as if the iteration of the phrase increased its efficacy, while others give equally formal thanks for deliverance, blindly arguing that, because no invader has yet "cast a bank against" the city (Isa. xxxvii. 33), their escape is assured, and they may go on practising all their old immoralities?

Jeremiah continues, still merging his own personality in that of his Divine Sender, and giving Jehovah's message,—

A den of robbers then has this house whereupon my name is called become in your eyes? I, even I, have surely seen it, is Jehovah's oracle.

To see with God is to punish. The lawless rich say in their hearts, "Thou wilt not require satisfaction." So one of the psalmists tells us, adding,—

> *Thou hast seen it, for thou lookest on mischief and vexation,
> To deal out (vengeance) with thy hand* (Psa x. 14).

No wonder then that Jeremiah next announces the punishment of those who thus abuse the holy name of religion. How he leads up to this, deserves an attentive study. A single verse doubtless condenses a fuller and more descriptive passage of an oral prophecy. Nearly the whole of the period of the Judges—or more exactly, between Joshua's latter days (Josh. xviii. 1) and Eli's death (1 Sam. iv 3), the ark found a "resting-place"—the name given to the Shiloh temple in the later tradition—in the famous Ephraimitish town of Shiloh. It is evident that a mere tent would not have sufficed for this long period; there must have been some kind of permanent "house" or temple. This is no mere presumption, but is confirmed by the language of the narrative books--see especially 1 Sam. i. 9, where Eli is represented as *sitting by the door-post of the temple of Jehovah*. For a long time this was the most honoured sanctuary of the Israelites [1]—its central shrine, in a different sense from that in which Jerusalem is sometimes called the centre of worship, for its existence did not exclude that of numerous *bāmōth* or "high places" But its "day of visitation" (Isa. x. 3) came at length. When, we cannot say with certainty, but from the fact that one of the psalmists introduces the catastrophe immediately before the accession of David to the

---

[1] In Jer xli. 5 "Shiloh" should be "Salem" (Sept. Cod. Vat.). Comp. John iii 23

throne (see Psa lxxviii. 59-72), we may plausibly infer that the temple was destroyed during the Philistines' oppression.[1] However this may be, it is probable that Jeremiah found in the history of Samuel and Saul current in his own time a full account of this great event.[2] I suppose that he also found there that prophecy of Samuel, which seems to refer, partly at any rate, to the destruction of the Shiloh-temple. For he announces in Jer. xix. 3 that Jehovah *will bring evil upon this place. which whosoever heareth, his ears will tingle,* evidently alluding to 1 Sam. iii. 11. So it appears that his "Book of Samuel" was similar in some respects to ours, though dissimilar in others. It was in fact a complete narrative, and was doubtless supplemented by a living popular tradition. Mothers told their children of the fate of the "house of Jehovah" at Shiloh, where God had revealed Himself to ancient prophets more distinctly if not more truly than to those of their own time, and the blood of the youthful listeners curdled in their veins. That "uncircumcised Philistines" should have laid low that most holy place, seemed too strange for aught but the fictions of the professional story-teller. The supernatural sanctions of prophecy guaranteed it, however, and more than one of the youths who heard that prophecy (1 Sam. iii. 11-14) never forgot it, but introduced its phraseology into works of their own [3]

In respect for the memory of the Shiloh-temple and horror at its end, Jeremiah and his fanatical hearers were agreed. As a doom, they both regarded its destruction by the Philistines. The latter, I make no doubt, confirmed themselves in blind self-righteousness by thinking of the wickedness which must have caused this awful judgment. "God, I thank thee that I am not as other men"—heterodox and schismatical ritualists, despisers of the house of David and of the more recent but

[1] From Judg. xviii. 30, 31 it may at first seem as if the Shiloh temple lasted till the captivity of the northern tribes. But any clear head will see at once that Judg. xviii 30 is a later addition (see Ewald, "History of Israel," ii 348 note ; Wellhausen's edition of Bleek's "Einleitung," p 199)

[2] See Wellhausen's "Prolegomena" (Germ ed), p 44, and his edition of Bleek's "Einleitung, ' § 103 (p 210) , also Maybaum, article in Steinthal's "Zeitschrift fur Volkerpsychologie," 1887, pp 290-315 , Vatke, "Biblische Theologie," p 318, &c , Graf's note on Jer vii 12 and his early treatise "De Templo Silonensi." Comp also Bertheau's note on Judg xviii 31.

[3] Another allusion to this prophecy occurs in 2 Kings xxi 12, 13

far worthier sanctuary, which has proudly withstood Egyptian, Assyrian, yes, and Israelitish invaders. This must have been their spoken or unspoken monologue with Jehovah; and Jeremiah, seeing through them, virtually answers them like our Lord, *Except ye repent, ye shall all in like manner* (ὁμοίως, "similarly") *perish* (Luke xiii. 3, R.V.). But he has his own way of expressing this. By a most effective turn in the discourse, he bids them come with him to Shiloh, and scan the desolate ruins of that once glorious shrine — glorious, not perhaps by its outward magnificence, but by the accumulated veneration of centuries. (Popular respect is indeed not always given to the symbols or the sanctuaries which are outwardly the most magnificent.) There was, it would seem, a special appropriateness in the time when this invitation was given For we cannot suppose that so sacred a place as Shiloh had been entirely without a sanctuary between the times of Saul and Josiah. There must have been an altar there, and at least a humble "chapel," though none that could bear comparison with the king's at Bethel (Amos vii. 13). But Josiah, not many years since, had broken down both altar and "chapel" (as he had done to those at Bethel), and it may well be that Jeremiah, on that visit to Shiloh [1] which (see Part I., Chap. V.) I ventured to assume, saw (like Dr. Robinson [2]) the owls fly off from the desolate spot. At any rate, all knew the two destructions of the sanctuary of Shiloh, the latter of which was but a re-affirmation of the original doom worked out by the abhorred Philistines. And now for the argument which Jeremiah builds upon the facts of past and present history. If the actual religion of Judah, now that Josiah's reforms have half collapsed, is in its idolatry and in its mechanical formalism so similar to that of its northern sister, and results in moral practices no better than those for which Hosea denounced the Israelites, and if the most ancient temple of Jehovah which lay within the Israelitish border was by His will profaned and destroyed,

---

[1] I know of course that "Go ye now," &c. in Jer. vii. 12 may be merely a rhetorical phrase, as in Amos vi. 2. But it may equally well be intended literally; and if so, one must suppose Jeremiah to have set the example in visiting Shiloh.

[2] "Biblical Researches," iii. 86 To this eminent American traveller belongs the credit of having discovered the true site of Shiloh (now Seilun), which, in spite of Judg. xxi. 19, had been forgotten since St Jerome.

does it not follow that the same fate must soon overtake Jerusalem and *its* sanctuary? Both temples were successively "places of the name [1] of Jehovah Sabáoth" (comp. Jer. vii. 12 with Isa. xviii. 7, Deut. xii. 5); how could one be punished and the other escape?

Thus far Jeremiah has addressed himself (see Jer. vii. 9) to the idolatrous party, who do indeed worship Jehovah, but do homage to "other gods beside" Jehovah, violating the first (or second) of the Ten Words of God (Exod. xx. 3). I do not say that the analogy between the Shiloh and the Jerusalem temple is as perfect as Jeremiah represents.[2] But his main idea is certainly correct. Throughout the history of Biblical religion we find righteousness described as essential to the true worship of God. *The wrath of God is revealed from heaven against all irreligiousness and immorality* (Rom. i. 18); "irreligiousness" and "immorality" describe different aspects of the same idea. No religious observances can "wipe out the old score," and give us liberty to break the commandments of God. And now comes the turn of those who worship Jehovah alone but in a purely formal way, who are free from the worst moral excesses of the others, but rest their hopes for Judah's future on the sacrifices for which the Deuteronomist cared so little and Jeremiah still less. This was in effect what he said to them: "If ye think to serve God by a multitude of sacrifices, ye do greatly err. Jehovah did indeed allow your fathers to offer Him sacrifices, but He gave no special directions concerning them." The Divine silence is significant; it means that nothing has an absolute value with God but an obedient heart.

I spake not unto your fathers nor commanded them, when I brought them out of the land of Egypt, concerning burnt offerings or sacrifices; but this thing commanded I them, saying, Obey my voice, and I will be to you a God, and ye shall be to me a people; and walk ye in all the ways that I have commanded you, that it may be well with you (Jer. vii. 22, 23).

Can we doubt that the speaker is thinking of Deuteronomy,

[1] Guthe has remarked that the expression "the name of Jehovah" is sometimes virtually synonymous with the ark. Certainly the special sanctity both of the Shiloh and of the Jerusalem temple arose out of the presence of the ark of the covenant.

[2] Jeroboam was apparently much opposed to heathenism proper and the introduction of new gods (Ewald, "History of Israel," iv. 27).

one favourite phrase of which he instinctively repeats, and more especially of that sacred Decalogue, adopted into the Deuteronomic *tōrāh*, which relates entirely to moral and spiritual duties, and not at all to ritual? As for your sacrifices, they would have been poor and imperfect things at the best (comp. Psa. l. 12, 13), and yet graciously accepted, as the expressions of childlike love. But *this is a nation that obeyeth not the voice of Jehovah their God* (ver. 28). Therefore—*put your burnt offerings to your sacrifices, and eat them as flesh* (ver. 21, Ewald), *i.e.,* throw all your offerings into a mass, and eat them at your pleasure; they have neither any inherent sanctity nor any secondary importance from the character of the offerers.

And what, the reader may ask, was the fate of this bold preacher of righteousness? We must turn to the parallel twenty-sixth chapter for a full description of the scene which ensued. The narrative is most effective in its unadorned simplicity; I need only recall its leading features. The priests, the prophets, and the people surrounded the prophet with angry looks and words. Like St. Stephen's audience long afterwards, *they were cut to the heart, and gnashed upon him with their teeth* (Acts vii. 54). Narrowly indeed did he escape St. Stephen's fate, for when they heard those echoing words of relentless doom, "This temple shall become like Shiloh," they *seized him, saying, Thou shalt surely die* (vers. 8, 9). But in the nick of time a fresh power appeared on the scene—the "princes," or high officers of the state, who came up from their place of deliberation in the "king's house" (*v.* 10, comp. xxxvi. 12), and apparently the "elders," some of whom had doubtless taken part in Josiah's reformation. Without the concurrence of these, the legal forms would not have been duly complied with; the prophet's violent death would have been a mere assassination. Jeremiah in dignified terms defended his own right to prophesy, and warned the people of the consequences of their act. *Then said the princes and all the people*—the crowd were as easily led by their superiors now as at Josiah's reformation—*to the priests and to the prophets, This man is not worthy to die, for he hath spoken unto us in the name of Jehovah our God* (ver. 16). "Certain of the elders" helped this view of the matter, and acted a truly patriotic part, by appealing to a fact in the past religious history of Judah (vers. 18, 19); and observe by the way, how much we are indebted to those who in our own

ON THE VERGE OF MARTYRDOM.

day bring to light half-forgotten facts in religious history. The fact about Micah (or, as he is here called, Micaiah, see *v.* 18, R V.) was not unknown, but its full significance had not as yet been seen. Micah may be called the morning-star of the evangelical movement in the Jewish Church. He saw that society needed to be reorganized on a new moral and spiritual basis, and that Zion must be *ploughed as a field, and Jerusalem become heaps, and the temple-mount as thicket-covered heights*[1] (Mic. iii. 12). This implies the essential reformation-truth that a temple is consecrated not merely by containing sacramental symbols of the Divine presence, but through being resorted to by holy worshippers. I do not say that no prophetic writer expressed this between Micah and Jeremiah ; for however Isaiah may vary his descriptions of Israel's future, he never fails to insist on the necessity of a judgment and the indispensableness of a righteous remnant. But Isaiah's truly evangelical teaching had to some extent been counteracted by the Deuteronomic compromise between Law and Gospel. And at any rate our prophet was the first to proclaim this great truth so distinctly as to strike even the dullest listener.

The glory of being the evangelical proto-martyr was, however, reserved for another prophet, named Uriah, son of Shemaiah, of the "town of the copses" (or thickets), Kiryath-Yearim.[2] In

---

[1] The word for "heights" (*bāmôth*) only has this general meaning in poetic style (so again in Mic. i 12), in prose, it has the specialized sense of "high places." That rendered "thicket-covered" (the Hebrew has "heights of thicket") is explained in the next note. The Jerusalem hills were anciently more overgrown with copse than they are now (see above) Hence we are not surprised that Judah the Maccabee and his brethren found (agreeably to the wide-reaching prophecy of Micah) *the sanctuary desolate, and the altar profaned, and the gates burned down, and shrubs growing in the court as in a forest or in one of the mountains* (1 Macc. iv. 38).

[2] The ancient "copse-town" has now become a "grape-town" (Karyet el-'Enab), if Robinson's identification be accepted. Conder's proposal to place Kiryath-Yearim on the site of the copse-enclosed ruin called 'Erma, "on the south side of the great ravine which is the head of the valley of Sorek," is in some respects plausible, though a philological connexion names does not exist. "Yearim" may however be explained, after the Arabic use of *wa'r*, as "rough, impracticable tracts of country" (comp. Isa. xxi. 13, where Wetzstein gives this sense to *ya'ar*, the singular of *yeārīm*) Thomson remarks that there are very rough "wa'rs" on every side almost of Karyet el-'Enab, and that the ark would have had a rough road from this village to Jerusalem ; Conder, that the dense thickets of

spite of the traditional connexion of his native city with the most sacred symbol of his religion (see 1 Sam. vi. 21–vii. 2), Uriah, possibly a disciple and doubtless a friend of Jeremiah, had the insight to discern the superstition and immorality which degraded the national religion, and the imminent danger which beset his country. He preached the truth, and paid the forfeit with his life. That he at first fled into Egypt, is not to be interpreted as an act of cowardice. Surely an inner voice had said to him, "Wait; it may be that Israel's God has more work yet for thee as well as for Jeremiah to do." The latter, at any rate, was saved for the Master's future use by the interposition of the "princes," and especially of Ahikam[1] (one of the deputation sent to Huldah the prophetess, according to 2 Kings xxii. 14), whose friendly interest in Jeremiah may remind us of that of the Duke of Lancaster in John Wycliffe.

See from the narrative which we have had before us the good results of the prophet's self-communings after his trouble at Anathoth. "Peace was not made for earth, nor rest for thee"— such was now his conclusion, like that of "New Self" in Hurrell Froude's poem.[2] He had fought his inner fight, not unaided by the sense of spirit-borne warnings and expostulations, such as these which he has ventured to clothe in words,—

If thou hast run with the footmen, and they have wearied thee, then how canst thou contend with horses? and though in a land of peace thou art secure, yet how wilt thou do in the pride of Jordan? (Jer. xii. 5, R.V.)

The "footmen" and the "land of peace" are Jeremiah's relatives and the town of Anathoth, where, but for secret machinations, he would have dwelt in peace. The "horses" and the "pride of Jordan" are the mighty multitude and the city where enemies beset the faithful prophet, who can only be compared to the fierce lions in the jungle of tamarisks on Jordan's banks. Looking back on his recent bitter experience, Jeremiah—that is,

copses must once have been more widely spread than they are now. I cannot discuss the geographical or philological questions further here. (See preceding note.)

[1] One of Ahikam's sons, Gemariah, lent Baruch his official room for his recitation of the prophecies of Jeremiah (Jer xxxvi. 10), another son, Gedaliah, showed himself Jeremiah's friend, and politically his disciple, when governor of Judah under Nebuchadrezzar (Jer xl 5-10).

[2] "Lyra Apostolica," lxxix, "Old Self and New Self."

his "Old Self"—complains of his sad lot; but looking forward to the trials which must, if he follows his conscience, be in store for him, he checks his weak complainings, and comforts himself with the inerrancy of the Divine justice. These thoughts were to his mind the direct suggestions of his ever-present Lord; hence their power—hence the wonderful transformation which ensued (strictly speaking, indeed, it had begun earlier, see Part I., Chap. III., end) in the prophet's character. At Anathoth, in a comparatively small danger, he gave way to impatient murmurs; at Jerusalem, amidst an infuriated mob led by priests and prophets, he is as calm as if he were amidst friends. Human nature was the same then as it is now. Are not many of us too ready to lose our self-command under small trials? And is there not still but one unfailing source of calmness—the presence of God in the soul?

Thus, from the point of view of the Christian, Jeremiah's message comes ultimately to this—that the lowly and believing heart is God's favourite temple, and the only one which has the promise of permanence. Full often has the course of history taught us the same truth. No need to point to Furness or to Melrose. "Go ye now to Shiloh"; or rather,

> "Go down with yonder abject few,
> In caftan green or dim white veil,
> Who hurry by to raise anew
> Their feeble voice of endless wail,
> Before Moriah's stones of might
> Scant beards are torn, old eyelids stream
> With many a sad, unhelpful tear;
> Man's weeping and earth's ruin seem
> To find their common centre here." [1]

But, thank God! there are more cheerful preachers than those of the Jewish "wailing-place." Elevating indeed must have been the sight of those five thousand French Protestants who gathered together the other day in the mountains of the Cevennes [2] to commemorate beneath the summer sky the stolen religious meetings of their forefathers. The gathering may indeed have partaken of the nature of a fast as well as of a

[1] St. John Tyrwhitt, "Poems," "The Jews' Wailing Place."

[2] Alluding to an impressive ceremony recorded in the newspapers, August, 1887. This passage is retained from a cathedral sermon.

festival ; for where are the moral representatives of the heroic though far from faultless Cevenols?

> "Cold mountains and the midnight air
> Witnessed the fervour of *their* prayer,"

who died even as they lived—the spiritual children of psalmists and prophets. Yet we may be grateful to those who, in celebrating the centenary of Louis XVI.'s edict of toleration, and praising the new virtue of religious tolerance, could not and did not withhold their homage to the more fundamental qualities which distinguished their ancestors. By this commemoration, the patriarchs and martyrs of the Cevennes, "being dead, yet speak," and hand on the lesson afresh to later ages that "God is spirit" (John i. 24, R.V. margin), and that the fairest contributions of art and of historic tradition to the outward forms of worship cannot compensate for the absence of spiritual religion, of an open Bible, and of hearts where Conscience reigns.

CHAPTER III.

KEEP THE MUNITION, WATCH THE WAY !

Progress of Neco—Accession of Jehoahaz, and soon after of Jehoiakim—Fall of Nineveh—Neco's defeat by Nebuchadrezzar—Dread of Babylon at Jerusalem—Jeremiah's new peace of mind—His prophecy on Egypt, &c.

SO Jeremiah was snatched from his enemies—delivered from that most terrifying of all dangers—the fury of a fanatical mob.[1] He was acquitted ; but his position was not thereby materially improved. The elders who so opportunely interposed may or may not[2] have been hearty believers in his special Divine mission ; but it is certain that the new king was not, that the bulk of the priests and of the prophets was not, and that the people had only a temporary access of superstitious awe at the troublesome preacher. It was indeed morally impossible that any but an elect few could tolerate such a violent reversal of received ideas. But how came the prophet to venture on such a step? What was it that so far altered the nature of this sensitive man that he could thus court opposition, and provoke the spirit of fanaticism ? Was it as a forlorn hope that he took up his station that morning in front of the assembled pilgrims and devotees? Was it the inspiration of despair at the strong backward current which had set in both in morality and in religion ? I reply that it was not this, though Jeremiah's "Old Self" may well have troubled his "New Self" with despairing suggestions.

[1] May I at least illustrate this by the vivid description of the mob at Charing Cross in "John Inglesant," chap xiv , and the remark of the officer to Inglesant, " You stood that very well. I would rather mount the deadliest breach than face such a sight as that."

[2] In their favour it may be urged that they treat Jeremiah's case as entirely parallel to Micah's But the low tone of their concluding words—*Thus should we commit great evil against our own souls*—may by some be taken to prove that they were merely afraid of the probable dangerous consequences of putting Jeremiah to death.

Listen to this—a favourite passage with our own sensitive poet Cowper,—

O that I had in the wilderness a lodging-place of wayfaring men, that I might leave my people and go from them ! (Jer. ix. 2, A.V.).

And then the prophet proceeds to describe the wickedness of the times in terms which remind us partly of his experience at Anathoth,—

Take ye heed every one of his neighbour, and trust ye not in any kinsman[1]*; for every kinsman useth trickery, and every neighbour goeth about with slander* (ver. 4).

Yes, Jeremiah's inner voices did not always appeal to his higher nature. And one of the psalmists who, as we have seen, thought themselves back into the soul of this prophet, was so moved by this passage that he amplified it in lyric verse,—

> *Fear and trembling have come upon me,*
> *And horror overwhelmeth me ;*
> *And I say, Oh that I had wings like a dove !*
> *Then would I fly away, and be at rest :*
> *Lo, then would I wander far off,*
> *I would lodge in the wilderness ;*
> *I would haste me to my safe retreat*
> *From the stormy wind and the tempest.*
>
> (Psa. lv. 5–8, De Witt.)

I am sure that those who agree with me on the subject of the porticoes of psalm-palaces (see p. 105) will enjoy this psalm more as the work of a writer circumstanced like Jeremiah and therefore drawn in an especial manner towards his life and character. The imitation is lovely, but the original passage is more vigorous. One feels that the speaker will not long remain in despondency. That he should be cast down, is only natural ; the prophetic call was not designed to kill nature, but to control and elevate it. And if, intelligibly enough, Jeremiah had his occasional moods of deep sadness, he had also, as I will presently show, his moods of lofty satisfaction at the providential ordering of affairs in Western Asia. These alternations are, in my opinion, clearly traceable in the changing tones of the prophetic strain, to

---

[1] I adopt the translation "kinsman," to bring out the chronological connexion of chap. ix with xi. 18–xii. 6 (see especially the last verse in this section). One might of course render or paraphrase "fellow-Israelite." The Hebrew has "brother."

account for which let us resume for a few minutes the thread of history.

Josiah had thrown himself, as it were, before Neco's chariot-wheels, and been crushed—to Israel a piteous tragedy, but a matter of supreme indifference to an Egyptian conqueror. Straight on went the proud Pharaoh towards the Euphrates, only halting before the renowned city of Kadesh,[1] now easier to take than of yore, when first one and then another Thothmes penetrated to the north of Palestine. He then continued his triumphal march, none venturing to check him, till once more after the lapse of nine centuries Egyptian garrisons looked down on that historic stream, and Neco could then return to secure his hold on Syria and Palestine. Three months after the battle of Megiddo he paused at Israel's ideal northern frontier (Num. xxxiv. 11, Ezek. vi. 14[2]), where, by the walls of Riblah, not many miles from the already captured city Kadesh, in a "deep and lazy stream" the Orontes flows, to receive the submission of the petty Syrian princes. There he learned that the Jews had lost no time in providing themselves with a new king —an act of rebellion, for which he summoned Jehoahaz (to whom I shall return later) to answer. At Riblah the unhappy

---

[1] This statement depends on the interpretation of a famous passage in Herodotus (II. 159). Neco is there said to have defeated the Syrians (i.e. the Jews) at Magdolus, and then taken Cadytis, "a large city of Syria." Magdolus is obviously an error for Megiddo, which Herodotus confounded with the Magdolus Egyptian frontier-city Migdol or Magdol, now Tell el-Hîr (Jer. xliv. 1). Cadytis in Herod. III. 5 means Gaza, which is Katatu or Kazatu in the Egyptian, Khazitu in the Assyrian inscriptions. The conquest of Gaza would, however, certainly not have been mentioned just after the battle of Megiddo, whereas that of Kadesh or Kodshu (the ancient capital of the Hittites) would be quite in order. In the accounts of the Syrian campaigns of Thothmes I. and III. the names Magidi (Megiddo) and Kodshu (Kadesh) constantly occur together. The Syrian chiefs, after being defeated at Magidi, generally retreated to Kodshu, and a second engagement took place beneath its walls. Is it not reasonable to suppose that Herodotus once more made a confusion of names (Katatu and Kadshu, or Kodshu)? The site of Kadesh has been identified by Conder with Tell Neby Mendeh (Laodicæa); see "Twenty-one Years' Work in the Holy Land," pp. 152-156. M. Maspero, the Egyptologist, however, is not fully convinced.

[2] Here we should evidently correct "Diblath" (or, "Diblah") into "Riblah" (see "Variorum Bible"). The mistake of the Massoretic text is repeated by the Septuagint in 2 Chron. xxxvi. 2, Jer. lii. 9, 27.

king was deposed, and an elder brother,[1] known to us as Jehoiakim, set up by Neco in his stead. Probably it did not take the Jews long to accustom themselves to the new state of things. A powerful philo-Egyptian party had long existed in Judah, and if a national choice had to be made, the Jews could not help preferring an Egyptian overlord to an Assyrian; the Assyrians were in fact the most cruel of all the conquering nations of antiquity. But soon another great piece of news startled the Jewish world. The Medes had long since given much trouble to the Assyrians. Once already indeed they had attacked Nineveh (Herod i. 103), and but for the invasion of Media by the Scythians would doubtless have taken it. Upon the withdrawal of the Scythians, they returned to the assault, and the Assyrian capital fell before the combined forces of Media and Babylonia. This was probably in the year 607. The remains of his hastily built and unfinished palace testify to the disquiet of the closing years of the last Assyrian king (Assur-êtihilâni).

It is an immense loss that we have no historical account of the details of this great event. The cuneiform records as yet discovered—even those which belong to the reign of Nabopolassar—are silent respecting them, while the classical writers confounded this final catastrophe with the temporary humiliation of Assyria in 788. But if a historian may be called a "backward-looking prophet," a prophet may surely be regarded in some degree as a "forward-looking historian." For the feelings of the Jews at any rate, as well as for the fact of the inevitableness of Nineveh's ruin, we may refer to Nahum the Elkoshite, who about 660,[2] when Assurbanipal was still at the height of his glory, predicts the destruction of the lion's lair. It was the cruel punishment of Thebes (No-Amon) for its defection to the Ethiopians which opened the eyes of Nahum to the necessity

[1] According to 1 Chron. iii. 15, Josiah had four sons—Johanan, Jehoiakim, Zedekiah, Shallum. Shallum is supposed to be the name of Jehoahaz before he became king. Though placed fourth, he was older than Mattaniah or Zedekiah (comp. 2 Kings xxiii. 31, xxiv. 18) On the changes of names I will speak later.

[2] The Assyrian inscriptions enable us to fix the date of Nahum in the most positive manner. They prove that the capture of Thebes, referred to by the prophet, took place about 663 Now as the event was still fresh in Nahum's recollection, he can hardly have written later than 660 (Schrader, "Die Keilinschriften und das Alte Testament," ed 1, p. 290)

of Nineveh's fall. History confirms not only the accuracy of his anticipation, but the principle upon which it is based. The Roman empire lasted, because it was based not merely on force, but on that unwritten covenant which Virgil has described in imperishable lines. The Assyrian fell, because the conquered provinces were only kept under by the iron heel of tyranny. I quote a passage in which, with a keen sense of retributive justice, the prophet argues from the cruelty of the Assyrian tyrants to the downfall of their capital :—

And all they that see thee shall flee from thee and say, Destroyed is Nineveh! who will condole with her? Whence shall I seek comforters for thee? Art thou (O Nineveh!) better than No-of-Amon, which was enthroned by the Nile-streams, surrounded by water; which was a fortress of the sea, whose wall was water?[1] *Ethiopia was her strength, and Egypt, and there was no end; Put and the Lubim were thy helpers. She however went as captive into exile; her children also were dashed in pieces at every street-corner, and for her honoured ones men cast lots, and all her great ones were bound in fetters. Thou also shalt be drunken, thou shalt faint away; thou also must seek a refuge because of an enemy* (Nah. iii. 7-11).

That there is no exaggeration in the atrocities here ascribed to Assyria, a glance at the monuments or at the translated inscriptions is enough to prove. Well might Nahum, as a representative of the petty states of Asia, draw breath in the striking words which conclude his prophecy,—

All that hear the rumour of thee clap the hands over thee;
For upon whom hath not thy wickedness passed continually ?
(Chap. iii. 19, comp. the delicate touch in the last line of chap. ii. 13.)

The burden of this grand triumphant strain was taken up by Jeremiah's contemporary Zephaniah, but with less ardour of passion. The fall of Assyria is to this prophet merely a detail in the general judgment of the nations, and the last feature in his description—"*every one that passeth by her shall hiss and wag his hand*—contains a reminiscence of the vigorous distich just now quoted from Nahum. We need not be surprised at this, for not only was Zephaniah a less original and effective writer than Nahum, but he lived at a time when Nineveh was

[1] I point *mayīm* with the Septuagint, the Peshitto, and the Vulgate.

no longer dangerous to the populations of Palestine. Whether spoken with more passion or with less, however, the maledictions of the prophets were accomplished to the letter. Xenophon and his Ten Thousand passed by the ruins of Nineveh in 401, and mistook them for the remains of Median cities laid waste by the Persians . the very name of Nineveh had been forgotten. In the lapse of years the ruins themselves became unrecognizable, and it is only in our own day that they have been discovered beneath their clothing of sand.

So colossal an event could not but involve grave consequences — it was destined to change the face of Asia. Not indeed all at once ; for the next two years Syria and Palestine continued to be attached to the empire of Egypt. But about 605 Nabopolassar (more correctly, Nabû-pal-uçur, *i.e.*, "Nebo, protect the son"!), originally a general sent out by the former of Assurbanipal's two successors to quell a Chaldæan revolt,[1] but too ambitious to resist the temptation of seizing the Babylonian crown, and now the conqueror of Assyria, sent his son to recover the southern provinces of the empire from Pharaoh-Neco :—it is the prince who bears the fatal name Nebuchadrezzar[2] (more strictly, Nabû-kudur-uçur, *i.e.*, "Nebo, protect the crown"). Neco too set forth once more on the way to Syria, and halted near Carchemish[3] on the Euphrates. In olden times this had been a great city as the capital of the Hittites, but its commercial prosperity dated from its conquest by Sargon in 717. To the Assyrio-Babylonian king, the possession of this point was of the utmost consequence, for it secured the passage of the River and the high road from Mesopotamia to Palestine. With a well-appointed army Pharaoh-Neco encountered his young rival ; but—oh the strange sight to all who knew Egyptian warriors !—*the heroes were beaten in pieces* (by the heavy Babylonian maces), *they fled away, and looked not back;* or rather, *the swift could not flee, nor the heroes escape*

---

[1] Tiele rightly regards this as the kernel of the strange account given by Abydenus. It is possible, however, that Nabopolassar was not merely a general sent on a special mission, but viceroy of Babylon. Assurbanipal had suppressed the viceroyalty ; the increasing peril of the empire may have induced his successor to restore it.

[2] So given in Jer xxi 2, 7 and twenty-four other passages.

[3] Identified by George Smith, in his last fatal journey, with Jerablûs or Jerabis, on the right bank of the Euphrates.

KEEP THE MUNITION, WATCH THE WAY! 131

(Jer. xlvi. 5. 6), because those swifter than the leopard (Hab. i. 8) were upon them. Nothing but the death of the old Babylonian monarch arrested his son's triumphant progress. Fearing to be absent from his capital, the young king committed the charge of his garrisons to his generals, and, with characteristic promptitude, dashed homeward with a small escort the shortest way across the Arabian desert.[1]

And now, what was the tone of mind in Judah during these eventful years? The reiterated references in Jeremiah to the "Peace, peace" of the flattering or false prophets[2] sufficiently show that, as in Isaiah's time, "they which should lead had caused Israel to err, and destroyed the way of his paths" (Isa. iii. 12). Putting aside a few individuals, the nation (*i.e.*, all those classes of the nation which counted) neither had nor wished to have any true conception of its position. Neither had, nor wished to have, I say designedly. For a long time past, prophecy had been a source of national danger. It had always been a regular and tolerably lucrative profession; but whereas in a simpler age, the prophets had "divined for money" and yet been conscientious, in the luxuriousness of the later regal period they had more and more laid themselves out for gain apart from conscience (see Mic. iii. 11). Their sole object was to please, and the way to please was to keep up all agreeable illusions. Listen first to Isaiah and then to Jeremiah.

For it is a disobedient people, lying sons, sons that will not hear the direction of Jehovah, who say to the seers, Ye shall not see [*truly*], *and to the prophets, Ye shall not prophesy unto us right things; speak unto us smooth things, prophesy illusions* (Isa. xxx. 9, 10).

The prophets prophesy falsely, and the priests rule at their beck, and my people love to have it so (Jer. v. 31).

It may be remarked by some reader of Wellhausen that the latter passage does not apply to the period which followed the Reformation. For the public recognition of the Deuteronomic Scripture must have greatly increased the authority of the priests, under whose care (comp. Deut. xxxi. 25, 26) it was placed. The prophet who was a joint-author of Deuteronomy gave up much for himself and his order that he might gain

[1] Berossus, *fragm* 11, in Josephus, "Ant." x 11.
[2] Jer. vi 14, viii 11, comp iv. 10 (all these passages occur in contexts referring partly to the Scythians, but partly no doubt to the Chaldæans)

more for the community. This is true, from whatever source the reader's insight may be derived. But we must remember that the Deuteronomic *tōrāh* was suffering a temporary eclipse. The old conditions of things were partly restored. Unity was lost, and the excited people must now more than ever have turned to the prophets for comfort. They at least could offer what no mere priests and no mere book could pretend to offer— a direct revelation from the Deity on matters of present moment. And so both statesmen and priests had to bend low before the prophets, or at least before the prophetic order. But the prophets (among whom I of course do not now include Jeremiah) could not afford to follow the inner voice. They were led by love of gain and of influence to ascribe a Divine authority to the blind instincts of the people, which received a fresh glamour from being expressed in the rhetorical style of prophecy. These instincts were at present those of self-complacent vanity. Three times over had God spoken in history, and loudly enough, one might think, to awaken all who had the power to reflect, but each of these unexpected events had but lulled the Jews in a deeper security. Again and again, one may suppose, Jerusalem gave itself up to the wild rejoicings of which Eastern nations alone are capable. Nineveh had fallen ; Neco had been defeated ; and now the prince who wielded the dreaded power of Babylon, had been turned back, as it seemed, by some supernatural hand.

Jeremiah at least saw more clearly. Not to him could those words of Jesus be applied, *Ye can discern the face of the sky, but ye cannot discern the signs of the times* (Matt xvi. 3). He saw once more the seething caldron ready to precipitate a flood of ruin over his dear country (Jer. i. 13, 14). You might think perhaps that the vision would strike him dumb with terror, as he thought of the fierce warriors streaming in from the north under the greatest general of the Semitic East before Hannibal. Listen to Habakkuk, who lived at Jerusalem about this time,[1] and see how awful the prospect really was :—

Look ye among the nations and behold, amaze yourselves, be ye amazed! for a deed doeth he in your days which ye believe not when narrated —For behold I raise up the Chaldæans, the rough and the restless nation which goeth through the breadth of the earth, to possess dwellings which are not his. Frightful

[1] That is, after the battle of Carchemish.

and terrible is it, from himself his justice and his majesty goeth forth, and swifter than leopards are his horses, and fiercer than evening wolves his chargers leap, and his horsemen go far away, fly as an eagle hasteth to gorging; each cometh to do wrong, the endeavour of their faces is towards assault, so that he collecteth prisoners like the dust; and at kings he mocketh, and princes are to him a laughingstock, and he laugheth at every stronghold, and throweth up dust and taketh it.—But he exceeded in daring and transgressed, and—becometh guilty: this his strength becometh his God[1] (Hab. i. 5–11, Ewald).

The rapidity of the rise of the new conquering power had evidently impressed Habakkuk. He compares the Chaldæan horses to leopards—meaning perhaps the chetah, or hunting leopard, still found in Palestine, "the rush of which on its prey is the most rapid of possible movements;"[2] and he gives the former the superiority in swiftness (comp. Dan. vii. 6). The thought of what is coming paralyzes him, and all the more because this physical energy of the Chaldæans is combined with a fierce and defiant assertion of their own standard of justice and their own all-surpassing majesty. But, as Ewald says, the prophet, commenting on the revelation which he has uttered, gives a hint of comfort to the true believer. The Chaldæan idolizes that strength which he owes to Another, and denies the true God. Then, in the next section, his tone becomes more pleading. The death of Israel as a nation would be equivalent to the death of Jehovah. There have no doubt been divine deaths. *Where is the god of Hamath and the god of Arpad* (Isa. xxxvii. 13)? But —*art thou not from everlasting, Yahvé my God? my Holy One, thou canst not die!* ... *Thou of too pure eyes to behold iniquity, and who to look at evil art not able, wherefore lookest thou upon the treacherous, holdest thy peace when the unjust devoureth the just, and makest men as fish of the sea, as the worm that hath no ruler!* (Hab. i. 12–14). Thus Habakkuk like Jeremiah (xii. 1) is troubled by the incompleteness of the Divine retribution. Judah, by comparison with Chaldæa, is righteous (Ewald, for greater vigour, shortens the literal rendering, which is, "the unrighteous devoureth him who is more righteous than he"); as for the covetous invader, *his inmost soul is puffed up, it is not upright* (or perhaps, *humble;* lit.,

[1] I have here followed Mr. J. Frederick Smith's accurate translation.
[2] Tristram, "The Land of Israel," p. 495.

"level"), *but the righteous shall live by his faithfulness*[1] (ii. 4). Such is the sure hope which pierces the clouds of trouble. Righteousness must outlive unrighteousness; and when we add to this the faith in a God *who only hath immortality* (1 Tim. vi. 16), what can the prophet need more to revive his courage? Alas that Habakkuk should have so far miscalculated the moral value of the two nations—Chaldæa and Israel, and seen so dimly into the abyss of the Divine purposes! Like Jeremiah, he "stood in the council of Jehovah" (Jer. xxiii. 18); why did he not "see and hear" better? He did indeed "see" that God loves and will have righteousness; but he did not see the moral and religious need of a complete subversion of the existing order of things. He saw that "law" (*tōrāh*)—even the incomparable Deuteronomic law—was *benumbed* (Hab. i. 4); but he did not see that bright spiritual landscape beyond the *sea of affliction* (Zech. x. 11), in which rises the mount of beatitudes and the second and better covenant. His fate reminds us somewhat of Josiah's. He trusted God implicitly, and his trust was not rewarded in the way that he expected. But he was probably spared Josiah's premature end; he may have lived to take to his heart of hearts the purer hopes and loftier aspirations of Jeremiah.

Or listen to the latter prophet's expressions of horror in one of his gloomier moods,—

Behold, as clouds he cometh up, and as the whirlwind are his chariots; swifter than eagles are his horses. Woe unto us! for we are spoiled (iv. 13).

O daughter of my people, gird thee with sackcloth, and roll thee in ashes; make thee an only son's mourning, most bitter lamentation; for suddenly cometh the spoiler upon us (vi. 26).

Oh that my head were waters, and mine eyes a fountain of tears, that I might weep day and night for the slain of the daughter of my people (ix. 1).

The last of these passages is surely a direct expression of Cassandra-like horror at the fate which impends over Judah. In some places the prophet may have husbanded his talent, and adapted old prophecies respecting the Scythians to the new and

---

[1] "Faithfulness" should be interpreted as in Jer. v. 1, where it is synonymously parallel to "right." There is an implied antithesis to the unfaithfulness of the Chaldæan invader, who acknowledges not God nor the Divine law.

greater Chaldæan crisis; but surely not here. But the fact that there are so few direct expressions of grief confirms the view that the sensitive Jeremiah was lifted up by a wonderful inspiration to a height like that which Christian poets love to describe —a height from which past troubles appear to be swallowed up in light. As soon as the prophet gained his first clear intuition of the future, what, think you, was his mood? The answer is given in chaps. xlvi.-xlix., a group of prophecies on the foreign nations (A.V.'s "Gentiles" is surely a most inappropriate rendering), written at various times during the period beginning 606-605. Here, more than anywhere else, is revealed Jeremiah's conviction that prophetic oracles are, not less than wind and storm, messengers of God, fulfilling His word, in destruction not less than in reproduction, and through this faith he obtains a profound repose for his throbbing heart. His own consciousness becomes more than ever absorbed in the divine —at least, in that aspect of the divine which at this moment forces itself upon him; and so he shuts up his heart's best treasure of love and pity (like Jehovah Himself, according to Isa. lxiii. 15, R.V.), and rejoices, not unlike the prophet-poet Dante, in the just judgments of God. Does not this suggest to us the true explanation of that calmness which surprised us in Jeremiah not long ago, and which contrasts so strikingly with his irritation at Anathoth? The prophet's intuition of the future was acquiring greater definiteness; and tired of his ceaseless anxiety, he was relieved to know that the end was so near. It is somewhat as when a man is told by his physician that he has not many months to live; the certainty has been known to bring to such an one a new, strange peace of mind. The fret and fever of life vanishes in a moment; troubles and disappointments assume another aspect, and he even welcomes weakness and pain as the harbingers of a change which, if God be faithful, cannot be for the worse.

In the opening oracle of the series referred to, Jeremiah's new peace of mind appears to be intensified into a kind of stern joy. I suppose that on this one occasion at least his words may have been echoed by the majority of his countrymen, who only remembered that it was by Neco that the nation's darling had been slain, and saw not that the Pharaoh's defeat did but prepare the way for a more severe master. Jeremiah's rejoicing, however, was not like that of his light-hearted people. He may indeed have hated Egypt only less than Assyria, and on much the same grounds as his countrymen, but this is not the whole secret of his triumph at its humiliation. He knew but too well the blow that was preparing from Jehovah's, not Nebo's, hammer [1]—Nebuchadrezzar. And this was to him the source of an inward transformation as remarkable as any in the New Testament. The Divine rebuke in Jer. xii. 5 was never required again. The prophet's sensitive nature was recast, and though traces of the old infirmity remained, yet, whenever there was a need for action, he was calm, adventurous, and resourceful.

I wish I had space to enter at length into the truly remarkable prophecy on Egypt, which should be read by all who would estimate the poetic capacity of Jeremiah. It falls into two parts, which cannot have been composed at quite the same time. In the former (vers. 3-12) the point of time assumed is immediately before the battle of Carchemish. It is a grand triumphal ode, describing this fatal blow as a Divine judgment from which Egypt cannot possibly recover. The latter (vers. 14-26 [2]) is a prediction in highly poetic imagery of Nebuchadrezzar's conquest of Egypt.[3] The date is not to be deduced with precision from the contents, but it is safest to refer both this and the following prophecies to the anxious time of Nebuchadrezzar's first Palestinian campaign. How striking is the picture which in the former passage unrolls itself before the prophet's imagination ! First, the setting forth of the splendid Egyptian army ; then the strange contrast—knights *sans peur et sans reproche* perishing miserably, their shields (to quote from an earlier poet) being "vilely cast away" (or perhaps, "defiled"—2 Sam. i. 21). Well for mankind, thinks our pro-

[1] Jer. l. 23, *How is the hammer of the whole earth cut asunder and broken !* The passage represents Jeremiah's view of Nebuchadnezzar, even if it be not written by him.

[2] I make this prophecy close at *v.* 26 and not at *v.* 28, because the two concluding verses of the chapter are evidently inserted at a later time from xxx. 10, 11, where they cohere far better with the context than they do here.

[3] Egypt certainly had more claims upon Jeremiah's sympathy than Moab. Had the prophet foreseen the hospitality accorded by Egypt to the Jews at a somewhat later time, and the important consequences which were to flow from this, he would perhaps have devoted more than half a verse to Egypt's happier future.

phet, that it was so! for the march of an Egyptian army is like nothing so much as a monstrous devastating river. But the day of vengeance is come. Gilead's costly balm, so prized in Egypt (Gen. xliii. 11, l. 2), has no healing virtue for Egypt's wound.

"To pluck up and to break down and to destroy" (Jer. i. 10) was no small part of Jeremiah's ministry at this time. We cannot however pause beside each canvas in this prophetic portrait-gallery. Suffice it to mention that what may seem repellent is mitigated by bright glimpses of the future. When the sword has done its work, it will be sheathed (Jer. xlvii. 6); Moab, Ammon, and Elam shall not always be *exiled from the eternal providence* (Wisd. xvii. 2), and even exhausted Egypt shall again support a teeming population. But what shall we say of chap. xxv., which gives the substance of chaps. xlvi.–xlix. in a more fearfully impressive form? Well, even here a bright prospect opens in vers. 12–14 to the nations (including Judah) which have drunk the wine of God's fury. It does not indeed commend itself to a Christian reader, but to Jeremiah's contemporaries it was only too congenial a picture (see vers. 12–14). "Fearfully impressive" is, I think, not too strong an epithet to use of this chapter as a whole. It deserves an attentive study on various grounds, historical, exegetical, and critical. As a survey of the Eastern world, in which Judah occupies no more than its due place, it reminds us of the prophecy of Zephaniah (see p. 33); as a list of the "nations round about" (vers. 19–26), it has even a geographical value; and from the peculiar arrangement of this chapter in the Septuagint interrupted as it is after ver. 13 by the insertion of xlix. 34–39, xlvi., xlvii., xlix. 7–22, 1–6, 28–33, 23–27, xlviii.) it presents the student with a curious critical problem. How much the early students of the Scriptures were interested in this chapter, is shown by several important interpolations,[1] evidently they

---

[1] Thus in *v.* 9 we should probably omit all between "saith Jehovah" and "and will bring them", in *v* 12, "the king of Babylon and," and also "and the land of the Chaldæans", and in *v* 26, "and the king of Sheshach shall drink after them" (most inappropriate, at the end of a list of the nations to be punished by Babylon, a little more elaborateness was surely required in the description of Babylon's retribution) See, however, Ewald's note on *v.* 9 in his "Prophets," vol ii., where a brave attempt is made to defend the Massoretic text (only changing *'el* into *'eth*).

had brooded deeply over it. Very different must have been the effect of this chapter on most of those who originally heard its substance. But was it ever publicly delivered? the reader may ask; for sometimes the denunciations of prophets would seem to have been elaborated in private for the reading of disciples or future generations. My own opinion is that it was, and that it is the prophecy which Jeremiah dictated to Baruch according to Jer. xxxvi. I find it difficult to believe that the roll referred to in that striking chapter contained the substance of all Jeremiah's prophecies from the beginning of his ministry. A complete reproduction of the prophecies would not have suited Jeremiah's purpose, and Jer. xxxvi. 29 expressly states that the obnoxious roll contained one great and terrible declaration—the very same which we find in Jer. xxv. But I am in danger of anticipating, and must now prepare to resume the thread of the narrative.

CHAPTER IV.

THERE BE GODS MANY, LORDS MANY.

Jeremiah's verdict upon the later kings—Nebuchadrezzar crosses the border—Duel between Jeremiah and Jehoiakim.

IT may have struck some readers that in hastening on to the great catastrophe which was to revolutionize Asia, I passed somewhat lightly over the fate of Josiah's successor. Let me now correct this involuntary injustice. In 2 Kings xxiii. 33, 34 we are simply told that Neco bound Jehoahaz at Hamath, and then took him away to Egypt, where he died in captivity. His melancholy end deeply moved his contemporaries, not, as that of another "king for a hundred days" has moved our generation, from its moral significance, but at least from its pathetic suggestions.

Weep ye not for the dead (said the tender-hearted man beneath one of the prophets of that day), *neither bemoan him: but weep sore for him that is gone away; for he shall return no more, nor see his native country. For thus saith Jehovah touching Shallum the son of Josiah, king of Judah, which reigned instead of Josiah his father, which went forth out of this place: He shall not return thither any more; but in the place whither they have led him captive there shall he die, and he shall see this land no more* (Jer. xxii. 10-12).

Jeremiah feels and writes in complete sympathy with his people; and so, it seems to me, does his younger contemporary Ezekiel, who perhaps (as Ewald suggests) has adopted one of the popular elegies upon Shallum or Jehoahaz in Ezek. xix. 1-4. "A young lion of royal strain, caught untimely, and chained and carried away captive,—this was how the people of

Israel conceived of Shallum."[1] Sooner would they have chosen for him the tragic but not dishonourable end of his father, than that he should be dragged with the rope of a captive to a foreign land, and be buried in the "house of bondage" far from the tombs of his ancestors. The words of Huldah to Josiah, *Thou shalt be gathered to thy grave in peace* (2 Kings xxii. 20), hardly seem an exaggeration in the light of coming events. Of the character of Jehoahaz, Jeremiah generously says nothing ; even if the report of this king's wickedness (see p. 104) be well-founded, yet he can hardly have done much good or evil in his short reign of three months. Of his elder brother Jehoiakim, however, the prophet speaks with great positiveness and patriotic resentment, drawing a pointed contrast between him and his noble father (Jer. xxii. 13-17). The same kingly virtues which were so conspicuous in David (2 Sam. viii. 15*b*) adorned Josiah ; covetousness and oppression and judicial murders disgraced the rule of Jehoiakim.

Woe unto him that buildeth his house by unrighteousness, and his chambers by injustice; that maketh his neighbour work for nought, and giveth him not his hire. . . . Shalt thou reign because thou viest with Ahab? did not thy father eat and drink (*i.e.*, enjoy life), *and do judgment and justice? then it was well with him. He judged the cause of the poor and needy; then it was well. Was not this to know me? saith Jehovah. But thine eyes and heart are only upon thy* (*dishonest*) *gain, and on shedding innocent blood, and on carrying out a crushing oppressiveness* (Jer xxii. 13, 15-17).

What a picture ! Josiah's model was David ; Jehoiakim's is Ahab, whose judicial murder of Naboth was the culminating sin of his life (1 Kings xxi.). Is it not an apostrophe worthy of the great Elijah, whose vigorous expression (suggested, it is true, by his antagonist) "disturber of Israel"—*i.e.*, subverter of the ancient social and religious order—is quite as applicable to Jehoiakim as to Ahab? We owe the genuine reading of Jer. xxii. 15*a* to two of our great Septuagint manuscripts (the Alexandrine and the Friderico-Augustan); the Massoretic read-

---

[1] Cox, "Biblical Expositions," p. 120. Tristram was reminded of Ezekiel's imagery in observing the rude Syrian mode of capturing a lion by driving it with cries and noises into a pitfall with spikes at the bottom ("Natural History of the Bible," p. 118).

ing is almost impossible to construe,[1] and the other Septuagint reading "with Ahaz" (so the Vatican MS.), though accepted by Ewald, is to be rejected (1, because "vying with Ahaz" has no historical basis; and 2, because "Ahaz" might easily be misunderstood to mean "Jehoahaz," of which name "Ahaz" is an abbreviation).

But the description of Jehoiakim is not confined to generalities. He is brought before us in *v*. 14 (which is a digression or parenthetic illustration) as a great builder, and as such receives severe censure. This is worthy of remark. The architectural tastes of Solomon are mentioned (1 Kings v.–vii.) without a word of blame; why should those of Jehoiakim be treated differently? At another time certainly no one could have blamed Jehoiakim and his nobles[2] for being discontented with the narrow, ill-lighted chambers of Syrian houses, and saying, *I will build me a wide house and spacious chambers, and cutting out their windows, inlaying the chambers with cedar, and painting them with vermilion* (Jer. xxii. 14). But was this the moment for beautifying Jerusalem when the land was still groaning under Neco's war-fine[3] (2 Kings xxiii. 33)? And how could a worshipper of Jehovah wrong his brother-Israelite by exacting labour for which he had neither the will, nor (we may fairly assume) the ability to pay?

The truth is that Jehoiakim was smitten with a passion for the pomp and splendour of an Oriental despot. He knew by hearsay of the great buildings of Egypt and Assyria which had been erected by forced labour, and may perhaps already have heard of some of the grand royal constructions of Nebuchadrezzar.[4] Another prophet may be taken to allude to these in

[1] R.V., however, attempts what is almost impossible; "thou strivest to excel in cedar" (*i.e.*, in cedar buildings), is at any rate good English, and masks the difficulty that Jehoiakim's self-chosen rival is not named. The reason why "with Ahab" has not met with more favour is that critics supposed his "ivory house" to be alluded to. But really there is no direct connexion between *v*. 14 and *v*. 15*a*.

[2] See Jer. xxii. 23 (quoted later on), which was addressed to the richer inhabitants of Jerusalem, including the king.

[3] It was a comparatively small fine (comp. 2 Kings xv. 19, xviii. 14); was the land already too impoverished to bear a larger one? One seems to feel in reading 2 Kings xxiii. 35 that the new king's mode of collecting it caused great dissatisfaction.

[4] On the building tastes of Assyrio-Babylonian kings, comp. Perrot-Chipiez, "History of Art in Chaldæa and Assyria," i. 51. For Nebuchad-

the following passage, the conclusion of which is closely parallel to Jer. xxii. 13, 17,—

Woe to him that gaineth evil gains for his house, that he may set his nest on high, that he may withdraw himself from the grasp of misfortune. . . . For the stone shall cry out of the wall, and the beam out of the timber shall answer it. Woe to him that buildeth a town with bloodshed, and establisheth a city with wrong (Hab. ii. 9-12). In fact, neither Solomon nor Nebuchadrezzar can have seemed to a prophet like Jeremiah or Habakkuk a much fitter model than Ahab, and to accuse Jehoiakim (whether directly or indirectly) of copying either of these kings was to pronounce his religious condemnation.

In their religious estimate of Nebuchadrezzar the prophets may possibly have done him some injustice; into this delicate question we must not refuse to enter at a more advanced point of the narrative. But we have no reason to question Jeremiah's verdict upon Jehoiakim, who, alike from a religious and a political point of view, appears to have been unequal to the crisis in the fortunes of Israel. It might indeed be urged in favour of Jehoiakim that in his own way he was as zealous for Jehovah as his father. Had he not even changed his original name Eliakim (with the Pharaoh's approval) into Jehoiakim,[1] to assure to himself, by a name compounded with Jehovah, the special protection of Israel's God? To apply the language of Prof. Milligan, "As in the case of so many of the Old Testament worthies, his name is the index to what he was,"[2] or at least to the religion which he professed. Now what does "Jehoiakim" mean? "Jehovah (rather Yahveh) raiseth up." It is an expression of faith that it is by Jehovah (Yahveh) that princes reign, and that not alliances, not defenced cities, not "the multitude of an host," can deliver a king, but the God in whom he trusts. Some, I know, have said that it was Neco who changed

rezzar's beautification of Babylon, see his inscriptions (*e.g.*, in "Records of the Past," vol. xii.).

[1] See 2 Kings xxiii. 34 (Dr. Lumby's note in the "Cambridge Bible" does not quite meet the difficulty). Eliakim's brother Shallum (Jer. xxii. 11) had also changed his name, as most suppose. Possibly the two names, Ilubid and Yahubid, of a certain king of Hamath in Sargon's reign may be accounted for on these analogies. On the Assyrian custom, see Sayce, "Hibbert Lectures," pp. 303, 304, and on Egyptian and Arabian parallels Goldziher, "Der Mythos bei den Hebraern," p. 351.

[2] "Elijah. his Life and Times," p. 43.

the name of Eliakim into Jehoiakim, and Nebuchadrezzar who altered Mattaniah's name into Zedekiah. They have on their side the meagre and perhaps hastily compiled Hebrew record of the reigns of the later kings, which in this one particular reads more like an Egyptian than a Jewish document. But if the names Jehoiakim and Zedekiah had been directly chosen by the Egyptian and the Babylonian king respectively, why is it that they have not an Egyptian and a Babylonian colouring (comp. Gen. xli. 45, Ezra v. 14, Dan. i. 7, and the names given to captured cities by the Assyrians)? To meet this, it has been suggested that the names of the Jewish vassal kings may have been compounded with the name of Israel's God, because they had been made to swear by Jehovah. This view is barely possible with regard to Zedekiah, because his oath of fidelity to Babylon had been sanctioned by Jehovah's prophets (2 Chron. xxxvi. 13, Ezek. xvii. 13), but hardly with regard to Jehoiakim. The prophets of this period were as a rule the advocates of a strong nationalistic policy; the higher prophets—those like Jeremiah—recognized the necessity of submission to Babylon, but none, so far as we know, were in favour of Egypt. But without the consent of prophets of Jehovah it is difficult to say how a king of Judah could swear allegiance to Egypt by the name of Jehovah. I think then that Shallum's and Eliakim's and Mattaniah's change of name must have had a religious motive; it was as if the king entered thereby into a special, personal covenant with his father-God (comp. Psa. lxxxix. 26). Assyrian, Egyptian, and Arabian analogies appear to me to confirm this view.

But was the religion professed by Jehoiakim identical with Josiah's? It was of course based on the worship of Jehovah; but then who was this Jehovah, and what amount of truth was there in his godship? Certainly he did not rank as high in the scale of divinity as either Merodach (Maruduk), in whose honour, and not simply for his own aggrandizement, Nebuchadrezzar strengthened and beautified Babylon, or Merodach's divine son Nebo (Nabû), whose "darling" the great king called himself—both of these deities were honoured by him with a worship only less pure and noble than the Hebrew psalmists' worship of their God.[1] And most certainly this Jehovah was not the

[1] For Nebuchadrezzar's prayers, see "Records of the Past," vol xii , Sayce's "Hibbert Lectures," p, 97. In all religiously important points, the interpretation of them is, I believe, secure.

equal of the holy God who spoke by Moses, by Elijah, by the Deuteronomist, by Jeremiah, by the psalmists, and who attached the enjoyment of His favour to compliance with strict moral conditions. No; the Jehovah in whom Jehoiakim truly enough professed his faith on ascending the throne was not He whom a great disciple of St. Paul so emphatically identifies with the Father of the Lord Jesus (Heb. i., ii.); rather he may be called, without any rhetorical flourish, a rival of the true God. A poor rival, some may say, for his dangerousness to Israel consisted in the fact that he too claimed the name Jehovah. But is there not often very much in a name? Was not the contest between the God of Elijah and the God of Ahab and Jezebel a contest between two rival claimants of the title "Lord" (Baal)?[1] May we not even venture to say that upon the death of Josiah a contest (or a new phase of a contest) began between two Jehovahs, not in the sense in which such a contest is carried on in the speeches of Job,[2] but in that in which in other countries besides Palestine a bitter but not doubtful contest has been waged between a partly moral God, who tolerates no rival, and claims the empire of the world, and a mere territorial divinity, the impersonation of the natural forces which the cultivator of the soil desires to propitiate. The true "son" or "servant" of Jehovah (for these terms are nearly equivalent; see 2 Kings xvi. 7, Mal. iii. 17, Gal. iv. 1) was no longer the Israelitish but—startling though most true paradox!—the Babylonian king. And this in a twofold sense: 1, because Nebuchadrezzar carried out the true God's providential purposes, and 2, because there are strong points of affinity between the religion of Merodach and that of Jeremiah's Jehovah. We have indeed no such prophetic glorification of Nebuchadrezzar as the "second Isaiah" gives of Cyrus,—*Thus saith Jehovah to his Anointed, to Cyrus, whom I grasp by his right hand,*—words which so strikingly

---

[1] We may legitimately infer this from Hos. ii. 16 (on which see my note in the "Cambridge Bible"). Ahab would not have confessed that he was an opponent of the worship of Jehovah. But to the great prose-poet who has described the contest on Mount Carmel it appeared as if Ahab had in very deed led the Israelites into forsaking Jehovah's covenant and throwing down His altars. The exaggeration was only natural, it reveals the true poet who delights in simple, direct issues, and the disciple of the later prophets

[2] See "Job and Solomon," pp. 31, 32.

remind us of expressions in the Cyrus cylinder-inscription (line 12), "whose hand he (Maruduk or Merodach) holds." But I see no reason why Jeremiah should not have used them as a direct contradiction to the misleading name of the preceding king (Jehoahaz, *i.e.* "he whom Jehovah holdeth"), except perhaps that he was unaware of the strong resemblance in character between Nebuchadrezzar's God and his own. At any rate, he does twice call the Babylonian king "my servant" (xxvii. 6, xliii. 10, *not* in xxv. 9, which is interpolated), and even if he means this in the lower sense of "one who, with or against his will, cannot help forwarding the designs of Me, who am God of Israel and of all the nations," we who read his words in the light of history know that they mean this, and more than this, viz., that Nebuchadrezzar's worship, however imperfect, was accepted by Jehovah, while that of Jehoiakim, nominally Jehovah's "son" and "servant," was rejected.[1]

To this battle of rival Jehovahs, there corresponds an antagonism between their respective representatives—Jehoiakim and Jeremiah, a specimen of which is presented to us in Jer. xxxvi. The date of the event is the fifth, or more probably, as the Septuagint of verse 9 says, the eighth year of Jehoiakim, *i.e.* the fifth year of Nebuchadrezzar. The king of Babylon has hitherto spared Judah, having more important work in other frontier territories. But at last he finds leisure to glance at its mountain fortress Jerusalem, which lies too near Egypt (then as now the coveted prize of ambition) to be left in the hands of a friend of Neco. He takes the field—or, as Bible language puts it, "goes up"—against Judah (2 Kings xxiv. 1), but he encounters no resistance, for Jehoiakim makes haste to swear the oath of fidelity.[2] How shall we account for the Jewish king's good resolution? Was he completely taken by surprise? Had he made no request for Egyptian aid? Or had the inflated self-conceit of the Pharaohs been so reduced by the disaster at Carchemish that Neco refused to listen to Jehoiakim's prayer? One or the other of these alternatives

[1] I fear that the "lower sense" is the one intended by Jeremiah, to whom the few spiritual believers in Israel formed, collectively, the only "servant of Jehovah" as yet in existence (Jer. xxx 10, xlvi. 27, 28).

[2] Note how even a Jewish prophet recognizes an oath of fidelity to Babylon (Ezek xvii 11-21), and contrast Isaiah's indifference to Hezekiah's breach of faith towards Assyria.

may be correct; but a third view is suggested by an attentive reading of the striking chapter referred to. The subject, as I have said, is a duel between Jeremiah and his bitter opponent the king—a duel, however, in which the combatants do not meet face to face. It is wonderful, let us notice in passing, how much could be done in the political world even then merely by pen and ink. Jeremiah was certainly no Cobbett, but he produced an effect with the help of his scribe wh ch even Cobbett would not have disdained. Let us try to picture the scene. Nebuchadrezzar and his army have crossed the Jewish border. The country-places are being deserted; Isaiah's description of a northern army (Isa. xi) is being verified to the letter. A temple fast is about to be proclaimed (just as the last Assyrian king at a similar crisis proclaimed one) for the citizens of Jerusalem, and for all who have flocked in from the cities of Judah (Jer. xxxvi. 6–9). Jeremiah seizes the opportunity to carry out a new plan. The people will not allow him to address them; then Baruch the scribe shall read the most relevant of his prophecies to them, especially that very important one (chap. xxv.) written in the fatal year of Carchemish, and containing a new and definite announcement of most serious import. The trumpet is blown in Zion (Joel ii. 1), and at the first notes citizens and refugees alike hasten to the temple. Soon sacrificial smoke ascends; suppliant processions go round the altar; penitential psalms are chanted, and those piercing cries of which Jewish throats are capable resound through the temple-courts. Baruch, too, the brave and faithful Baruch, betakes himself to God's house; or rather, for how should he win the attention of this busy multitude?— to one of the many chambers of different sizes attached to the temple. A fellow scribe, whose duties bring him into constant relations to the king, and who is the brother of Jeremiah's patron Ahikam, offers him hospitality. Probably he is acquainted with Baruch, who himself has a family connexion with the court, being the brother of one high functionary (Jer. li. 59, see "Variorum Bible") and the grandson of another (2 Chron. xxxiv. 8).[1] In this large room Baruch recites one or more prophecies to many of the people, declaring that "this

[1] The respectful behaviour of the princes to Baruch in *v.* 15 confirms the view that he was of good social rank, comp. Josephus, "Ant." x. 9, 1. This illustrates Jeremiah's caution to Baruch in Jer. xlv. 5a.

house shall become like Shiloh," and that "Nebuchadrezzar shall destroy this land and all the countries round about" (Jer. xxvi. 6, xxv. 9; comp. xxxvi. 29), but doubtless adding a strong appeal to them to "return every man from his evil way that I (Jehovah) may forgive their iniquity" (Jer. xxxvi. 3).

Not a very attractive sermon for those who think to move Jehovah by forms and ceremonies! The next to hear it, by their own request, are the princes in their council-chamber. They too are startled at its boldness. They know Jeremiah, but a prediction quite so definite as this they have not yet heard from him. They also know Jehoiakim, and how passionately he resents the least infringement of his royal rights. As politicians, too, perhaps they partly sympathize with him, even though, as fellow-converts of Josiah, the oldest and gravest of them revere Josiah's prophet. *They turn trembling one to another, and say unto Baruch, We have to tell the king of all these words* (ver. 16). We all know the sequel! it is one of the scenes in the Bible-story which has engraved itself the most deeply on the memory. Jehoiakim sends for the scroll. It is December; Jehoiakim is sitting in the "winter house," *i.e.*, in that part of the royal palace which was arranged for use in winter (comp. Amos iii. 15), and there is a fire burning in the fire-pan or brasier—still, as I know by experience, commonly used in Syria, and called by a name (*kānūn*) which also designates the months of December and January. How piercingly cold these months can be, even to those who have come from temperate climes, is well known. One remembers, too, how in Ezra's time, on the twentieth day of the ninth month (*i.e.*, some time in December), *all the people sat in the street of the house of God, trembling because of this matter, and for the great rain* (Ezra x. 9). A group of courtiers stands in the background. Jehudi (a courtier; but, being the son of an Ethiopian, not a Jewish citizen) comes forward and reads first one column, then another, and then another. But the proud king can bear it no longer; he rises— he steps forward—three high officers in vain attempt to check him—he snatches the scroll from the reader's hands—he cuts it, with a cruel kind of pleasure, into piece after piece, and throws it into the fire. Then, as he watches the curling fragments, he despatches three other high officers, to arrest the prophet and the scribe on a charge of high treason.

The fortunes of spiritual religion hang upon the escape of Jeremiah.

CHAPTER V.

BRIGHT VISIONS IN THE DEATH-CHAMBER.

Jeremiah's Wartburg period and its results—The drought—The problem of Israel's spiritual condition—The new covenant—Jehoiakim's rebellion—The Rechabites—Two symbolic actions—Jehoiachin's captivity—His character and Nebuchadrezzar's.

THE duel between Jehoiakim and Jeremiah reminds us to some extent of that between Ahab and Elijah. Differences of course there are, but both at any rate agree in this, that a prophet singlehanded overmatched a king and his false prophets. Take Jeremiah for instance. Even if he had paid for his boldness with his life, yet he had effectually thwarted the advocates of the insane policy of resistance. You remember the complaint of the enemies of Jeremiah some time after this, *He weakeneth the hands of the men of war and of all the people in speaking such words unto them* (Jer. xxxviii. 4). This was precisely what the prophet did, with truest patriotism, on this occasion. The stern oracles recited by Baruch produced such an effect that no one either would or could lift a hand against Nebuchadrezzar. Thus a brief respite was gained for earnest preachers to renew God's conditional offers of mercy, and a last chance presented to the Jews for repentance. Do you not admire the loving craft by which Jeremiah accomplished this? Said I not rightly that he was fertile in resources?

Elijah and Jeremiah were both for the moment successful, but each of them had to flee from his defeated antagonist. Of the latter we are told that *Jehovah hid him*[1] (Jer. xxxvi. 26).

[1] The princes had already told Baruch to go into hiding with Jeremiah (*v.* 26), but how easy it should have been for the king's officers to track them, as they tracked Urijah (Jer. xxvi. 20-23)!

BRIGHT VISIONS IN THE DEATH-CHAMBER.

May there not be an allusion to this in a psalm plausibly ascribed to Jeremiah, *In the covert of thy presence dost thou hide them from the plottings of man; thou keepest them secretly in a pavilion from the strife of tongues*[1] (Psa. xxxi. 20, see R.V.)? One loves to linger on such sweet words, and even to hope that they may often be verified in lives far humbler than Jeremiah's. To be kept in a pavilion from the strife of tongues —oh how much one needs this amidst the jangling controversies of our time! Oh how hard it is to preserve the attitude of the peace-maker, of one who does justice to the elements of truth in contending parties, a Falkland in theology and in politics! How hard, nay, how impossible, without a special benediction not vouchsafed to those who do not seek it. *Keep me, as the apple of the eye; hide me under the shadow of thy wings*—not that I may evade my share in the work of the age, but that, being in heaven with my heart, I may work the better with head and hands upon earth. Fairness and charity are sure tests of this heart-communion with heaven, and these perfumes of the soul cannot be long preserved unless we come sometimes into a desert place apart, and rest awhile. There we repent of having followed human leaders, instead of Him whose name is Truth, and whose "banner over us is Love." There we bathe in the waters of life, and lose the morbid craving for earthly excitements, the joy of battle and the fame of achievement. Too seldom have we collectedness enough for this spiritual transfiguration; and so God Himself gently draws us apart into solitude. This was now the case with our prophet, who had indeed acquired a new peace of mind, but who was still ignorant of that sweet charity which believeth and hopeth all things. Perhaps "the Lord hid" His faithful servant, in order to guide him to this loftier height. Jeremiah should not die knowing no more than a Moses or an Isaiah. It was not enough that he had lost the irritation of conflict, and accepted God's will as in some uncomprehended way the best; not enough that he loved God and God's people with a pure heart fervently. A great thing was to happen. Jeremiah was to be taken into God's secrets, as no other prophet had been; and as a consequence of this, he was to realize the capacities of the individual soul as he had not done before. He was to learn to love, not merely Israel, but each Israelite.

[1] See also Psa. xxxi. 21, and cf. Jer. i. 18.

And the king commanded to take Baruch and Jeremiah; but Jehovah hid them. The first result of this enforced seclusion reminds us of Martin Luther's Bible-work in the Wartburg. Jeremiah too betook himself to Bible-work. The first prophetic roll had been destroyed; but, as in the case of Tyndale's New Testament, a new and improved edition issued, as it were, from the flames. Jeremiah cared intensely for his people; he might win a deeper love for individuals, but no man could love Israel more than he. And if love—if even *his* love, anxious, importunate, and sometimes disguised under threatenings—was powerless to move his people, yet a stronger appeal to the motive of self-interest might perhaps do so. Therefore, we are told, he not only reproduced the old prophecies, but added thereto "many like words" (Jer. xxxvi. 32). Only for the king, though a son of his friend Josiah, he had no love and consequently no hope left. He foresaw that Jehoiakim's vow of fidelity was only a momentary shift, and spared no circumstance of horror in foretelling his end. But we must not think that the oracle in Jer. xxxvi. 30 is simply retaliation on Jeremiah's part. It is no doubt called forth by a personal offence against Jehovah's prophet, but the same awful details come before us again in a different setting (Jer. xxii. 19) as the punishment of a life of consistent transgression of God's law. Jeremiah was already moving towards the individualistic view of morality implied, as we shall see, in his great final discovery in the sphere of religion, and which a prophet considerably influenced by him (Ezekiel) expresses in these striking words,—

The soul that sinneth, it shall die. The son shall not bear the iniquity of the father, neither shall the father bear the iniquity of the son: the righteousness of the righteous shall be upon him, and the wickedness of the wicked shall be upon him (Ezek. xviii. 20; "soul" = person, cf. Ezek. xvi. 5, A.V.).

Among the prophecies written in the strict privacy of this period I am tempted to include at any rate chaps. xiv., xv. (or xiv. 1–xv. 9). The softer side of the prophet's nature comes out finely in the first of these chapters, which brings vividly before us the painful "searchings of heart" which accompanied the exercise of his prophetic ministry. One of those terrible droughts which so frequently visited Palestine had caused acute suffering among all classes, as well as among the cattle—with whom psalmists and prophets never fail to sympathize. Jeremiah's picture of it is "like some of Dante's in its realism, its pathos, and its terror." Twice he intercedes for his people on the ground of the covenant, but in vain. How pathetic is the pleading in *v.* 8!—

O thou hope of Israel, the saviour thereof in time of trouble, why shouldest thou be as a stranger in the land (a μέτοικος, who had no civic rights, and no interest in the commonwealth), *and as a wayfaring man that turneth aside to tarry for a night?* (Jer. xiv. 8, A.V.) The first verse of chap. xv. connects it very clearly with that which precedes.

"On receiving a revelation (xv. 2-9) of the bitter fate in store for his people, Jeremiah bursts out into a heart-rending complaint that his destiny should throw him into such a whirlwind of strife. His Lord at once corrects and consoles him (xv. 10-21)." So I have myself explained the connexion,[1] though not concealing my strong doubts. Surely we cannot appreciate chap. xvi. unless we read it in close connexion with xv. 7-9. Could we venture on a rearrangement of the prophet's discourses, we should, I think, be justified in placing this thrilling passage (xv. 10-21) immediately before the section xl. 1-6, which relates the prophet's decision to remain with the Jews at home, and not to go to Babylon with the exiles. At any rate, it is this passage of Jeremiah's life which seems to me to be best illustrated by it. I do not think that Jeremiah's newly gained acquiescence in the will of God concerning his people was so quickly lost. But how his heart must have bled that even the comparatively small trouble of the drought could not be taken away in answer to his prayers! In this respect again he reminds us of Elijah, who, charitable as he was by nature (1 Kings xvii. 17-24), and fervent and effectual as his supplications were (James v. 16, 17), could not help his people till it turned back to Jehovah.

The drought in Jehoiakim's reign, however, was but a "beginning of pangs," a prophecy of severer judgments, a sign that Jehovah's longsuffering was exhausted. The northern Israel, when gathered in a national assembly, returned from "the error of its way." Till Judah did the like, what hope was there for its future? And this is partly why Jeremiah from the very first is so earnest in attacking the moral abuses

---

[1] "Jeremiah" (in the "Pulpit Commentary"), i 372.

of his time. Jehovah could not be to His people that which He wished to be until they had offered Him that to which He could respond. *I said, Obey my voice, and walk in my ways, and I will be to you a God* (Jer. vii. 23). Nevertheless—*they proceed from evil to evil, and know not me, saith Jehovah* (Jer. ix. 3). Therefore. *O Jerusalem, wash thine heart from wickedness* (Jer. iv. 14).

But can such a great thing be? The prophet has heard of physical but not of moral miracles. He thinks with Zophar in the Book of Job—written as some think at this very time—that an *empty man will get understanding, when a wild ass's colt is born a man* (Job xi. 12, R.V. marg.). *Can the Ethiopian change his skin, or the leopard his spots? . . . Woe unto thee, O Jerusalem! how long yet ere thou become pure?*[1] (Jer. xiii. 23, 27). You see the prophet is like a man without a clue in a maze. The intricacy of the problem baffles him. It is not Job's difficulty of the righteous man suffering, but the still greater one of the want of means for breaking the force of habit, and giving the will a new bias.

I venture to suppose that Jeremiah began to make the discovery, or, speaking religiously, to receive the revelation, which threw a flood of light on this spiritual problem, during his enforced seclusion,[2] and that this is why Jehovah hid Baruch and Jeremiah. It takes long to bring a great thought to maturity. The process was certainly completed in Jeremiah's case at the fall of Jerusalem; when did it begin? Surely on the day when the last hope of Judah's repentance began to fade away—when the faithful prophets had either been killed (like Uriah) or driven into hiding-places (like Jeremiah), so that the work of preaching could only be done by obscure disciples at the peril of their lives. The last hope had not yet quite disappeared; but it was as feeble as the last gleam of departing day. What, then, is this sublime truth which visited the prophet's mind, and enabled him to look forward to the dread future with more than calmness, to bear up under the personal perils of

[1] R.V.'s rendering, in some respects an improvement upon A V., retains the faulty "be made clean." "Allow thyself to be made clean" would be better, but this is too lengthy.

[2] I do not deny that in their present form Jer. xxx., xxxi. belong to a later period than the reign of Jehoiakim. See Kuenen, "Onderzoek," ii. 207, but comp. Graf, "Jeremia," pp. 365-368.

the siege and the privations hardly less painful which followed?

The problem which besets Jeremiah is not quite the same as that which beset St. Paul, when he wrote those three memorable chapters, Rom. ix., x., xi. St. Paul's problem is twofold,—first, how the apparent fact of Israel's rejection is to be accounted for; and next, how, in spite of this fact, the ancient promises to Israel are to be fulfilled. The first part of St. Paul's problem is discussed by him at great length. He answers it both upon theological and anthropological or psychological grounds. *Hath not the potter a right over the clay, from the same lump to make one part a vessel unto honour and another unto dishonour?* (Rom. ix. 21, R.V.) This question gives the kernel of his theological argument: God predestines. *As to Israel he saith, All the day long did I spread out my hands unto a disobedient and gainsaying people* (Rom. x. 21, R.V.). This quotation from Isaiah gives the substance of his psychological argument: man is free to obey or disobey. The second part of his problem the apostle does not discuss at all; it was unnecessary after the many glimpses which he had given into his Divine philosophy. *A hardening in part hath befallen Israel, until the fulness of the Gentiles be come in; and so all Israel shall be saved* (Rom. xi. 25, 26, R.V.). The judicial blindness from which the Jews suffer at present shall in God's good time be taken away, and then the gospel will find an entrance into their heart; or, to quote from an earlier Epistle, *Unto this day, whensoever Moses is read, a veil lieth upon their heart; but whensoever it shall turn to the Lord, the veil is taken away* (2 Cor. iii. 15, 16).

Our prophet would not have sympathized with St. Paul's theological use of the figure of the potter. Very different is his own application of it in chap. xviii. Jehovah, according to him, has not the sovereign right to do as He will either with individuals or with nations, His action being strictly limited by a regard to character. Israel was, no doubt, in these latter years, like clay in the hand of the potter: its fate is about to be determined. But Jehovah has endowed His creature with the power of choosing its own lot. No threat of punishment can be unconditional. *One instant* (such is the Divine voice in our prophet's heart) *I may speak concerning a nation and a kingdom, to pluck up and to pull down and to destroy, but if that nation, against which I have spoken, turn from their evil, I repent of the evil that I thought to do unto them* (Jer. xviii. 7, 8). Nor would Jeremiah have laid such a stress on the judicial hardening of Israel's heart. If it be true that *Jehovah hath rejected them* (Jer. vi. 30), it is because *they are all grievous revolters* (Jer. vi. 28). Isaiah may introduce Jehovah saying, *Go on hearing, but understand not, and go on seeing, but perceive not* (Isa. vi. 9), but Jeremiah accounts for Israel's rebellion simply and solely by a spontaneous action on Israel's part.— *This people hath a revolting and a rebellious heart; they are revolted and gone* (Jer. vi. 23). It is therefore not difficult to Jeremiah to take in the idea of the rejection of Israel, considered apart from the Divine covenant; but it is an enigma how Jehovah's sure word of promise is to be fulfilled. Let us see how light dawns upon the prophet. The record of it is to be found in chaps. xxx, xxxi., which represent, as xxx. 4 states, "the words which Jehovah spake concerning Israel and concerning Judah." It is clear that Jeremiah can never have delivered this prophecy before a mixed audience; it is an anticipation of Isa. xl.–lxvi., and meant for the comfort of penitent believers during the Exile. The later seer's prophecy of Israel's Restoration may be, poetically regarded, finer than Jeremiah's, but except in chap. liii (the chapter of the Sin-bearer, and in the passages relative to the Church), is less original; so that the earliest "evangelical prophet" is, not the Babylonian Isaiah, but Jeremiah, and chaps xxx, xxxi., are the casket in which the evangelical truths are enshrined. The prophecy falls into two parts, the first reaching from xxx. 5 to xxxi. 14, the second from xxxi. 15 to xxxi. 40. Part I. itself has four sections, in each of which the prophet (or shall I say? the seer) reveals himself as a master of picturesque imagery. His usual practice is to begin a section with a picture of the calamitous present, but this is only to enhance the effect of a prophetic description of the glorious future. Yes; the prophet has come to the end of his jeremiads; he can almost welcome calamity in the strength of his new faith in the Divine promise. As one of the later psalmists wrote from the point of view of at least an initial fulfilment, *He hath sent redemption unto his people; he hath appointed his covenant for ever; holy and reverend is his name* (Psa. cxi. 9). Redemption! A short time ago Jeremiah would not perhaps have thought it possible; but now he builds upon it as an assured certainty. With the eye and ear of faith, he discerns Jehovah approaching to redeem Israel, and saying, *I have loved thee with an everlasting love; therefore do I continue lovingkindness unto thee.*

In the fourth section (*vv.* 7–14), transported with joy, the prophet breaks through his custom, and at once gives an idyllic sketch of the future prosperity. Specially beautiful is the opening of the second part,[1] which, as Matt. ii. 16–18 shows, found a home in the Jewish heart. The prophet seems to hear Rachel weeping for her banished children, and comforts her with the assurance that they shall yet be restored. For Ephraim has come to himself, and God, who has overheard his soliloquy, advances towards him with gracious promises. Then another voice is heard calling Ephraim home. See the generosity of a true prophet—a statesman in the kingdom of God. Should Jeremiah's prophecy fall into the hands of the recently acquired subjects of Judah, how they will contrast his treatment of them with Isaiah's! The older citizens of the enlarged state sufficiently know their prophet's passionate love for his people. Well may they be content with the few but radiant lines given them in Jer. xxxi. 23–25. Alas! too soon the sweet vision vanishes; but it continues to supply food for his Spirit-guided meditations. How this strange reversal of Israel's fortunes (Israel's, not less than Judah's,—the "ten tribes" cannot be lost) can possibly be, is as yet a moral mystery to Jeremiah, just as it was to the psalmist who wrote those two strangely-contrasting verses,—

> *Lord, where are thy old lovingkindnesses*
> *Which thou swarest unto David in thy faithfulness?*
> *For thou hast said, lovingkindness shall be built for ever;*
> *In the heaven* (*itself*) *wilt thou stablish thy faithfulness.*
> (Psa. lxxxix 49, 2.)

But the fact, to both writers, is not less certain than the existence of God. The first helpful idea that occurs to him (Jer. xxxi. 29, 30) is that God cannot, strictly speaking, be said to

[1] At that most interesting place Eleusis, I could not help comparing Demeter, sitting on the mystic stone, and weeping for her daughter, with the poet-prophet's Rachel. May not both be fitly taken as symbols of Humanity weeping for its children carried off into the "land of the enemy"? Surely this is in the spirit of St. Matthew (comp. Dante, "Convito," ii 1). We all of us find such higher meanings in Shakespeare, why not in Jeremiah?

"visit the iniquity of the fathers upon the children." If the children are punished, it must be because human sin has a natural tendency to perpetuate itself in succeeding generations; no transgressor is punished simply for the sin of his ancestor. As Barabas asks the cruel governor in Marlowe's "Jew of Malta" (act i., scene 2),

> "But say the tribe that I descended of
> Were all in general cast away for sin,
> Shall I be tried by their transgression?
> *The man that dealeth righteously shall live.*'"

A comforting idea, doubtless, during the Captivity, but one which does not clear up the difficulty—how an ungodly nation is to be made godly. Hezekiah and Josiah had cut the Gordian knot, but to the little band of advanced religious thinkers a violent reformation had become intensely repugnant. Even Deuteronomy did not meet the wants of the time; it was a compromise between two opposing principles—the legal and the evangelical. Jeremiah felt that if the problem were to be solved, it must be on the evangelical and not on the legal principle; in short, that he must work out the germinal ideas found in the prophetic not the legal part of Deuteronomy. Obedience, according to this part of the book, is based, not upon compulsion, but upon love (see Deut. xi. 1), and in one remarkable passage (Deut. x. 16—for I exclude Deut. xxx. 6, as not in the original book) we find the strangely new phrase "to circumcise the heart." But was this "evangelical" enough? Had not Israel lost (if it ever possessed it) the faculty of loving God? What great things God had done in the past! and yet Israel had never felt more than a slight tingling of gratitude comparable to morning dew. And how could Israel "circumcise" his own heart? *The virgin of Israel is fallen; she can no more rise; she is cast down upon her land; there is none to raise her up* (Amos v. 2). Moses has not sympathy enough; he broke the two tables of stone at the sight of Israel's very first sin, and what means of help has he in his covenant? Surely the thunders of Sinai do but sound the knell of condemned sinners. And so with the boldness of despair, and the intensity of a love like St. Paul's (Rom. ix. 3), Jeremiah dares to proclaim that the old covenant is superseded by a new one which more completely meets the wants of poor human nature.

BRIGHT VISIONS IN THE DEATH-CHAMBER.

Its contents may be summed up thus. God, of His free grace, will make the people what He would have them to be, by first forgiving their sins in so absolute a manner that it shall seem as though He had forgotten them, and then as it were writing His requirements on the tablets of their hearts (comp. Psa. xl. 8). Neither priests nor sacrifices will therefore be henceforth necessary—the one for making known to men the details of Jehovah's *tōrāh*, and the other for expiating sins and transgressions. A written *tōrāh*, too, will become superfluous, and there will be no longer the terrible fear that the copies in circulation may be "handled deceitfully" (see Jer. viii. 8).

Some one, however, may ask, Is not this going too far? Does the promise of the new covenant really anticipate that priesthood and sacrifices will be abolished?—But did I use the word "abolished"? Jeremiah's words do indeed appear to me to point to a time when a regenerate people will, as the hymn says,

> "——see Thee face to face,
> In peaceful, glad Jerusalem, thrice holy, happy place,
> When Sacrament and Temple shall never more be known,
> When Thou art Temple, Sacrifice, and Priest upon the throne."

But neither here nor elsewhere does the prophet explicitly announce such wonderful things; nor do I say that the last line was within the range even of his thoughts. All that he affirms here is that there shall be direct relations between Jehovah and each member of His people (individuality shall come to its rights); all that vii. 22 declares is that the Sinai covenant related not to sacrifices but to obedience; all that xvii. 12, 13 and iii. 16, taken together, say is that Jehovah is Israel's true sanctuary, so that the presence of the ark in the earthly temple was unimportant.[1] We may safely assume that Jeremiah's disciples consisted of two classes of men—those who could rise to the sunlit heights of spirituality (comp. Psa. li. 17), and those who into their pictures of the future could not help introducing temple and ark, priests and sacrifices (see xvii. 26, xxxi. 11, 14, and comp. Psa. li. 19). In truth, Jeremiah's predictions of the Messianic age were all the more stimulative

---

[1] The Deuteronomic *tōrāh* (apart from its setting) does not mention the ark. Josiah, to prevent superstition, forbade it to be carried about in processions (2 Chron. xxxv. 2). A late legend says that Jeremiah afterwards hid it in a cave on Mount Pisgah (2 Macc. ii. 4, 5).

because of their real or apparent inconsistencies. It would not have been well that one class of thinkers alone should be able to appeal to Jeremiah; he shines out more gloriously as the author of a movement than he would have done as the founder of a sect. If Isa. lxvi. 1 is inspired by Jeremiah, so also is Ezek. xxxvii. 26-28,[1] and, may we not add, the prophecies on the Church and on the Sin-bearer due to that great prophet, who was "hidden" in Babylonia (like Jeremiah in Jerusalem) that he might brood deeply over the spiritual problem of Israel. Not Jeremiah, but the Second Isaiah, had the first dim intuition of the "mediator of the new covenant," but the "new covenant" itself was first foreseen by Jeremiah.

Said I not right that "the fortunes of spiritual religion hung on the escape of Jeremiah?" But in fact his life is a series of escapes. He was soon to exclaim—whether he wrote the words or not, they must express his feeling, *Blessed be Jehovah! for he hath shewed me passing great kindness in a besieged city* (Psa. xxxi. 21). Wishing himself back under the Pharaoh's supremacy, Jehoiakim in B C. 597 broke his oath to Babylon, three years after he had taken it. The neighbouring peoples refused to join him Following the example of "the Chaldæans" (*i.e.*, those left in garrison in Syria), they made raids upon the country districts of Judah (2 Kings xxiv. 2, 2 Chron. xxxvi. 5 Sept.), driving a crowd of fugitives before them to Jerusalem. One dramatic scene in Jeremiah's biography, well versified by Dean Plumptre, belongs to this period (Jer. xxxv.). Venturing forth in this great crisis, he noticed among the refugees a group of men of strange aspect, seldom or never seen before in Jerusalem. These men belonged to the tribe of the Rechabites, who were a branch of the Kenites, and therefore bound by an ancient alliance to the Israelites, and who stood, both socially and religiously, exactly where the Israelites stood during their wanderings, after they had consolidated their union on the basis of Jehovah-worship.[2] They had had, as it seems, a great reformer, who had restored the purity of their social and religious customs, one Jonadab, whose zeal for Jehovah is described in 2 Kings x. 15-27, and whose personal influence on

[1] Note, in this connexion, Ezekiel's fondness for the term "covenant" (see Ezek xi. 20, xiv 11, xxxiv 24, xxxvi 28, xxxvii. 23, 27).

[2] Probably enough, the Rechabites adopted into their clan many who, like the Essenes afterwards, were disgusted with a too sensuous civilization.

his clan exceeded, as Jeremiah declares, that of even the greatest prophets on the Israelites. Jeremiah knew the religious constancy of these Rechabites, and put it to a severe test, in order to contrast it with the religious inconstancy of the Israelites. According to their law, these simple folk ought not to have entered a walled city like Jerusalem. If they had broken their vows in one respect, why should they not in another? There were the wine-bowls and the drinking-cups; why not enjoy one of the sweetest and most valued products of civilization? Plainly and even bluntly the Rechabites refused to drink. Jeremiah was prepared for this result, and at once pointed the moral.

Jonadab had tied up his people to a life of hardship; Jehovah had done the opposite, simply requiring obedience to certain precepts, chiefly moral, which would set Israel on high above the nations of the earth. Yet Jonadab's precepts were obeyed and Jehovah's were not. Therefore all the threatenings conditionally pronounced against Israel must be fulfilled, whereas *Jonadab, the son of Rechab, shall not want a man to stand before me for ever* (Jer. xxxv. 19). What does this closing promise mean? "To live long in the land" is the reward of filial obedience in Exod. xx. 12. The Rechabites therefore are to continue in Judah, while the Jews are carried captive to Babylon. Nor will their life be useless. They will go on witnessing to the divinity of Jehovah in Jehovah's land. Although without any but the simplest ritual, they will be, what Israel ought to have been, a "kingdom of priests" (Exod. xix. 6); for "to stand before Jehovah" is specially the function of priests.[1]

The ceaseless inroads of the "bands" of divers nations were almost worse to bear than a regular invasion. What such "bands" could do, we may see from 1 Sam. xxx. 1, 2 (comp. *v.* 8). Even the Rechabites fled before them in dismay. The land of Judah was passing through a similar experience to that of Babylonia during the Scythian invasion. Was Jehoiakim, then, defenceless? Yes; the warriors were paralyzed by dread of the Chaldæans, and Neco's troops, on which (comp. Jer. xvii. 5, 6) the king probably relied, were slow to appear. In the midst of this confusion the chief author of it all died. How, we cannot say for certain. Did he, like Joash, fall by the assassin's

[1] Was Jeremiah thinking of the favourite phrase of Jonadab's great predecessor Elijah, *Jehovah, before whom I stand?*

hand, and was his dead body thereupon cast out unburied, as Jeremiah had threatened? Or does the Septuagint correctly report (2 Chron. xxxvi. 8) that "Joakim slept with his fathers, and was buried in *ganozan*" (*i.e.*, the garden of Oza or Uzza)? The latter view is at any rate much the easier.[1] Jehoiakim died in peace, and upon his unoffending son was visited the collective sin of his family. It was a short reign which fell to the lot of Jehoiachin—just as long as Napoleon's after his landing in March, 1815, or as that of his own uncle Jehoahaz, and then—more bitter weeping than even for his ill-fated uncle. But I must not anticipate; for Jeremiah has left us an ample record of his prophetic activity during these three months.[2]

We know the prophet's tone of mind already. He was no longer called upon—

> "To watch with firm, unshrinking eye
> His darling visions as they die."

The old visions had long since died away; new and more divine ones had taken their place. One of his first actions was to renew the terrible announcements familiar to us already from chap. vii. To emphasize this, he had recourse to that sign-language in which the heroes and prophets of Israel delighted (1 Sam. xi. 7, Amos vii., viii.), although the words of the Hebrew tongue were as full of expressive figure as they could be. Once more, it was the work of the potter which he chose for a symbol, but not the still soft though moulded clay (as in chap. xviii.), but the already definitely formed vessel. With this he went with certain elders into the glen of Hinnom, and, as a Syrian *fellah* still does when under the dominion of violent passion, shivered the jar to atoms.[3] Need I repeat the prophet's sermon, or need I add that it drew down upon him the wrath of the priests? The instrument of torture applied to him (Jer. xx. 2) was doubtless more painful than our "stocks"; and his punishment was equivalent to a declaration that he was a madman and a pretender to the prophetic office (see Jer. xxix. 26). It was the duty of the "second priest" (comp. Jer. lii. 24) to keep

[1] The statement in the Greek version runs directly counter to the terms of the denunciation in Jer. xxii. 19, xxxvi. 30, and must therefore be founded on tradition

[2] 2 Kings xxiv. 8 says "three months"; 2 Chron. xxxvi. 9 adds, "and ten days."

[3] Similar actions are ascribed to early Quaker zealots.

BRIGHT VISIONS IN THE DEATH-CHAMBER.

an eye on such; in fact, the guild of the prophets was subject to a certain official control on the part of the priests.[1] Jeremiah, though in the "stocks," will not be hindered from uttering his revelations. He answers Pashhur very nearly as Amos answered Amaziah the priest of Bethel in like circumstances (Amos vii. 16, 17). I do not think, however, that because of this bitter utterance I need modify what I said just now of Jeremiah's tone of mind. It is true that Jer. xx. 7-18 contains expressions which are not in harmony with the heroic temper which I have ascribed to him. But this section is almost entirely out of chronological order; probably it was placed where it now stands simply because the phrase *Māgōr-missābīb* occurs both in *v.* 4 and in *v.* 10.

This was not the prophet's only use of sign-speech. He is deficient in that fine taste which distinguishes a greater than the prophets in His parables from common life. But when we see his meaning, I think we shall excuse him for the symbolic text of his sermon against Judah's pride. Evidently his mind was much exercised by the dissolution of the bond between Jehovah and Israel. This is what he says elsewhere, in a choicer style, of the new king,—

As I live, saith Jehovah, though Coniah, the son of Jehoiakim, king of Judah, be a signet upon my right hand, surely I will pluck thee thence (Jer xxii. 24).

The humiliation of course is greater when the object of comparison is a rotting linen apron. I cannot help thinking that the choice of this symbol was dictated by a proverb like the Arabic, "He is unto me in place of a waist-wrapper[2];" it will be noticed that the second part of the discourse actually has a proverbial saying for its text. The strangeness of Jer. xiii. 1-11 will now perhaps offend the reader less, especially if I add that "Euphrates" in A.V. and R.V. is probably a mistake; the Hebrew has *P'rāth*, which may be a name, or a corrupted name, of a place near Anathoth, still known, as our maps show, by the name Fārāh.[3] It was not, then, by the Euphrates (which is not

---

[1] W. Robertson Smith, "The Prophets in Israel," p. 389.

[2] We have no more dignified equivalent for *'ĕzōr* = Arab. *'izār* (on which see Lane, "Arabic Lexicon," i. 53; Dozy, "Dictionnaire détaillé des noms des vêtements," p. 24, &c).

[3] See Robinson, "Biblical Researches," ii. 288. Should not *P'rath* be *Parah* (Josh. xviii. 23), as Birch suggests ("Palestine Fund Statement," Oct. 1880, p. 236)?

a rocky stream) that Jeremiah hid his apron, but in a rocky and yet even in summer verdant retreat, not so far from the famous Michmash, close to one of the torrents which unite to form the Kelt (Cherith?). How he must have suffered as he walked alone to this spot, perhaps repeating the words, *But if ye will not hear it, my soul shall weep in secret for your pride* (Jer. xiii. 17); or, *Is this man Coniah a despised broken pot? is he a vessel wherein is no pleasure?* (Jer. xxii. 28, comp. xiii. 14).

Soon after Jeremiah's return the second time, may we not suppose that his worst previsions began to be realized? Up to the last he had cried, *Hear ye, and give ear;* but now—*the Destroyer of the nations is on his way. The cities of the Southland are shut up* (blocked up with ruins), and *the daughter of Zion is left . . . as a besieged city* (not yet beleagured, but cut off from communication with the provinces).[1] Neco seems at length to have despatched troops in aid of Judah, but it was of no avail. A part of the Destroyer's army was detached to invest Jerusalem, while he himself (probably) met and defeated the Egyptians, so that *the king of Egypt came not again any more out of his land* (2 Kings xxiv. 7). *The harvest is past*, cried Jeremiah, *the summer is ended, and we have not been saved* (Jer. viii. 20). Nebuchadrezzar's arrival determined the young king and his mother and his court to surrender at discretion; *and the king of Babylon took him in the eighth year of his reign* (2 Kings xxiv. 12). Never again did Jehoiachin see the land of Judah or Judah's last great prophet. But was there no mitigation of his lot? Yes; a sad one indeed, but one for which Jehoahaz might have envied him. All that was best and worthiest in the old capital city went with Jehoiachin to Babylon. Most of the trained warriors (who were doubtless also the proprietors of the soil), 7000 in all, most of the artisans, amounting to 1000, and 2000 more heads of families, including doubtless many refugees from the provinces, were carried away from their own dear hill-country to the monotonous but fertile plain between the Euphrates and the Tigris. Of the two greatest religious thinkers of that time, one (Ezekiel) was taken and the other (Jeremiah) was left. The numbers indeed are not quite certain. Some think that the passage, 2 Kings xxiv. 13, 14, has been misplaced.[2]

[1] Jer. xiii. 15, iv. 6, Isa. i. 8

[2] Stade thinks that these two verses properly refer to the deportation of the year 586, and points out that they interrupt the flow of the narrative ("Geschichte," p. 680, and see the reference there given).

BRIGHT VISIONS IN THE DEATH-CHAMBER. 163

I do not see that this makes much difference (see vers. 15, 16); but the total number of the captives must have been larger than that mentioned in the narrative. We may be sure that sons and daughters very often (not always; see Ezek. xxiv. 21) accompanied their parents. This was the beginning of the "displantation" (to use a word of Sir Walter Raleigh's) of Judah— the first great fulfilment of the ancient prophecy in Isa. iii. 1–3.

Let us pause here to contrast the two men thus strangely brought together — Jehoiachin and Nebuchadrezzar. Both indeed are called lions, the former in Ezek. xix. 6; the latter in Jer. iv. 7, xlix. 19; but if Jehoiachin had really shown a warlike and ambitious character, would his offended overlord have spared his life? From Jer. xiii. 18 it would almost seem that he shared the supreme power with his mother Nehushta.[1] If he did so, we may be sure that Nehushta had the reality and he the semblance of power, according to the old saying, *A child is my people's tyrant, and women rule over it* (Isa. iii. 12). Add to this the friendly feelings which he inspired alike in Babylonian kings, contemporary Hebrew prophets, and the later generations of the Jews,[2] and I think we may safely describe Jehoiachin as a man of mild and probably (even from the higher point of view) not irreligious character. I cannot, however, go to the length of ascribing to him (with Ewald) the composition of Psalms xlii., xliii., lxxxiv.; the "last sigh of the royal exile," as he gazed from the hill above Bâniâs, was one of those which "cannot be uttered," least of all in lyric poems which soar so high into the regions of faith. Perhaps, indeed, Nebuchadrezzar could have appreciated these psalms better than his captive. Energy and force of will sit upon the brows of the young hero in the cameo portrait of him at Berlin;[3] there is, however, a

[1] Great stress is laid on the fact that the queen-mother accompanied her son into exile (see Jer. xxii. 26, xxix. 2; 2 Kings xxiv. 12, 13).

[2] See 2 Kings xxv. 27–30; Ezek. i. 2; Lam. iv. 20, Josephus, "De Bello Jud." vi. 2, 1 (where an annual commemoration of Jehoiachin is spoken of). One of the gates of Jerusalem bore his name (Mishna, "Middoth," ii. 6).

[3] The type of features might no doubt be accounted for if Nebuchadrezzar could be shown to have had (like the Assyrian king Shashanq) an Egyptian mother. But Babelon's view (in the large edition of Lenormant's "Histoire," iv. 394) does violence to Herodotus, who may himself have credulously adopted a mere legend On the Berlin portrait, my friend Prof. Schrader has learnedly commented in the "Transactions of the Berlin Academy, 1879," pp. 293–298.

refinement of feature which suggests that he is above the savage inhumanities of the Assyrian kings. Even if we hesitate to accept the evidence of this portrait, there is the undeniable evidence of facts. Nebuchadrezzar could indeed be severe (like the Asmonæan princes among the Jews, and like the chivalrous Saladin himself) to those who rebelled against his divine King,[1] but he willingly tempered the lot even of those whom he regarded as rebels. He was cruel, according to our ideas, to Zedekiah, but that unhappy king had broken his pledged word, and even to Zedekiah he was less cruel than Saladin to Raynald after the battle of Hattin. How gentle he was to the Jews left in Judah, and how respectful to Jeremiah in particular, the sequel of this story will show. "Such treatment," remarks an American Assyriologist,[2] "is a beautiful contrast to the way in which Saul or David would have dealt" [four centuries earlier].

Both these men, therefore, come out better in a historical picture than they did in the Scripture handbooks of our youth. The shock, so far as Nebuchadrezzar's character is concerned, will be mitigated by remembering that Jeremiah honoured him as "Jehovah's Servant," a distinction which carries more weight than the blame of a too patriotic, too sanguine contemporary, Habakkuk[3] (Hab. i. 13).

[1] For a case in point, see Jer xxix. 22. The punishment referred to there was not arbitrarily chosen, but common both in Assyria and in Babylonia (see "Records of the Past," ix. 56, and comp. Bertin in "Babylonian and Oriental Record," vol. 1. No 2).

[2] Prof. Lyon, "Israelitish Politics." p. 10.

[3] That "the wicked" here means the Babylonians collectively is certain. But we must not with Hooker, in his second sermon, give the same sense to "the wicked" in Hab. 1. 4, which, as the context shows, means the lawless men in Jerusalem.

CHAPTER VI.

IF THOU HADST KNOWN, EVEN THOU!

Zedekiah; his accession and character—Ezekiel, the prophet of the exiles—
The lower prophets at home and in Babylonia—Zedekiah's revolt—
First siege of Jerusalem—Imprisonment of Jeremiah—His purchase of
family-property—He is again in danger of his life—Cast into the
cistern—Ebedmelech's help—Fall of Jerusalem—Book of Lamentation.

IN spite of his virtual abdication, Jehoiachin (like Edward II. in Berkeley Castle) still wore a crown, at least in the eyes of his fellow-exiles. Doubtless they bewailed his hard fate, and the elegy, based probably on a popular song, in which Ezekiel laments over "the princes of Israel," contains this verse on the sad termination of Jehoiachin's reign,—

And they put him into a cage with hooks, and brought him to the king of Babylon, that his voice might no longer be heard upon the mountains of Israel (Ezek. xix. 9).

Deeply too must Ezekiel, and all true priests and worshippers, have mourned their removal from the holy city, though as yet sobs must have stifled the utterance of their grief. Not less bitter must have been the mourning in Jerusalem, not only for the material losses to church[1] and state, but for the vanished familiar faces. What an official mourning meant to a Semitic race, we know from the cuneiform inscriptions; and what a national mourning was in Judah, the last sad page of Josiah's

[1] The temple vessels, remarks Ewald, were the things most regretted at Jerusalem in the next few years Comp 2 Kings xxiv. 13 with Jer. xxvii. 16, 18–22, xxviii. 3–6, Dan. i. 2, v. 2, &c., Baruch i. 8.

story tells us. This new lamentation was a national one indeed.

A phantom-king had meantime been set up by Nebuchadrezzar, but his want of maturity of character must already have excited the fears of religious patriots both at home and in Babylon. His name was Mattaniah—he was "Jehovah's gift" to Josiah in the memorable year of the finding of the lawbook ; but on his elevation to the throne he was allowed to take the name Zedekiah or Zidkia,[1] *i.e.*, "Jehovah is righteousness." Was he already (like his namesake in Jer. xxix. 22) cherishing dreams of a "righteous" interposition of Jehovah for Israel, or even applying to himself the great prophecy of the Branch (rather, Shoot) in Jer. xxiii. 5, 6 ?

I doubt it ; the name of this poor *roi fainéant* (see Jer. xxxviii. 5) must have been chosen for him by others. Personally, he would have been content with the "base kingdom" given him (Ezek. xvii. 14). It was not repugnant to him to be like a vine trailing along the ground (such as any one may see in the Lebanon), watered, as it were, by the favour of Babylon ; Ezekiel's parable, so far as he was concerned, might have been comprised in the first six verses of his seventeenth chapter. It was Zedekiah's "environment" (if we may use a word of recent coinage) which was the chief source of his trouble. The Jewish princes may have had their faults, but at any rate they formed a true aristocracy ; and when most of them had been removed to Babylon, it was as if a fair garden-land (Jer. ii. 7 Heb.) had been robbed of all its good fruit (Jer. xxiv.). There was no wisdom left to direct, no strength to carry out, no moral principle among the governors or the governed. *Woe unto the shepherds*, cries Jeremiah to the wretched "princes" of this period (Jer. xxiii. 1, 2). All the old evils had, under their utterly selfish rule, suddenly gathered to a head ; *both prophet and priest are profane ; yea, in my house have I found their wickedness, saith Jehovah* (Jer. xxiii. 11). Jeremiah alludes to practices specially inconsistent with the holy place, and one of the Jewish captives explains what they were (Ezek. viii. ; comp. *v.* 11, and 2 Chron. xxxvi. 14). There was—1, an image of Ashérah ; 2, totemistic animal emblems on the wall of a temple-

[1] Zidkia was the name of a king of Ashkelon in Hezekiah's time (see Schrader on Josh. xiii 3) What the relation is between the Israelitish Yahveh and the Canaanitish Yahu, I will not attempt to decide.

chamber; 3, weeping for "Thammuz yearly wounded"; 4, sun-worship and the rite of holding up "the twig" to the nose.[1] Side by side with these heathenish usages, some of them of a low type, there was the self-righteousness and formalism of a large number of Jehovah's worshippers, who still trusted in the inviolable sanctity of the temple, and perhaps thought that, in spite of a few violations of the Law,[2] they could still claim the fulfilment of Deuteronomic promises. The popular discontent was fanned by the arrival of ambassadors from the neighbouring nations, who had come to draw Judah into a confederation against the common foe.[3] Jeremiah thought that he could give no better expression to the Divine warnings entrusted to him than by a symbolic act like that ascribed to Isaiah in Isa. xx. 2. This was probably in the fourth year of Zedekiah (comp. Jer. xxvii. 1, " Var. Bible," xxviii. 1), the year to which chap. xxviii. refers the episode of Hananiah "the prophet," who with a light heart made promises in Jehovah's name, inconsistent with the moral condition of the people, and therefore not to be realized. It was Jeremiah's own symbolic action which in the same signspeech Hananiah contradicted; the prophetic denunciation of the former followed the next day, and was literally fulfilled. Perhaps this awful fact gave a temporary weight to Jeremiah's warnings. At any rate Zedekiah became anxious to dissipate the rumours of his infidelity, and either journeyed himself or sent an embassy to Babylon to give fresh assurances to his strict overlord. According to Jer. li. 59-64, it was on this oc-

[1] This reminds us of a precept respecting a twig called *baresma* in a Zoroastrian Scripture ("Vendidad" xix. 64), and of a custom (Sir Monier Williams says that it still exists among the Parsees) of holding up a veil to prevent impurities of breath from passing into the sacred fire.

[2] I do not think we can take *all* Ezekiel's descriptions of the heathenism of Judah in their most obvious sense. Ezek. viii. seems to say that the "high-places" were resorted to in Zedekiah's reign; but surely he throws himself back into Manasseh's reign, the abominations of which he cannot recall without a deeply felt *woe, woe unto thee* (Ezek. xvi. 23; comp. 2 Kings xxiv. 3).

[3] It has been supposed that troubles in Elam may have favoured these projects of revolt. But, as Tiele remarks, in the division of the Assyrian empire Elam (or the Assyrian claims upon Elam) passed to Media. The conqueror pointed to in Jer. xlix. 34-39 may be Teispes (*Tsheispa*) of the Achæmenid family, the ancestor of Cyrus II. and Darius Hystaspis, of whom Jeremiah may have heard through the Jewish exiles in Babylon ("Babylonisch-assyrisch Geschichte," p. 435).

casion that Jeremiah committed the long prophecy in Jer. l., li. to the friendly prince Seraiah, who, after reciting it, was to bind it to a stone and cast it into the Euphrates, with the words of doom, *Thus shall Babylon fall.* I have elsewhere given the reasons for holding these chapters to be wrongly ascribed to our prophet,[1] just as Isa. xl.–lxvi. and certain parts of Isa. i.–xxxvi. are erroneously assigned to Isaiah. They furnish a welcome addition to our already large collection of literary products dating from the close of the Exile.

Let us pause a moment, for this reference to Jer. l., li. suggests the thought of the great intellectual refreshing for which Israel's genius was indebted to the sojourn in Babylonia. The first great writer of this period began his career in the year following Zedekiah's journey or embassy. After passing his first four years of expatriation by one of the many canals of the Euphrates (called the Chebar), Ezekiel the priest *saw divine visions* (Ezek. i. 1), and came forward among a people, whose God seemed to it to have been defeated, to show how great and wondrous and righteous and yet merciful Jehovah was. With this object in view, he scrupled not to press into his service the novel and stupendous imagery of Babylonia, and became a great imaginative writer. But alas! his fellow exiles "refused to hear the voice of the charmer;" the poetry of Ezekiel was too enigmatical and his prose too coldly judicial in tone to produce much immediate impression. His influence, like Jeremiah's, was most felt by individuals; his conception of religion, though churchly, was also individualistic, and it was his task to gather out of the corrupt mass those who might in time form the nucleus of a Jewish Church. As a poet, he has sometimes been overrated; it is absurd to compare him, with De Quincey, to Æschylus. As a teacher, he has been equally underrated. He owes, indeed, much to Jeremiah, whose very phrases, as Movers has shown (in his work on the two recensions of Jeremiah, part iii. sect. 16), he sometimes reproduces, but he has added much from his own Spirit-led meditations. His book is more distinctly literary than those left by Isaiah and Jeremiah, but, though written long after the latter had passed away, is of the

---

[1] Orelli, a good scholar, still holds out against this result of criticism. But this half-hearted critic regards Isa. i. -xxxvi. as altogether the work of Isaiah!

utmost value for the period which we are studying ; would that my limits permitted me to draw more from it !

How constant the intercourse was between Jerusalem and the Jewish colonies in Babylonia, we may see, not only from Ezekiel, but from Jeremiah. In Jer. xxix. we have the substance of a letter sent by Jeremiah through two royal officials to the exiles, exhorting them to resign themselves to the will of God, and obey their foreign lords, in spite of the misleading advice of the lower prophets. On the receipt of this, one of the latter wrote letters to the Jews at home, especially to Pashhur's successor in the office of "second priest," named Zephaniah, but only to his own confusion. *Build ye houses, and dwell in them; and plant gardens, and eat the fruit of them, . . . and seek the welfare of the city whither I have sent you as captives, and pray unto Jehovah for it,*—such was Jeremiah's advice. Nebuchadrezzar was, at present, Jehovah's commissioned Servant (Jer. xxvii. 6), and as Bossuet says, applying Jer. xxvii. to Oliver Cromwell, " Quand ce grand Dieu a choisi quelqu'un pour être l'instrument de ses desseins, rien n'arrête le cours ; ou il enchaîne, ou il aveugle, ou il dompte tout ce qui est capable de résistance."[1] If the Jews could only be persuaded of this, there might yet be two Judahs, a greater and a lesser ; the one in Babylonia, the other in Judah—to be reunited after seventy years,[2] by which is perhaps meant a long and indefinite period (comp. Jer. xxv. 11, xxix. 10, with Jer. xxvii. 6). It appears certain that chaps. xxvii.–xxix. have not come down to us as their author left them (among other peculiarities, note the spelling Nebuchadnezzar[3]); the section xxvii. 16-22 ought certainly to be restored to its original purity from the Septuagint.[4] But the historical statements of the chapters are above suspicion. How interesting, although painful, are the notices of prophets like Hananiah, who was not exactly a " false prophet " as the Septuagint calls him (Jer. xxxv. 1), but rather a fallen prophet, one who devoted

[1] "Oraison funèbre de Henriette Marie de France, reine d'Angleterre."

[2] "Seventy" is a symbolic number both in Jeremiah and, partly at least, in "Daniel" (Dan. ix. 24).

[3] " Nebuchadrezzar" only occurs once in these three chapters (Jer. xxix. 21). The only other places where " Nebuchadnezzar" occurs in Jeremiah are xxxiv. 1 and xxxix. 5.

[4] See Movers' Latin treatise on the recensions of Jeremiah, part ii. sect. 13, Matthes, *Modern Review*, 1884, p. 428.

his natural prophetic gifts to the service of a Jehovah who was not the true one, because not "the God who ruleth in righteousness," and who had "sent" Jeremiah to warn His people of their too sure punishment. Stationary or retrograde prophets could only do harm to Israel. Hence Ezekiel compares such to jackals burrowing in ruins, and says that in fostering Israel's blind self-love, they do but give a coating of plaster to mud-walls (Ezek. xiii. 4, 10). No good word can either Jeremiah or Ezekiel find to say for them, and the only palliation of their conduct is that though the true Jehovah *hath not sent them*, and, as we are told, *hath deceived* (or, *enticed*) *them*, they *expect the confirmation of the oracle* (Ezek. xiii. 6, xiv. 9.)—they are honest though misguided enthusiasts.[1] Why, indeed, may not such prophets, however blameable, as having fallen from their "high calling of God," yet have been fanatically sincere in their patriotism and their religion? Superficially regarded, does their prophesying differ from that of Isaiah in some of his discourses (comp. Hananiah's expressions in Jer xxviii. 11 with those of Isa. x. 25, xxix. 17)? If this leading prophet refused to "bate a jot of heart or hope" in Judah's extremity, and grew still bolder in faith, why should not his successors copy him in this respect? The answer is, that Isaiah's encouraging promises were combined with a resolute maintenance of the highest moral standard, whereas our only authorities distinctly assert that the lower prophets (and, as one of them says, prophetesses) of their time lived evil lives themselves, and "strengthened the hands of the wicked" (Jer. xxiii. 14, xxix. 23 ; Ezek. xiii. 19, 22). If, like Habakkuk a few years earlier, they had been equally earnest for moral and for political salvation, Jeremiah and Ezekiel would not have opposed them so bitterly as "conspirators" (Ezek. xxii. 25) against the common weal. May we take all their vehement expressions literally? It matters not ; whatever the lower prophets were in private, they neglected their public duty when they might perhaps have saved the state. And though the exiles as a body may have been superior to the home-community (comp. Ezek. xiv 22, 23), there is no evidence that the prophets of Babylonia were wiser or better than their fellows at Jerusalem.

[1] For a fair view of these lower prophets, see Rowland Williams, "Hebrew Prophets," ii 56, 57, and Matthes' valuable monograph "De pseudoprophetismo Hebraeorum" (Lugd. Bat. 1859).

"Like prophet, like people," we may say, applying Hos. iv. 9. It is clear that, from the point of view of the higher religion, the Jews both at home and in Babylonia had not been brought nearer to God by calamity, but driven farther from Him. Singularly enough, whereas it is prosperity which too often makes *us* forget God, it is adversity which had this effect among the early Jews, brought up in the narrow belief that Israel's God was bound to be Israel's protector. God had His own purposes, however; Ezekiel believes in the "new covenant" as much as Jeremiah (Ezek. xi. 19, 20, xxxvi 25-27), and knows that the next generation will confess, *It is good for me that I have been afflicted* (Psa. cxix. 71). But the vine-stock of ancient Israel, half-consumed already, has no possibility of usefulness. Let it be again consigned to the purifying flames (Ezek. xv). Did the Jews believe this? No; they only said, *Doth he not make fine parables* (Ezek. xx. 49)? Was there not a new Pharaoh, whom men praised already for his energy and ambition (Uahibrî, called Hophra in the Hebrew of Jer. xliv. 30, Οὐαφρῆ in the Sept., Ἀπρίης in Herodotus)? So the people had their way, and Zedekiah rebelled against Babylon, Tyre and Ammon joining him, and Egypt promising "horses and much people" (Ezek. xvii. 15). At once Nebuchadrezzar takes the field, but against which adversary? *He stands where the ways divide to use divination; he shuffles the arrows*[1] (Ezek. xxi. 21), and decides for Jerusalem. How could he hesitate? Strategically the capture of Jerusalem was too important to be postponed. In January 587 the siege began. Had Zedekiah done nothing to avert this? No; the experience of Jehoiakim was repeated. *They have blown the trumpet, and made all ready; but none goeth to the battle* (Ezek. vii. 14). An attempt was indeed made to increase the number of Jerusalem's defenders, by reviving a neglected law, not long since adopted and expanded in Deuteronomy, which directed that every enslaved Hebrew or Hebrewess should be emancipated after seven years. To atone for their previous neglect, the princes did more than fulfil this law, for they set *all* their slaves and handmaids free. And behold! a wonder happens, which seems like a blessing upon their obedience, and a repetition of the great deliverance in Hezekiah's reign. The approach of an Egyptian army compelled Nebuchadrezzar to raise the siege,

[1] See Lyall, "Ancient Arabian Poetry," p. 106; Lenormant, "La divination," p 18; Wellhausen, "Skizzen," iii. 127.

and go to meet it. In vain did Jeremiah try to sober the excited minds of his people. At once the freedmen were enslaved again, and the one true patriot—Jeremiah—was arrested at one of the city-gates on a charge of "falling away to the Chaldæans." The poor weak king had probably nothing to do with either transaction (comp. Jer. xxxiv. 8 with *v.* 15). Certainly he had a superstitious veneration for Jeremiah, to whom he had not long before sent a deputation of priests, hoping to obtain through him another "wonderful work" like that granted of old to the prayers of Isaiah.[1] The excuse for those who arrested Jeremiah on a false charge is that the prophet had actually said (Jer. xxi. 9), *He that goeth away and falleth away to the Chaldæans, he shall live;* and judging him by the ordinary standard, was it not (so his accusers may have said) only too clear that he was basely deserting his post in the hour of danger? The grounds were doubtless insufficient; for had not the Chaldæans raised the siege? But the prophet's old friends among the princes were now in Babylonia, and he was as helpless before his low-minded adversaries as a suspected aristocrat before a French revolutionary tribunal. He was consigned to an unhealthy prison, until the king, with whom, upon the return of the Chaldæans, he had a private interview, gave orders for his removal to the "court of the guard," which adjoined the palace (Jer. xxxii. 2, comp. Neh. iii. 25). Soon after this, he received a visit from his cousin Hanameel, who, strange to say, invited him at this dark moment to purchase the family property at Anathoth. To Jeremiah this was clearly the hand of God. He called witnesses, paid the price of the land, had the purchase-deed prepared, subscribed and sealed it, and then gave it to Baruch to keep securely, and all this in spite of a mental struggle which even he, the prophet of the "new covenant,"[2] could not escape. Yes; even after his great victory on Carmel, Elijah must have his doubting time in the wilderness, and Jeremiah's bright visions must once more be renewed to him in his cap-

---

[1] To obtain a full account of this episode, we should, with Stade, connect Jer. xxi. 1, 2, xxxvii. 4–10, xxi. 4–14. The more original form of the prophecy is that given in Jer xxxvii 7–10.

[2] The form of chap. xxxi. may here and there (*e g.* in *v.* 15, on which see my note) have been affected by later experiences, but the kernel of the prophecy I regard as earlier How can we understand his prophecies or account for his development otherwise?

tivity. So once again he is assured that a new and better covenant will be given to Israel, and that as one consequence of this, *houses and fields and vineyards shall yet again be bought in this land* (Jer. xxxii. 15).

So the days went by in prayer and prophecy (notice the connexion of these in Jer. xxxiii. 3) and intercourse with those who like Zedekiah retained some belief in the prophet. But the bitter end of the struggle was visibly approaching, and the princes, to whom the defence of the city was committed, thought that Jeremiah was playing an unpatriotic part by counselling surrender. We can hardly wonder at this. Rightly or wrongly, the princes had decided on resistance, and felt bound to enforce at any rate silent acquiescence. Surely any modern government would do the like. Jeremiah had "despaired, not merely of his country, which any man may innocently do : but also for her, which no man has a right to do" (if I may apply Thirlwall's words, spoken of Phocion), at least from the point of view of a politician. We, who are free from their illusions, can pity the princes, and partly even respect them. But still more can we respect and admire the prophet. Alone among these desperate men he persisted in advocating what was then the only "way of life" (Jer. xxi. 8), though, as Niebuhr remarks, he would doubtless have spoken differently in the days of the Maccabees. Such lonely heroism was worthy of a type of Christ. Imagine the scene ; recall the faces in Munkacsy's "Christ before Pilate," and compare the psalmist's words in Psa. xxii. 12-17 (written perhaps with more thought of Jeremiah's trouble). Neither Christ nor Jeremiah could soften unwelcome truths nor, at the supreme crisis, look to God to hide him from his enemies (comp. Jer. xxxvi. 26, Luke iv. 30). Jeremiah fell a victim to his cowardly foes—"cowardly" I call them, because they were too superstitious to kill Jeremiah, as Jehoiakim killed Urijah ; they would rather that famine should do their work for them. So, like Joseph in the fine old story, he was cast into a cistern, *and Jeremiah sunk in the mire* (Jer. xxxviii. 6).

Now, thought the princes, we may safely forget Jeremiah. But they overlooked one thing, that the cistern was near the palace, and that about the king's person were some who by the accident of birth were free from the prejudices of Israelites. (Need I say that none of the cisterns under the floor of the so-called Grotto of Jeremiah can be that intended, for the simplest topographical reasons;[1] mediæval traditionalists have indeed much to answer for !) Assistance prompt, courageous, and effectual was on its way when the prophet least thought it. Three men ("thirty," Jer. xxxviii. 10, is a scribe's error), with "old cast clouts" to ease Jeremiah where the cords might cut him, were sent to draw him up out of the cistern. That dark form which bends over the pit is, not the angel of death, but a friendly Ethiopian who has used his influence with the king in favour of the prophet. His true name we know not; he passed among the Jews as "King's slave"—Ebedmelech; but he ranks in the Bible with the eunuch of queen Candace (Acts viii. 27) as one who feared God and was accepted by Him. "*Can the Ethiopian change his skin?*" (Jer. xiii. 23). True; but where is whiteness of soul to be found—in Ebedmelech or in the Jewish princes? in Livingstone's tender-hearted African bearers or in the Arab slave-merchants? Jeremiah at any rate knew who was his true "neighbour." A short prophecy in his works is devoted to Ebedmelech, closing with the words (with which compare Psa. xxxvii. 40), *because thou hast put thy trust in me* (Jer. xxxix. 18).

One person there was whose "feet were sunk in a mire" worse than that of Jeremiah's cistern; this was king Zedekiah. His character at this period seems a bundle of inconsistencies. He deserves credit for bravery in sitting at the gate of Benjamin, where Ebedmelech found him (Jer. xxxviii. 7); for this, being in the north of the city, was the point most exposed to the besiegers. He has also relieved himself from the imputation of cruelty by assenting to the transference of Jeremiah from the cistern to his old safe lodgings. But he is now to be tested again for the last time, and fails shamefully. *I am afraid of the Jews that are fallen away to the Chaldæans, lest they* (*i.e.*, the latter) *deliver me into their hand, and they mock me* (Jer. xxxviii. 19). What unkingly cowardice and selfishness! Why should Zedekiah fear taunts or ill-treatment from these deserters, when he would rather deserve thanks, for having justified their own course of action? And how could he think of himself when the fate of his country and, as it might seem, of his religion was in question? Especially when, as he probably thought, Jeremiah had guaranteed his own personal safety and comfort,

---

[1] See Thomson, "The Land and the Book" (1881) p. 555.

IF THOU HADST KNOWN, EVEN THOU! 175

by prophesying (as Zedekiah might easily infer from Jer. xxxii. 5, xxxiv. 5) that after a short stay in Babylon, he would return to "die in peace" in his own country. With kindly earnestness Jeremiah presses the king, whose weakness he pities, to listen to his advice, but in vain. Zedekiah cannot bear the thought of being ridiculed, but can with calmness picture Jerusalem in flames and its inhabitants, except himself, exposed to every outrage. Let him be; vengeance is on its way; the oracles concerning him will be fulfilled, but not as he thinks. Let us keep our sympathy for worthier objects. Oh for a solemn symphony to attune the mind! For the end of the first part of Israel's tragedy is at hand. *Thus saith the Lord Jehovah: An evil, an only (i.e., unique) evil; behold it cometh. An end is come, the end is come, it awaketh against thee; behold, it cometh* (Ezek. vii. 5, 6). Primitive Israel is about to pass through its supreme agony. Good may come out of this great "evil"; yet we can but sympathize with those upon whom the ploughshare of captivity made such "long furrows" (Psa. cxxix. 3).

The siege had now lasted for one year, five months, and twenty-seven days. It was early in July,[1] 586, and the wheat harvest ought to have been near. Provisions had long since begun to fail; indeed, but for this we might never have heard of the capture of Jerusalem. There was still no thought of surrender. Zedekiah stayed within the walls from pure weakness of mind; the "princes," because they would sooner starve than see their proud city laid low. Some homes there were in which (as in the later siege) sights of horror were seen (Lam. ii. 20, iv. 10), which I will merely hint at in the reticent words of Ugolino's poet, "*Then even grief by hunger was outdone.*"[2] The famished warriors could no longer defend the one weak point in their fortifications. With a wild shout, the besiegers poured in through a breach in the northern wall. It was night, and under cover of the darkness Zedekiah and his little army hurried in the opposite direction. By the rocky ravine of the Kedron they fled as far as the "plains of Jericho"; doubtless they hoped to cross the Jordan, and elude their pursuers in the

[1] The exact day is chronicled — the ninth of the fourth month. Like the other "black days" of this period, it was afterwards observed as a fast (Zech. viii. 19).

[2] "Poscia più che' l dolor potè il digiuno," Dante, "Inf." xxxiii. 75. Above, I have followed Dean Plumptre.

mountains of Moab. But it was too late; the Chaldæans were upon them. The army melted away; the king was captured, and carried to the headquarters at Riblah (see p. 127), where, as a punishment for his perfidy (Ezek. xvii. 16), his eyes were put out, his sons and "all the nobles of Judah"[1] having been previously executed (Jer. xxxix 6,7 ; 2 Chron. xxxvi. 13). Ruthless Nebuchadrezzar! some one may say. But it was the just reward of Zedekiah's perfidy (Ezek. xvii. 16), according to the ideas of those times; Nebuchadrezzar was of a more refined character than any of the Assyrian kings (see p. 146). Jeremiah foresaw this gloomy issue of the building extravagances of Jehoiakim's reign. In an impassioned address to the nobles of Jerusalem (collectively described as a maiden dwelling in Lebanon, because of their houses inlaid with cedar-wood) he says,—

O inhabitress of Lebanon that makest thy nest in the cedars, how wilt thou groan[2] *when pangs come upon thee, the pain as of a woman in travail!* (Jer. xxii. 23).

A month of passive submission to the outrages of the soldiery followed. The officers of the king of Babylon had posted themselves by the so-called "middle gate," from which they doubtless commanded both parts of the city, the upper and the lower. The names of the two chief officers[3] are preserved (Jer. xxxix. 13), showing that the narrative (which, of course, is not Jeremiah's work) is based on a contemporary record. On the seventh day of the fifth month came the chief of Nebuchadrezzar's bodyguard, Nebuzaradan by name,[4] and burned all the

---

[1] More complete details are given in 2 Kings xxv. 18-21. The chief priest and the second priest were included.

[2] So the Septuagint, which is followed by the Peshitto and the Vulgate. The text-reading gives, according to the Revised Version, "How greatly to be pitied wilt thou be", this, however, is improbable. The difference of readings is slight.

[3] V 3 should be corrected in accordance with v. 13,—"Nebushazban (*Nabû̂ēzibanni*) the chief eunuch, and Nergalsharezer (*Nergalšaruçur*) the chief Magian " " Chief Magian " is, however, an uncertain rendering of "*Rab-mag*." "*Mag*" is probably a synonym for *rubû*, Assyrian for "prince." Tiele, "Bab.-ass Geschichte," p 430.

[4] *Nabûziriddin* would be the Babylonian form, his office may be more strictly defined as that of "chief of the executioners." Dr. Lansing's objection (*Expositor*, Sept. 1888, p. 224) cannot stand, Ass. *tabikhu* = "executioner."

IF THOU HADST KNOWN, EVEN THOU! 177

houses of the city, and with them the palace and the house of Jehovah. The sacred vessels still remaining, together with the two splendid pillars (1 Kings vii. 15–22), were carried away. How many of the inhabitants were carried away, we know not; Nebuchadrezzar's library is likely to be more precise on this point than the fragmentary Jewish narrative. One day we shall doubtless have it; till then, we must rest content with a few facts and possibilities.

Certain it is that agriculture was not entirely interrupted by the calamities of the state. Besides the incidental notice in Jer. xli. 8, we have the definite and trustworthy statement in Jer. xxxix. 10 that Nebuzaradan *left of the people the mean ones who had nothing, and gave them vineyards and fields.* From Jer. xliv. 2, Ezek. xxxvi. 4, Isa. li. 3, &c., it is clear that the remaining inhabitants of Judah were comparatively few; this was only too natural, for the previous calamities had reduced the land of Israel to a waste condition, as Ezekiel testifies (Ezek. xxxiv. 23, 27). But it would be hasty to infer that these few were entirely composed of the lowest class. Criticism has shown it to be not impossible that the educated class was to some extent represented among them.[1] To members of this literary class in Judah some critics have ascribed the Book of Obadiah and the prophecy which now forms chaps. xxiv.–xxvii. of Isaiah, also the Lamentations. Yes; these touching elegies, which have so long been ascribed to Jeremiah, are now generally denied to him on grounds which no archæological research can deprive of their force. Poems like these cannot, it is urged, have been produced till the worst misery of conquest had been mitigated by time. The technical artificiality of their form proves this. In the first four it is noteworthy that each verse begins with one of the Hebrew letters, according to the alphabetical order. Even in the fifth, in which this strict "alphabetic" structure is not found, there is at least an approximation to it; the number of verses being the same as that of the Hebrew letters, viz., twenty-two (comp. Psa. xxxiii., xxxviii., ciii.). To assert, with Dean Plumptre, that the born poet "accepts the discipline of a self-imposed law just *in proportion* to the vehemence of his emotions," still seems to me incapable of proof from modern European poetry, and, if possible, still more opposed to the facts of Hebrew literature. Some of the examples which the

[1] See Kuenen, "Religion of Israel." ii. 176.

dean adduces, in the introduction to Jeremiah in Bishop Ellicott's series of commentaries, "are merely the rhetorical exercises of poets learning their craft ; others merely concessions to the taste which every now and then prevails for superfine elaboration in every branch of art ; others again (and these few examples are alone in point), the attempts of the artists to help Nature to recover her balance, when the recovery has already begun, and emotion has already lost its overpowering vehemence."[1]

Surely we ought to be glad and not sorry at this result, the critical grounds for which I have explained in detail elsewhere. We are introduced through it to three writers. One is the author of Lam. i., ii., iv. ; a second, of Lam. iii. ; and a third, of Lam. v. The second, who is acquainted with Job as well as with Jeremiah, may have lived either in Judah or in Babylonia ; the first and third are most naturally regarded as resident in Judah. Jeremiah was apparently the favourite book of all these poets, though the second seems also to have been well acquainted with Job (written most probably in the exile period). If therefore a title had to be given by way of defining the authorship, we might perhaps style the entire collection, on the analogy of portions of the Psalter, "The Book of the Lamentations of the Sons of Jeremiah."[2]

The author of the Septuagint version may therefore be excused for representing the Lamentations to have been indited by Jeremiah, seated (like another Job) on the dustheaps of Jerusalem. He says (and this notice is repeated with a few additional words in the Vulgate), "And it came to pass, after Israel was taken captive and Jerusalem made desolate, that Jeremias sat down weeping, and lamented with this lamentation over Jerusalem, and said." Some account for this preface by supposing the writer to have followed 2 Chron. xxxv. 25, which states (see p. 97) that Jeremiah "lamented for Josiah," and also "all the singing men and singing women," and that these lamentations are written down in a collection called *qīnōth* ("elegies"). If this view were correct, the Chronicler must have absurdly interpreted Lam. iv. 20 of Josiah. It is quite enough, however, to suppose that the Septuagint translator was struck by the affinities of phraseology between Jeremiah

[1] "Lamentations" (in "Pulpit Commentary"), Introduction, p. vii.
[2] *Ibid.* Comp my crit. note on Psa. xxix. 1.

and the Lamentations, and also found a certain poetic propriety in ascribing the authorship of the latter to Jeremiah, just as some Hellenistic Jew actually assigns Psa. cxxxvii. to this prophet,[1] because of the words "sat down and wept," although Jeremiah never saw the "rivers of Babylon," at any rate with his outward eyes. More elaborately imaginative than the Septuagint translator of Lamentations were the traditionalists who fixed upon a cave near the Damascus Gate for the abode of the weeping prophet. The "savage wildness" of the spot "may well seem," as George Williams thinks, "to have caught the gloomy colour of the desolate heart that pours forth its plaintive melody"[2] in the Lamentations. I cannot myself see that "savage wildness" of which the learned archæologist speaks. It was natural for a Jew to seek refuge in a cave, and Jeremiah could hardly have found a grander or a more convenient hermitage than the cave which bears his name. According to Thomson, it extends about 120 feet under the cliff, and I can well believe it. In fact, but for the much more extensive quarries close by, it would be reckoned among the wonders of Jerusalem. A vast column of rock, left and indeed produced by the quarrymen, supports the roof and adds to the impressiveness of the place. But the elliptically shaped cave which you see first is not the whole of the excavation. To the left of the column you enter a second cave, not so large, nor so light and pleasant, as the first, and forming as it were an inner chamber. Clearly this is no common hermit's cell, but worthy of the large-hearted prophet, to whom it would have afforded both space and quiet for his poetic toils. Nor is it incredible that some of the inhabitants of Jerusalem should have found refuge both here and in the larger quarries. Addressing Moab, Jeremiah says (and he may well have thought of his own advice when the "day of Jerusalem" came)—

O ye inhabitants of Moab, leave the cities and dwell in the rock; and be like the dove that maketh her nest in the sides of the hole's mouth (Jer. xlviii. 28).

In later times these quarries were used, like the catacombs, for graves. It is not an ignoble fancy that Jeremiah "sat down and wept" over the grave of his youthful hopes in this grand natural hermitage, the rock-doves round about him cooing in unison with

[1] The Septuagint has a conflation of two titles, Τῷ Δαυιδ 'Ιερεμίου.

[2] Supplement to vol. i. of "The Holy City," p. 67.

his elegies. Yes; it is not an ignoble fancy, and even Dean Stanley sees no strong objection to accepting it.[1] But truth must prevail over mere imagination. Jeremiah could not have stayed long in a cave in the "day of Jerusalem." We mistake the result of providential training when we suppose that he all at once forgot his highest intuitions, and his far-seeing religious patriotism. His words are not, as Stanley thinks, "preserved to us in the Book of the Lamentations." We wrong him by too exclusively picturing him with the "awestruck figure" and "attitude of hopeless sorrow" attributed to him by Michel Angelo. It is a touching idea of a Jewish Rabbi (Eleazar) that though the gates of prayer are closed, the gates of tears are not, but though suggested by the Lamentations (Lam. iii. 8, comp. Psa. xxxix. 12), it does not express the mind of Jeremiah. This spiritual hero is not rightly styled the weeping prophet. There was a time, no doubt, when he really was that which poor Matthew Arnold so much disliked; it was when his intuition was clear enough to show him the swiftly approaching judgment, but not the buds of peace and holiness blossoming on the fields of ruin. Jeremiah's anguish in his helpless wisdom, when he alone—a grander Demosthenes—saw how the judgment could be stayed, and no one would give heed to him, when he wished that "his head were waters and his eyes a fountain of tears, that he might weep day and night for the slain of the daughter of his people" (Jer. ix. 1), is indeed a subject worthy of a painter's hand, but is there not a still nobler theme—the same once sad man taking up his cross and bearing it aloft, strengthened (like his great antitype) by "the joy that was set before him" (Heb. xii. 2)?

Of this I shall be called to speak in the next chapter. Meantime let me not withhold the truest and most admiring sympathy from those "sons of Jeremiah," who followed the prophet in his weakness rather than in his strength, but who so sweetly struck the keynote of captive Israel's mourning.[2] Is

[1] "Sermons on Special Occasions," p 311. Comp p 317, "We are with Jeremiah on the rocky mount, weeping over Jerusalem." Truly we could hardly imagine that even a weeping prophet always remained in his cave-dwelling.

[2] These elegies were the forerunners of a large body of synagogue poetry. The most famous of the later *qīnōth* is that of Yehuda Halevi (twelfth century A D.), known even to general readers by Heine's poem in the *Romanzero*.

there another such book in the whole world—such an "almost unalloyed expression of unrestrained anguish, and utter, inconsolable desolation"? Well did Stanley draw out the permanent elements of human interest which it contains, and find a pathetic present-day illustration of them in the Siege of Paris, 1870-71. But there is that in the circumstances of the original writers to which, from the nature of the case, there can be no complete parallel. The tragedy of Israel is greater than that of any other people : *Behold and see if there be any sorrow like unto my sorrow* (Lam. 1. 12).

CHAPTER VI.

A PASTOR'S STRANGE FAREWELL.

Gedaliah becomes viceroy—The prophet stays with him at Mizpah—Ishmael's outrages—Flight from Mizpah – Migration into Egypt—The heathen festival—The stormy colloquy.

"BUT have you not been somewhat too hasty in rejecting the help of tradition? Have you not expressly accepted the help of imaginative conjecture in filling up the scanty notices of contemporary records (see p. 13)? Why should you refuse the co-operation of those early traditionalists, who were themselves so imaginative?" So some one may ask, dismissing with a wave of the hand the reasons which I have offered, and pointing triumphantly to the four verses which follow the account of Nebuzaradan's displantation of the "remnant of the people" (Jer. xxxix. 11-14). In this paragraph we are in fact told that Nebuchadrezzar gave special injunctions to his high officer to "set his eyes on Jeremiah, and do him no harm," in consequence of which the prophet was brought from the "court of the guard" into "the house" (*i.e.*, perhaps the royal palace), and given perfect liberty of movement. Is it likely that Jeremiah would feel happy in the home of fallen greatness? Why may we not suppose that, while the captives were awaiting the order to remove, Jeremiah "sat down and wept" in the dim seclusion of the cave,

> "Still round and round that strange old alphabet
> Weaving his long funeral chant of woe?"
> (Alexander, "The Waters of Babylon.")

I am afraid that this imaginative inference from those four verses will not hold, for we have an express statement in Jer. xl. which militates altogether against it. There we are told that the prophet was taken with the other captives, bound with chains, to Ramah, where he was set at liberty by Nebuzaradan.[1] This is much more likely than that Jeremiah received any special attention in the turmoil of the capture, and most of all improbable is it that Nebuchadrezzar himself had anything to do with his liberation. Let us then accept the historical picture suggested by Jer. xl. Jeremiah, who doubtless passed at first for one of the dependents of the palace, went with Ebedmelech and the rest to Ramah.[2] That conspicuous hill-town, five miles north of Jerusalem, now became the meeting-place of bands of exiles from all quarters. It was there that Jeremiah, in the greatest of his prophetic visions, had seemed to hear "ancient Rachel" (as Dante calls her) weeping for her captive children (Jer. xxxi. 15), and there that, in sober, waking reality, he now saw and heard the bitter grief of the last representatives of the true people of Israel. It is in a dreary, lonesome country—only interesting to us from its historical associations, and surely the saddest of these is that connected with the starting of the Jewish exiles for Babylonia. Not far off, to the south-west, was a still more strikingly situated hill-town called Mizpah,[3] where in the period of the Judges popular assemblies had been held (Judg. xx. 1 ; 1 Sam. x. 17). This place had been selected for the residence of the newly appointed governor of "the cities of Judah," himself a Jew, and bound by family ties to Jeremiah—Gedaliah, the son of Ahikam (comp. Jer. xxvi. 24). It now became the duty of Nebuzaradan to consider the special circumstances of any particular captive, and Gedaliah appears to have called his

[1] It will be noticed that two remarkable expressions in Jer. xxxix. 11-14, "set eyes upon" and "dwell among the people," occur also in Jer. xl. Probably therefore the shorter account in Jer. xxxix. is not to be regarded as a distinct tradition.

[2] Ramah (now the village er-Ram) was on the frontier of the two kingdoms (see 1 Kings xv. 17, 22) Hence the reference in Jeremiah's vision.

[3] I do not see how the well-known Mizpah of Benjamin can be identified with Nob (so Conder). Neby Samwîl, where traces of an ancient town are still found, answers all requirements (see Robinson, "Biblical Researches," ii. 144). It has a grand view, "the most comprehensive in southern Palestine," thus justifying its name.

attention to Jeremiah. There was much in the character and previous history of the prophet to command even a Babylonian's respect. We know how susceptible of reverence for all that was good and spiritually noble Nebuchadrezzar was, and we cannot doubt that Nebuzaradan acted in the spirit of his master when he gave Jeremiah the choice of either going to Babylon with the exiles, or dwelling with the Jews who remained under the native governor. In an impassioned section of his prophecy (Jer. xv. 10–21) Jeremiah (as some think) reveals the state of mind in which his difficult decision was made. "He tells his friends that the resolution to go to Gedaliah costs him a severe struggle. He longs for rest, and in Babylon he would have more chance of a quiet life than among the turbulent Jews at home. But he has looked up to God for guidance, and, however painful to the flesh, God's will must be obeyed. He gives us the substance of the revelation which he received. The Divine counsellor points out to him that He has already interposed in the most striking manner for Jeremiah, and declares that if he will devote himself to the Jews under Gedaliah, a new and fruitful field will be open to him, in which, moreover, by Divine appointment, no harm can happen to him."[1] Yes; in these trying circumstances Jeremiah may have wavered for a moment, and longed that "this cup might pass from him." How much he had suffered from the intense strain of the last few years! Would it be wrong to live in comparative ease in Babylonia, varying the elegies of the mourner with the bright visions of the heaven-taught prophet? No; it would not be wrong in another; but it would be inconsistent with his unselfish character. There was Ezekiel for the exiles; the poverty-stricken remnant at home[2] could not dispense with Jeremiah. So he bade farewell to the captives, and went to Mizpah. It is a noble example, and those who can follow it

[1] "Jeremiah" (in "Pulpit Commentary") i. 373. In this view I follow Grätz. It is no doubt only a conjecture, but it enables us to realize the words of the prophet more vividly. There are some great difficulties in the text, and apparently one interpolation, verses 13, 14 being probably an incorrect copy of xvii 3, 4

[2] I see no reason to suppose with M. Clermont-Ganneau that the "remnant of Judah" consisted merely of "serfs of the Israelitish aristocracy, themselves not of pure Israelitish blood" (see his lecture, translated in "Palestine Fund Statement," 1875, p. 206). Observe that princesses of the blood royal were among those who were left behind.

may miss much that is pleasant in life, but show that they have the true prophet's spirit.

It was a bold experiment which was about to be tried, and Nebuchadrezzar deserves credit for the kindness which prompted it. The newly organized subject people might perhaps be less fickle than the primitive Israel now numbered with the dead, but there was certainly a risk of disappointment. There was also not a little danger from the small neighbouring peoples, which had looked with malicious pleasure on the calamity of Judah, and hoped to increase their territory at its expense (see Lam. iv. 22, Ezek. xxv., xxxv, Obad. 10-16). The governor, however, had been carefully selected; his views (see Jer. xl. 9) were precisely those which Jeremiah had so long vainly inculcated in Jerusalem. General confidence appears to have been reposed in his upright character, and crowds of Jewish fugitives resorted to him from their temporary hiding-places in foreign lands. Even the leaders of the Jewish guerilla bands condescended at his entreaty to engage in husbandry. Nature did her best to efface the sad marks of invasion; we are told that the husbandmen (most of them now for the first time proprietors, Jer. xxxix. 10) "gathered wine and summer fruits very much" (Jer. xl. 12). No doubt they took this for a favourable omen, and ventured to hope that He, who had not forgotten His covenant with the land, would yet call to remembrance His covenant with His people (Hos. ii. 21-23). Our prophet would be the last to blame them; but he would warn them not to forfeit these blessings by disobedience to the authority which had Jehovah's sanction. A certain chastened happiness must have been Jeremiah's at this time; he had the governor on his side, and the other prophets (who *found no more vision from Jehovah*, Lam. ii. 9), had left the field free to their "despised and rejected" colleague. For about four years[1] all went smoothly; but in the fifth, grave events took place. It was now Tisri, the month of the Feast of Booths—

[1] Comparing Jer xli 1 with 2 Kings xxv. 8, we might infer that only two months elapsed between Nebuzaradan's arrival at Jerusalem and the massacre at Mizpah This is in itself improbable, besides, in lii. 32 a third deportation of Jews is mentioned, which certainly stands in some connexion with the murder of Gedaliah and the Chaldæans. Such an open insult to Babylon would surely not wait nearly five years for a severe punishment It is only fair to mention that Jer xli 1 does not mention the year in which the events to be described took place.

the annual thanksgiving for the crops. Ishmael, a prince of the injured royal house, had determined to spoil this year's celebration for all peaceable Jews. He obtained the support of Israel's bitter foe, Baalis, the Ammonite king, and began to seek an opportunity ot wreaking his vengeance on the Babylonian viceroy. One of the old guerilla-leaders—Johanan by name—heard of it, and gave notice to the governor; but he in the simplicity of his heart refused to credit such baseness. The warning was repeated,—*Why should he slay thee, that all the Jews which are gathered unto thee should be scattered, and all the remnant should perish?* (Jer. xl. 15)—but in vain. Gedaliah refused to give leave for Ishmael to be slain; "*thou speakest falsely,*" he said, "*of Ishmael.*"

And now we hear no more of the Ammonites; the story of accumulated murders which follows has for its central figure the inhuman Ishmael. With ten companions he reaches the hill-town where Gedaliah resides, and is entertained by the governor at a meal. Generous, simple-minded Gedaliah! how could he dream that even the law of hospitality was no longer sacred to his guest, and that he who had, from the purest patriotism, accepted the unenviable position of head of a ruined house (Isa. iii. 6), would be called to account for misfortunes which none more than he deplored? *Then arose Ishmael, and the ten men that were with him, and smote Gedaliah the son of Ahikam the son of Shaphan with the sword, and slew him whom the king of Babylon had made governor over the land* (Jer. xli. 2). Too significant words! Gedaliah, the innocent Gedaliah, suffered the vengeance intended for Nebuchadrezzar, and with him all the trained warriors who were about him, including, we are expressly told, "*the Chaldeans who were present there.*" Whether the interests of Judah were promoted or not by these murders, was not a question which occurred to Ishmael. Perhaps he would have been content himself with the position of a chieftain of a small Israelitish tribe under the suzerainty of the Ammonites. As yet, however, his predominant feeling was that of rage at any Israelite who recognized "the logic of facts," and submitted to the Babylonians. The second day after the murder, "while no one knew it" (had Ishmael, then, closed the gates of the town?), there came eighty men from Shechem, Shiloh (or perhaps rather Shalem or Salem [1]), and Samaria—places

[1] See p. 116, note 1.

which, probably through Josiah's exertions, still maintained their religious interest in Jerusalem, on their way to the site of the destroyed temple. They had all the outward signs of mourning; it was no joyous festivity which they thought to celebrate; but, so far as they could, they wished to observe the accustomed forms by bringing oblations (*minkhāh*) to Jehovah. Truly a noteworthy phenomenon! How great is the power of sacred spots, even apart from the buildings essential, as one might think, to religious observances! The temple has been burned, but the temple-precincts are not less sacred to these faithful worshippers. And now that the sad procession has almost reached Mizpah, they can clearly see these precincts, and weep anew.[1] Perhaps it was evening; at any rate, one more halt would be necessary. Hence the men were not surprised at the seemingly hospitable invitation, "Come to Gedaliah the son of Ahikam." But the speaker was the ruthless Ishmael; of those eighty men only ten returned home. Unchanging East! still dost thou nourish the same hot, revengeful natures as of yore; still does thy revenge accept the help of treachery in the execution of its fell designs. Cawnpore and Mizpah stand together in the annals of Oriental passion.

There was a "great cistern" in the middle of the town which king Asa had constructed during his war with Baasha king of Israel (comp. 1 Kings xv. 22); into this Ishmael threw the dead bodies of the murdered seventy. And what of the ten? Was it pity which saved them? No; it was greed. Then, as now, husbandmen who feared robbers stored the rich products of the soil where no one would suspect them—in carefully concealed openings in the rocky hill-side. These ten men were more prosperous than the rest, and ransomed their lives by their wealth.[2] Ishmael was doubtless a poor adventurer, and material means were wanting to carry out his plans. The greatest difficulty, however, still remains to be explained. How could Ishmael venture to touch the sacred persons of pilgrims? I suppose that he was one of those whom Jeremiah

[1] Following the Septuagint (see "Variorum Bible").

[2] There is a Zulu formula for deprecating death on the ground of some important work which cannot be done without the person whose life is in danger. Bishop Callaway compares this with the story before us ("Zulu Nursery Tales," i. 242), but it is not a very close parallel.

addresses in that indignant strain, *What? steal, murder, and commit adultery, and swear falsely, and burn incense unto Baal?* (Jer. vii. 9). Possibly too he thought that Jehovah had deserted his land, and that now less than ever were those moral laws, of which Jeremiah was the exponent, binding upon an Israelite. These eighty men were carrying oblations to Jehovah; he, for his part, was satisfied with the less exacting religion of Baal. But why were the people of Mizpah spared? Did he think that those poor northern people could be better dispensed with than the inhabitants of his own native Judah? Or that seventy was about the number of those Jewish nobles whom Nebuchadrezzar had slain in Riblah (Jer. xxxix. 6), so that the avenger of blood could now afford to be merciful? At any rate, the people of Mizpah, including, besides Jeremiah, kinswomen of Ishmael belonging to the royal house, were being carried off by these few bold adventurers in the direction of the land of Ammon.

The route which they adopted led them at first northwards. Before they had got far, they paused to drink by "the great waters that are in Gibeon."[1] How natural! Remember that they had started in haste. One can still observe an ancient broken reservoir on the west side of the hill of Gibeon (*el-Jîb*); and in the wet season, says Thomson, there is a considerable pond in the plain below the modern village. While the caravan halted, Johanan and his fellow-captains came up with them. What could Ishmael and his ten warriors[2] do against this superior force? Blows were exchanged, and Ishmael lost two of his men, and made off with the rest to the Ammonites. What was Johanan to do now? Had he been able to deliver up the arch-conspirator to the Chaldæans, he might perhaps have hoped for a continuance of Nebuchadrezzar's favours. But appearances were against him. He had (so it would be said at the court) allowed a few bold men to subvert the existing organization, to kill the representatives of Babylon, and to escape unpunished.

---

[1] In 2 Sam. ii. 13 these "waters" are called "the pool of Gibeon."

[2] In Jer. xli. 16 "men of war" must surely be an interpolated gloss. According to *v.* 3 the warriors had all been slain by Ishmael. The Hebrew *g'bărîm* (represented in A.V by "mighty") simply means "men" as opposed to "women." In Jer. xliii 6, where the sexes and classes of the people of Mizpah are again catalogued, we have simply *g'bărîm* (comp. xliv. 20).

Vengeance would assuredly be taken for this, and among the
leading sufferers would be Johanan and his fellows. So they
thought it most prudent to make for the Egyptian frontier, and
without stopping at Mizpah, pressed on to the hospice or khân
of Chimham (if the reading is correct[1]), close to Bethlehem.
Here they halted to hold a fresh council of war, and more
especially to obtain supernatural light from the prophet of
Jehovah. It was indeed no slight matter for the choicest part
of the remnant of Israel to return to the very land out of which
their fathers had been divinely guided. So they (*i.e.*, the whole
community) approached Jeremiah in suppliant guise, as one
who, like Moses and like Samuel, had power with God to turn
the destinies of his people. Jeremiah agreed to this request,
and Johanan promised in return that, whatever the oracle
should be, they would cheerfully obey the commandment of
Jehovah. "Methinks he doth protest too much," was perhaps
the unspoken thought of Jeremiah.

Nine days the prophet passed in meditation and prayer.
Knowing him as we do, we cannot doubt that he sustained a
severe mental conflict. His dear friend and patron, who
seemed to have been raised up "for such a time as this,"
had been brutally murdered, and Jehovah had not warned
him of it. Common sense seemed to bid acquiescence in the
policy provisionally adopted by Johanan. Jeremiah knew as
well as any one what Babylonian vengeance meant; could he
imperil the lives of so many of his countrymen by advising
them to remain? It was hard no doubt to condemn themselves to exile; but in all material respects might they not hope
to be the gainers, and if Isa. xix. 18–25 was really written by
Isaiah, did it not indicate that, even religiously, Israelites might
have all their cravings satisfied in Egypt? And yet the prophetic spirit had distinctly assured him that in Babylon alone
could the regeneration of Israel be effected. Had not the
silence of Jehovah in the recent crisis proved that the delight-

[1] Chimham (rather, Kimham) is most probably a personal name. To
found a khân for the accommodation of travellers was a most natural expression of public-spirited liberality. Possibly it is the son of the rich
Gileadite Barzillai (2 Sam. xix. 37–40) who is meant. But Josephus and
Aquila appear to have read "by the hurdles of Chimham," which is almost
more probable. Gederah, Gederothaim, and Gederoth, are the names of
three places belonging to Judah in Josh. xv.

ful project of a small home-community was not from Him?[1] And was He not the God of the innocent, and the helper of the friendless? So faith spoke louder than policy, and on the tenth day the prophet had a clear intuition of the Divine will, or, in the consecrated phrase, *the word of Jehovah came unto Jeremiah*. He sent word to Johanan, and the whole community again met before the great prophet. No longer, however, in the same submissive spirit. These ten days had not been spent idly by the captains and their companions. The more they considered the question, the less they could regard it as an open one. Jeremiah was in a difficult position. Never was the need more obvious of a class of teachers distinct from the prophets, who could inculcate prophetic ideas in a more conciliatory style. Such a class had never existed at Jerusalem, though some of the "wise men" had down to the time of the death of Josiah helped to predispose suitable individuals in favour of the prophetic point of view.[2] There was certainly no one to stand by Jeremiah now—no one to go in and out of the tents, preparing the people to receive his address, and explaining it kindly and wisely after it had been spoken. So the words of the "allocution" fell upon unfriendly ears, and the increasing sternness of its tone suggests that clouds of wrath were visibly gathering on the brows of the excitable audience. This is what Jeremiah in effect said: "I know that ye are sick of the trumpet's blare, and of the never long absent fear of famine. I know that ye long to live together under a mild sovereign. All these things that ye desire shall ye have, if ye will only dwell in this land. Jehovah is satisfied with the chastening which Israel has received, nor does He wish to root up His people altogether. Be not afraid of Nebuchadrezzar; he is the instrument of God's purposes, and God will turn his heart like the water-courses. But if ye obstinately disobey, I warn you that the evils which ye dread shall overtake you there; ye shall see this land no more. Do ye scowl at me? Infatuated men! Ye deluded yourselves[3] when ye protested such willingness to obey God's word. Ye have

---

[1] In imagining such a thought to have passed through Jeremiah's mind, I assume that Jer. xlii. 10 does not accurately represent the point of view of Jeremiah. See below.

[2] See p. 90.

[3] In Jer. xlii. 20, we should render, "Yea, ye misled your own selves," &c.

made your choice; know, then, that sword, famine, and pestilence await you in Egypt."

It is a striking narrative. The writer does not conceal from us that he has taken his side. Azariah [1] (who seems now to have pushed himself to the front) and Johanan are the leaders of a band of disobedient apostates.[2] Their reply to Jeremiah is preserved; it places us in the very midst of the religious party-struggles of the day. *Thou speakest falsely*, they say; *Jehovah our God hath not sent thee, saying, Go not into Egypt to sojourn there.* Their point of view is precisely that of the priests and prophets on an earlier occasion. When Jeremiah prophesied, "This house shall be like Shiloh," they arrested and condemned him to death, not on the ground that he was a false claimant of the prophetic gift, but that he had mistaken his private opinion for the "word" of Jehovah. So his opponents argued now, though they cast a part of the blame on one of whom we should never have thought—the prophet's faithful scribe: *Baruch the son of Neriah setteth thee on against us, to deliver us into the hand of the Chaldæans* (Jer. xliii. 3). Was there any foundation for this story? It is possible. From the special oracle to Baruch, spoken in the fatal fourth year of Jehoiakim, we may gather that Baruch was inclined by nature to paint things in rose-colour. *And seekest thou great things for thyself? seek them not.*[3] *Behold, that which I have built will I break down, and that which I have planted will I pluck up, even this whole land* (Jer. xlv. 5, 4). Taking this passage in connexion with Jer. xlii. 10, I infer that Baruch, though his moral standard was as high as Jeremiah's, believed that, even after its heavy losses, Israel as a nation could yet be "built up" in its own land. No doubt the oracle in Jer. xlv. weakened his illusion for the time; indeed, the logic of facts had already *added sorrow to his grief*. But, as is the wont of human nature, his personal bent reasserted itself, and the establishment of Gedaliah at Mizpah seemed a providential confirmation of his hopes. Will it not help us to understand Jeremiah's attitude,

---

[1] Azariah, whose name appears in Jer. xlii 1 by mistake as Jezaniah (Sept. gives "Azariah"), is not mentioned among the captains, Jer xl 8.

[2] "All the proud men." The word (zēdīm) is one which occurs repeatedly in Psa. cxix. (see the author's note on v 21) Compare the antithesis between restless pride and composed humility in Psa cxxxi.

[3] Gentle Bishop Ken's motto (in his copy of Grotius "De Veritate").

if we suppose that Baruch really did influence him during this period? The prophet does not appear to have remonstrated with Gedaliah for accepting the responsibilities of a vassal chieftain, nor to have given him any prophetic counsel, nor to have received any prophetic warning of his death: in short, so far as we can see, his communion with his God was not as vivid nor as direct as it had been formerly. May we not ascribe this to some shade of human reason intervening between the prophet and his Sun, and probably enough, to his intercourse with Baruch? I cannot help thinking that we not only may, but must; and considering that these chapters, as they stand, cannot be the work of Jeremiah, my loyalty to the prophet suggests the conjecture that Jer. xlii. 10 embodies ideas for which Baruch is chiefly responsible—Baruch, whom the prophet has already described as being (in no ignoble sense, of course) ambitious of great things, and as listening with a heavy heart to the oracle, "I will break down, and I will pluck up"

Angry as the captains were, they made no attempt on the life either of Jeremiah or of Baruch. They had not that class-jealousy of the prophet which doubtless animated his enemies in the temple at Jerusalem (Jer. xxvi.). They carried the prophet with them to Egypt. If he could not protect them by his presence, he should at least share their fate. Beyond the frontier they doubtless found other Jewish fugitives already settled (Jer. xxiv. 8), and it would seem from Jer. xliv. 1 that they separated into two bands, some going to the two northern frontier cities Migdol and Tahpanhes (inhabited to a great extent by foreigners), others further south to Noph and Pathros (or Upper Egypt).[1] From these havens of rest they looked with a pity mingled with self-satisfaction on their less

[1] Migdol (comp. xlvi. 14, Ezek. xxix. 10, xxx. 6, R.V. marg.) is the Magdolon of Herodotus (ii. 159, see above, p. 96); it is also mentioned in the Itinerary of Antoninus, as being twelve Roman miles from Pelusium. It derived its name from one of the forts connected by a wall on the Asiatic frontier. (This is not the Migdol of Exod. xiv. 2; see Naville, "Pithom," p. 25) Tahpanhes is doubtless Daphnæ (comp. Septuagint), Noph is more probably Memphis than Napata (comp. Jer. ii. 16, xlvi. 14, Ezek. xxx. 13, 16, 18). Pathros (pa Hathor, "place of the goddess Hathor") means first the nome of Thebes, and next the whole of Upper Egypt. See Ebers, "Aegypten und die Bucher Mose's," i. 81–83, 115, 120, and comp. Mr. Stuart Poole's excellent little volume, "The Cities of Egypt" [At the last moment, I can add Part II. of Mr. Petrie's "Memoir on Tanis."]

fortunate fellow-countrymen in Judah, some of whom were at this moment perhaps being carried off by Nebuzaradan out of vengeance for the recent outrage to the majesty of Babylon (Jer. lii. 30). Jeremiah was now at Tahpanhes. There he laid a fresh prophetic burden on the land of Egypt, which calls for attention (Jer. xliii. 8-13). It is introduced by another specimen of sign-speech. A prophetic impulse bade him take great stones and imbed them in the mortar (not "clay," as A.V.) in the pavement at the entry of the royal palace. This means that Nebuchadrezzar, who all men thought would stop short at the Palestinian frontier, would soon set up his throne here, and from here penetrate into Egypt, slay or lead captive its inhabitants, destroy its obelisks and temples, and *go forth from thence in peace*. An indefatigable English explorer (Mr. Flinders Petrie) is the best commentator on this "sign-speech" of Jeremiah. In the year 1886 he found at Tell Defenneh the ruins of a fort built by Psametik I., and now called "the palace of the Jew's daughter," and could identify Jeremiah's "pavement" with "a great open-air platform of brickwork, a sort of *mastaba*, such as is now seen outside all great houses, and most small ones, in this country."[1] Little, however, he says, is left of the palace. But have we gained as much as some of us thought when the news of this interesting discovery reached us? Not unless further corroboration of the details of Jeremiah's prophecy comes from contemporary inscriptions. As to the burning of the temples spoken of (Jer. xliii. 12), that of course is a prophetic hyperbole, which is simply useful as giving us a measure of the feeling which animated the speaker. On the other hand, the particular instance of Divine vengeance specified by the prophet is true to fact. Of the obelisks of the Sun-god's temple at Heliopolis (in Egyptian, "Pe-Ra" or "Ra's Abode"; in Hebrew, "Beth-Shemesh" or "House of the Sun"), only one remains, to prove the venerable antiquity of the fallen religion.[2] But what of Nebuchadrezzar and his desolating invasion of Egypt? Did he erect his tribunal at Tahpanhes? We shall return to this later; Jeremiah himself will give us the best of opportunities. But we must, even here, carefully notice the difference between this and the other prophecies of the calamities of Egypt (Jer. ix. 25, 26, xlvi. 2-26), viz., that

[1] "Memoir on Tanis," Part II. "Egypt Exploration Fund," 1888, p. 50.
[2] Mr. Stuart Poole states that "it was set up at least 4000 years ago."

Jeremiah is here thinking as much of his fellow-countrymen as of the Egyptians. It was by the Divine will that Jacob and his sons went down into Egypt; but there is no "land of Goshen" for those who go there of their own will. When the "woe to Egypt" is fulfilled, let not the foreign refugees expect to be mere spectators. "Death, captivity, and sword" in Jer. xliii. 11 correspond to "sword, famine, and pestilence" in Jer. xlii. 17; comp. xliv. 12–14.

The last discourse of Jeremiah which is preserved to us (chap. xliv.) is in several respects an interesting one. We might have thought that the change of the old order of things would have brought some peace and quiet to the harassed prophet. But no—the great Huguenot's motto, *repos ailleurs*, might have been Jeremiah's. Not yet could he put off Elijah's mantle; the close of his ministry was to be as full of rejected calls to repentance as the beginning. No more bright and original ideas, but sad reminiscences of a past which must have seemed to Jeremiah far more distant than it really was. Must we not admire him for thus calmly resuming his thankless task, and renewing offers only too sure to be despised? Where the scene of the prophecy is laid, and what was its occasion, we shall see presently. It falls into five sections. In verses 2–10 Jeremiah reminds his hearers of the terrible judgment upon Judah. Surely this part of the discourse at any rate must have been modified by the hand of Baruch, for the description of the state of Judah is a very exaggerated one.[1] Suicidal, continues the prophet, is the conduct of the refugees in continuing their polytheistic practices even after such a warning. How contrite they ought to be! With what trembling hope they ought to approach Jehovah, remembering that *with thee there is forgiveness, in order that thou mayest be feared*. But what a different tale is told by these unmoved countenances (see Jer. xliv. 10)!

In verses 11–14, the doom already proclaimed (Jer. xlii.) is repeated with a terrible particularity. Did Jeremiah really use

[1] We are only told that the citizens of Mizpah and their families went to Egypt; the farmers (as we should call them) of whom Jer xxxix. 10, xl. 10, speaks remained to cultivate the soil, and kept certain "cities" from absolute desolation. In a subsequent passage (Jer. xliv. 22) the exaggeration is still stronger, unless "without inhabitant" be an interpolation (see Septuagint).

these words? Or may we not ascribe some of them, as well as the parallel expressions in chap. xlii., to the editor, Baruch? I for my part can with difficulty realize the relapse of Jeremiah into his old, too vehement manner, considering the Pisgah-view which he has taken of a better and happier age. The section concludes with the words, *for none but* (single) *escaped ones shall return* (comp. *v.* 28). At this point an explanatory statement is inserted, with reference to the speech of the Jews which follows. Isaiah at the close of two of his greatest prophecies (Isa. iii. 16–iv. 1, xxxii. 9–12) turns to the women, "gathered, we may suppose, at a little distance from the rest, and testifying their indifference."[1] So Jeremiah appears to have done—at least he distinctly addresses his answer (*vv.* 21–30) to the women who had boldly addressed him as well as to the men. This is the note in question,—

Then all the men who knew that their wives burned incense unto other gods, and all the women who were standing by, a great assembly, even all the people who dwelt in the land of Egypt, in Pathros, answered Jeremiah (Jer. xliv. 15).

"Great assembly" (comp. 1 Kings viii. 65) is clearly a religious phrase; these men and women had resorted to some central place in Upper Egypt to celebrate the worship of the "queen of heaven." Not an encouraging circumstance for Jeremiah, some one may say. No, truly; he carried his life in his hand, and thought perhaps of that other "assembly" (Jer. xxvi. 17) when he had had such a hairbreadth escape from danger. He now ventured again before a crowd of religious enthusiasts, who had not indeed cast off the worship of Jehovah (see especially verse 26), but had placed other gods beside the true God of Israel. They were among those who had taken the Deuteronomic Torah in its most obvious but not its highest sense. And the consequence of recent events was a strong reaction in their minds against the God who, in His impotence, as it seemed, had let them be driven out of their own land. Jehovah had promised prosperity, they said, to those who observed the Law; *they* had observed it, and see what the result had been. They must now, in common prudence, revert to those old idolatries which Deuteronomy had forbidden, and especially to the worship of that gracious divinity, the "queen of heaven." And who was

[1] "The Prophecies of Isaiah," i. 186.

the "queen of heaven"? We must first of all see the issue of the controversy.

As for the word that thou hast spoken unto us in Jehovah's name, we will not hearken unto thee: but we will perform all our promises to burn incense unto the queen of heaven, and to pour out drink offerings unto her, as we did, we and our fathers, our kings and our princes, in the cities of Judah, and in the streets of Jerusalem, and so we were satisfied with bread, and were happy, and saw no evil. But since we left off burning incense to the queen of heaven, and pouring out drink offerings unto her, we have wanted all things, and have perished by sword and famine.

Let us not be too severe on these unhappy men. At any rate, they are in some sense patriots; the fate which has befallen so many of their countrymen they make, by sympathy, their own. It is probable enough, from the prominence given to the women, that the wives had really been all along hankering after this *feminine* cultus, in the rites of which they were, by old custom, important persons. (Is it not the fact that women are everywhere a conservative religious influence?) But see, one of the women steps forward to speak to Jeremiah, who may perhaps suppose that they forced their wishes on their unwilling husbands. Not so. *If we burn incense to the queen of heaven, and pour out drink offerings unto her, is it without our husbands that we have prepared cakes for her to pourtray her, and poured out drink offerings unto her?*

Verses 20–23 form the third section of the prophecy. The prophet himself puts his own point as forcibly as possible in *v.* 23. *Because ye burned incense . . . therefore this evil happened unto you* (*v.* 23). He admits the facts, but interprets them in a diametrically opposite sense. By so doing, he shows how hopeless it was to make any progress along the traditional lines of Jewish religious thought. That true piety must lead to earthly prosperity, was an illusion which had become positively harmful. Jeremiah knew this, but had not the power to set it forth in a logical manner; and yet it was a logical explanation which was imperatively called for by the circumstances. And so in the fourth section (verses 24–28) he endeavours to make up for his logical deficiency by expressing more earnestly than ever his prophetic intuition that Jehovah cannot permit such insults to the higher and the only true view of His "name" or essential nature to pass unpunished.

A PASTOR'S STRANGE FAREWELL. 197

Behold, I swear by my great name, no more shall my name be pronounced by the mouth of any man of Judah that saith " By the life of the Lord Jehovah." Such is the oracle; it means that all the Jewish refugees shall perish but a very small number (comp. *v.* 14), who shall have to take refuge in their old land (*v.* 28). Never did Jeremiah (if the report be correct) commit himself more definitely to the literal fulfilment of a prediction than now. He knows the Jewish fondness for "signs," and so, that his opponents may recognize him as a true seer of the future, he offers them two "signs." First, those few who do ultimately escape shall know by sad experience *whose word standeth, mine, or theirs* (*v.* 28). Next, to quote the prophet's own words in the last section, *Behold, I give Pharaoh Hophra king of Egypt into the hand of his enemies, and into the hand of them that seek his life, as I gave Zedekiah king of Judah into the hand of Nebuchadrezzar king of Babylon, his enemy, and that sought his life* (*v.* 30).

One cannot but be distressed, first, that Jeremiah in spite of himself accepted the old "tendency argument"; and next, that he staked his prophetic character on the circumstantial fulfilment of certain predictions. The argument was of course inconclusive; the circumstantial fulfilment, even if it can be proved, cannot now contribute—did it indeed ever greatly contribute?—to increase the influence of Jeremiah. Granting that we find a prediction in Jeremiah of some event which actually took place, yet how easy it is for a prophet or his editor to manufacture predictions after the event. And how difficult it is to prove such fulfilments. It appears certain that Jeremiah's and Ezekiel's prediction of the Babylonian conquest of Tyre (Jer. xxv. 22, xxvii. 3, xlvii. 4; Ezek. xxvi. 1–xxviii. 19) was not ratified by the event; Ezekiel himself seems to say as much (Ezek. xxix. 17–21). Is it probable, so a rationalist might well argue, that the conquest of a country like Egypt should have been really foreseen in its details by Hebrew prophets? I think that from the highest point of view prophecy neither gains nor loses by having received a circumstantial fulfilment; the moral and spiritual element is that by which alone it lives. Let me not then be thought biassed by theology if I hold,[1] in opposition to M. Maspero, that in all essential points the prophetic references to a Babylonian con-

[1] See my discussion of this question in "The Pulpit Commentary."

quest of Egypt are accurate. Putting together two cuneiform records and a hieroglyphic inscription, it appears that in his 37th year Nebuchadrezzar penetrated into Egypt as far as Syene. There he was met and repulsed by the Egyptian troops (comp. Ezek. xxix. 10). Two years later the Babylonians renewed the invasion, and by their complete success forced Egypt to pay tribute. It has not however been shown (see Herod. ii. 169) that Hophra (the old ally of Zedekiah) was slain by the Babylonians, though this seems almost required, if Jer. xliv. 30 is to have the character of a "sign."

Certainly Jeremiah and Ezekiel spoke a true "word of the Lord" when they uttered these prophecies. What sufficient moral safeguards had these ancient states? A temporary exception may be made for Babylon, the religion of which, with all its imperfections, was, as we have seen, a noble one. But of all the communities of that time the most miserable was this Jewish one in Egypt. Less endowed with physical advantages, it was also, through the operation of causes which we have studied, at a lower moral and spiritual level than any other. In the religion of Babylon at any rate there were elements akin to that of the prophets and psalmists. Even the worship of the "queen of heaven" may in some countries have had a moral tinge; but it was not so among the Jews of Pathros. The children gathered wood, the fathers kindled the fire, the women kneaded the dough, to make sacrificial cakes, as they had done in Jehoiakim's time (Jer. vii. 18), simply as a propitiatory rite which would keep off sword and pestilence. Who was the "queen of heaven"?[1] Was she the moon? or the planet known to the Babylonians as Istar and to ourselves as Venus (not the masculine deity referred to in Isa. xiv. 12, but the feminine)? Some have preferred the former, reminding us that cakes were offered to Artemis at the Eleusinian Mysteries. But Wellhausen has pointed out[2] that a similar

[1] See Schrader's paper in the "Transactions of the Berlin Academy," 1886, pp. 477-491, Kuenen, "De Melecheth des Hemels" (Amsterdam, 1888), and articles by Stade in his "Zeitschrift," 1886, pp. 123-132, 289-339, and comp. Norris, "Assyrian Dictionary," i. 86. "Melecheth" is doubtless wrongly vocalized, the punctuators explained the whole phrase "(God's) work in the heaven" (comp. Gen. ii. 1, 2). They meant the starry host.

[2] "Skizzen und Vorarbeiten," iii. 38, 39. The worship of different planetary divinities was widely spread among the Arabian tribes.

rite formed part of the cultus of the Arabian goddess al-Uzza (Venus), and Kuenen that in the Targum of the prophetical books the Hebrew phrase is rendered "star (fem.) of heaven," *i.e.* the planet Venus, while Isaac of Antioch, who wrote in the same century (the fifth A.D) in which that Targum was finally shaped, infers from this passage of Jeremiah that the Jews sacrificed to "the Star" (which he identifies with the Arabian al-Uzza or Venus).[1] Finally, Schrader has given evidence that the Assyrians called the feminine Istar *malkatu* "queen," and that in Assurbanipal's reign (*i.e.* not so long before Jeremiah's prophecy) the northern Arabs worshipped a deity called Atar-samain (*i.e.* Atar [2] of heaven).

It is a tempting theme which Jeremiah's last prophecy suggests to us. Many writers have dealt already with the "vestiges of ancient manners and customs discoverable"[3] in Christendom. The phrase "Regina Cœli" can now be dealt with as one of these "vestiges" with more fulness than before. It belongs not only to the Virgin Mary, and to the Ephesian Artemis, but in the Semitic countries (probably) to the goddess of the Moon and of Venus. Yes; it is a tempting study, and if pursued a little farther, might lead us to sympathize in some sense with the myth-makers. Why, then, did Jeremiah hate the "queen of heaven"? Because these fair but inwardly exhausted mythologies did dishonour to Him who is the true "king of heaven" (Dan. iv. 37), and of whom it was said, *Hear, O Israel: Jehovah our God is one Jehovah* (Deut. vi. 4).

[1] To the passages from St. Isaac cited by Kuenen, add Carm. x. *v.* 343 (Bickell i. 220, 221), where boys and girls are said to have been sacrificed to "the Star."

[2] Atar is the Assyrian Istar. See Schrader's note on Jer. vii. 18.

[3] I quote from the title of an early work by Prof. J. J. Blunt, of Cambridge.

CHAPTER VII.

PER CRUCEM AD LUCEM.

Legendary accounts of Jeremiah's death—His sufferings and compensations—Jeremiah compared with Milton and Savonarola—The spring foreseen by the Israelite and the Italian still future.

THE heathen festival proceeds. But where is the grieved, the broken-hearted protester? What was the prophet's subsequent history? When Nebuchadrezzar conquered Egypt, did he, as some later Jewish writers say, carry Jeremiah and Baruch with him to Babylon? Or, as a Christian legend, possibly referred to in Heb xi. 37, asserts, was he stoned to death at Tahpanhes by his unbelieving people? Certainly the latter is psychologically a probable view of Jeremiah's closing scene. Once and again, when death stared him in the face, Jehovah had "hidden" Jeremiah; but why should Providence baffle the designs of his persecutors, now that his work was done, and their malice could but add fresh flowers to the faithful servant's crown? His God "hid" him this time in a far more secret place, if we may trust our sense of the fitness of things. Already (see p. 112) I have invited my readers to follow this legend. Already the narrative of St. Stephen's martyrdom has helped us to imagine how—

> ". . . . some strong pathetic
> Face of a wounded prophet gazed, and then
> Sank in God's darkness grandly
> From out the infinite littleness of men," [1]

---

[1] Alexander, "Death of the Earl of Derby."

and to infer the feelings of Jeremiah. May we venture on a still bolder step, and, with the great Jewish scholar Saadya (who died 942 A.D.) and with the versatile statesman-critic Bunsen, consider Isa. lii. 13–liii. Israel's penitent confession of its guilt in having slain this great teacher? Certainly Jeremiah likens himself to the *gentle lamb that is led to the slaughter* (xi. 19), and might, even by one who knew his slight regard for the sacrificial system, have been called metaphorically a sacrifice for his people. But to me it seems clear that if a historical martyr is referred to in that great monologue, it must be some one who was judicially murdered, and whose death was remembered afterwards. Jeremiah's death was forgotten; so indeed Isaiah's had been. At an earlier age some prose-poet might have projected from his divinely illumined imagination chariots and horses of fire to carry them up to heaven; and at a later period the rising Church would have chronicled the minutest facts of the "new births" of such heroes of faith. Their earthly fame suffers; but *dear shall their blood be in his sight*.

"In Jeremiah," as the most sympathetic of critical interpreters has said, "the kingdom lost the most human prophet it ever possessed. His heavy sorrows and despair, his noble yet fruitless struggles, and his fall, were those of prophetism, and, so far as prophetism constituted the inmost life of the ancient state, of the state itself. If any pure soul could still save the state, that soul was Jeremiah's, whose period of greatest vigour fell in these three and twenty years of its dying agony: but even for the noblest of the prophets the time was now gone by; and the last great prophet, and all the remains of the ancient kingdom of Israel, which had been preserved amid the storms of centuries, were engulfed in a common ruin."[1] Three and twenty years, however, is not the whole duration of Jeremiah's career. He saw not only the dying agony, but the last stage of the disease which prepared that agony. If he was martyred five years after the fall of Jerusalem, and if he began to prophesy in the thirteenth year of Josiah's reign, we get forty-four years as the duration of his ministry, so that his age at his death cannot be less (comp. Jer. i. 6) than sixty-four. He was therefore an old man, and my comparison of his glimpse of the "new covenant" to the prospect

[1] Ewald, "History of Israel," iv. 249

which Moses enjoyed upon Nebo is justified. "Few and evil" were his days. Nor had he the blessing which Israelites prized so dearly—a wife and children (Jer. xvi. 2), in this respect less favoured than Moses. But can we say that his sun went down in unmitigated gloom? Had he no compensations but his posthumous influence and his early friendships? Surely he had, if, "speaking as a man," the Saviour had any. Jesus, too, was old in experience and perhaps in countenance (John viii. 57), and was without the closest of earthly ties. Jesus, too, was, except by a few friends, "despised and rejected." Still the Saviour had not only "unknown griefs," but unknown comforts—*the joy that was set before him*, and Jeremiah, I think, must in some dim way have enjoyed a similar spiritual happiness. Yes; Jeremiah is not unfitly called a "type," an unfinished sketch as it were, of the unique, the incomparable One. It is true that only once [1] does he (perhaps) refer to a personal Saviour of Israel, and even then he uses a symbolic expression which circumstances were proving to be wholly inadequate to its object. But if he did not predict the true Christ in words, he did so by his life. Rightly did the Crusaders erect a church at *their* Anathoth dedicated to *Saint* Jeremiah.[2] It is true the later Jews had in their fashion already canonized him (see the touching narrative in 2 Macc. xv., and notice the homage paid to him in the land of his martyrdom by Philo [3]).

A long characterization of our prophet is needless. If this book does not present a living, growing character, it has missed its aim. I have no space to speak of his literary merits, which have been depreciated perhaps somewhat too much. He was not an artist in words; he is given to repetition and the use of stereotyped formulæ; he is too often diffuse and always imita-

---

[1] Jeremiah has but one undoubted reference (xxiii. 5) to royalty as the organ of God's future government of His people—it is the famous prophecy of the "Shoot" or perhaps "Shoots" (*i.e.*, either a Davidic king or a succession of Davidic kings). This shows that, while on the one hand Jeremiah will not neglect the symbol of his gifted predecessor, he is fully conscious of its inadequacy in the decadence of the royal house. As for Jer xxxiii. 14–26, it is extremely probable that it is an accretion on the text It is not contained in the Septuagint.

[2] *Their* Anathoth was Karyet el-'Enab (on which see p. 121, note 2). The church (now in the possession of the French) is one of the most interesting in Palestine.

[3] See Drummond, "Philo Judæus," 1 16.

tive. But how could he soar, when there was so much to depress his imagination? He at any rate can touch the heart, and is free from affectation. His greatest poem is his own fascinating character. In the earlier chapters I have taken much pains to detect the germs of subsequent developments; I must not repeat myself. Suffice it here to mention two persons with whom Jeremiah may be profitably compared.

The first is our own Milton, whose greatness both as a poet and as a public man is so inextricably connected with his fervent spiritual religion. There have been few who could more fully enter into Jeremiah's first chapter than Milton (from whom the motto for my own opening chapter is taken), or who have equally experienced that loneliness which fell upon Jeremiah when, as Wellhausen puts it, "the true Israel was narrowed to himself."[1] Neither was wholly free from the bitterness of strife, but to neither was refused an emancipating heavenly vision. A literary critic has recently said that "the love of country in its most creative and passionate form was the outcome of Puritanism;"[2] but the same passionate spiritual ardour which we find in the patriotism of the Puritans existed long before in that of Jeremiah.

But at the close of his ministry I would rather compare Jeremiah with one who was *mighty both in words and in deeds* (Acts vii. 22), and whom a sympathetic poetess has painted perhaps more truly than her sister-artist in prose.[3] Need I mention his name?

> ". . . . This was he,
> Savonarola, who, while Peter sank
> With his whole boat-load, cried courageously,
> 'Wake, Christ; wake, Christ!'
> Who also by a princely deathbed cried,
> 'Loose Florence, or God will not loose thy soul!'
> Then fell back the Magnificent and died
> Beneath the star-look shooting from the cowl,
> Which turned to wormwood-bitterness the wide
> Deep sea of his ambitions."

---

[1] "Encyclopædia Britannica," xiii. 417*a*.

[2] *Spectator*, June 16, 1888 (review of Mr. Harrison's "Cromwell").

[3] Mr. G. W. Cooke well remarks that George Eliot's Savonarola is "always much more of an altruist than of a Christian." Prof. Creighton, I think, would reject the version of Lorenzo de' Medici's death accepted by Mrs. Browning. But the general impression given by the above lines is, I hope, correct.

I admit that Jeremiah had not the hopefulness described in the opening lines; Jerusalem was a less promising field of work than, with all its faults, Florence was in the age of Lorenzo. But do not the closing lines give almost a reflexion of Jeremiah's attitude towards Jehoiakim? Savonarola had, I suppose, a richer nature than Jeremiah. In him several of the old Hebrew prophets seemed united. He had the scathing indignation of Amos, and the versatility of Isaiah, as well as the tenderness of Jeremiah. He differs most from the latter in two respects—in his emphatic reassertion of the principle of theocratic legislation, and in his ultra-supernaturalistic theory of prophecy, which disturbed the simplicity of his faith in his own inspiration. Again and again, however, in his latter days, his preaching reminds us of Jeremiah's. "Your sins," he cries to the Florentines, "make me a prophet. . . . And if ye will not hear my words, I say unto you that I will be the prophet Jeremiah, who foretold the destruction of Jerusalem, and bewailed it when destroyed." Like Jeremiah, he had many a sore inward struggle; "an inward fire," he says, "consumeth my bones (comp. Jer. xx. 9), and compelleth me to speak." Like Jeremiah, he was no respecter of persons; he fought bravely, and outwardly at least was defeated. Like Jeremiah, he foresaw the end of the struggle "If you ask me in general"—so he said, shortly before he was burned at the stake, in the convent-church of St. Mark's—"as to the issue of this struggle, I reply, Victory. If you ask me in a particular sense, I reply, Death. For the master who wields the hammer, when he has used it, throws it away. *So He did with Jeremiah, whom He caused to be stoned at the end of his ministry.* But Rome will not put out this fire, and if this be put out, God will light another, and indeed it is already lighted everywhere, only they perceive it not."

It was winter both in Jeremiah's time and in Savonarola's. Which was the more favoured of these two heralds of spring? *I* think, Jeremiah, because his prophecy of spring was fulfilled, after a brief interval, to his own people. Not so fortunate was Savonarola. Germany, France, and England—not Italy— were the theatre of the promised Reformation. Italy still waits. Still Jeremiah's advantage was not so great as it might seem. Israel had indeed its bright spring (thanks to the Second Isaiah), and its disappointing but still brilliant summer (thanks to Ezra), but it passed only too quickly into another winter. Israel waits again, and seems to say, *How long, Jehovah, wilt thou forget me for ever?* But why be impatient? Winter is not death. We know that there is a real though concealed life around us in the winter-time, and that mighty forces are at work, which will restore to us first, spring's fair promise, then summer's fulness of growth, and then autumn's golden fruitage. And we know that mighty spiritual forces are at work in Israel and among the Italians, and that, though not with the voice of Jeremiah or of Savonarola, yet with such power as God has given them Israelitish and Italian reformers are continuing the work of those prophets in Italy and Israel. True sons of the prophets are they—

> ". . . men, whose spirit-sharpened sight
> Foreknows the advent of the light."

www.ingramcontent.com/pod-product-compliance
Lightning Source LLC
Chambersburg PA
CBHW051922160426
43198CB00012B/2006